© Copyright 2021 by Mark Davis

TRADING BIBLE
For Beginners

-3 books in 1-

Forex Trading + Options Trading Crash Course + Swing and Day trading. Learn the Powerful Strategies to Start Creating your Financial Freedom Today

Written by **Mark Davis**

BOOK 1

FOREX Trading For Beginners

Discover the Psychology of A Successful Trader. Learn How to Make Money By Investing in Forex. Start Creating Your Passive Income Today with Powerful Secret Strategies - **Written by Mark Davis**

Table of Contents

Introduction 11

Chapter 1: Mentality of a Trader 13

Chapter 2: Emotions in Trading 23

Chapter 3: What You Need to Trade on Forex 29

Chapter 4: The Basics of Forex 37

Chapter 5: Macroeconomic Analysis 49

Chapter 6: Forex Correlations 59

Chapter 7: Technical Analysis of Forex 67

Chapter 8: The Habits of a Successful Trader 87

Conclusion 97

BOOK 2

OPTIONS Trading Crash Course

Discover the Secrets of a Successful Trader and Make Money by Investing in Options. Start Creating your Passive Income Today with Powerful Strategies for Beginners - **Written by Mark Davis**

Table of Contents

Introduction 103

Chapter 1: How to Get Started in Options Trading 105

Chapter 2: Mindset and Secrets of a Trader 109

Chapter 3: Learn the Purpose of Options and When to Use Them . 117

Chapter 4: Advantages and Disadvantages of Options Trading 121

Chapter 5: Overview of Options 127

Chapter 6: Simplified Examples of Options Trades 133

Chapter 7: Myths About Options Trading 139

Chapter 8: Puts and Calls 143

Chapter 9: Technical Analysis 149

Chapter 10: Chart Reading 157

Chapter 11: Candlestick Common Patterns 163

Chapter 12: Wave Analysis: Elliott Wave Decomposition 177

Chapter 13: Tools and Indicators for Options Trading 183

Chapter 14: Strategies for Options Trading 193

Chapter 15: Money Management 209

Chapter 16: Risk Management 217

Chapter 17: The Market Environment 223

Chapter 18: Options to Pursue If Your Options Aren't Working 229

Chapter 19: Creating an Options Trading Plan 233

Conclusion 239

BOOK 3

$WING & DAY Trading for Beginners

The Best Strategies for Investing in Stock, Options and Forex With Day and Swing Trading. Make Money and Start Creating your Financial Freedom Today – **Written by Mark Davis**

Table of Contents

Introduction 245
Chapter 1: Overview of Day Trading 247
Chapter 2: Pros and Cons of Day Trading 253
Chapter 3: Day Trading Orders 257
Chapter 4: Best Markets for Day Trading 263
Chapter 5: Technical Analysis 271
Chapter 6: Introduction to Candlesticks 285
Chapter 7: Fundamental Analysis 293
Chapter 8: Basic Day Trading Tips 299
Chapter 9: Strategies of Day Trading 303
Chapter 10: More Day Trading Strategies 313
Chapter 11: Best Platforms for Day Trading 321
Chapter 12: Stock Management 327
Chapter 13: The Dos and Don'ts of Day Trading 333
Chapter 14: Swing Trading 339

Chapter 15: Swing Trading Rules 345

Chapter 16: How Does Swing Trading Work? 349

Chapter 17: Swing Trading Vs. Day Trading.. 355

Chapter 18: Advantages and Disadvantages of Swing Trading 361

Chapter 19: Strategies of Swing Trading.. 363

Chapter 20: Swing Trading Psychology 367

Chapter 21: How to Manage Your Funds When Swing Trading 371

Conclusion 377

© Copyright 2021 by Mark Davis- All rights reserved.

The content contained within this book may not be reproduced, duplicated or transmitted without direct written permission from the author or the publisher.

Under no circumstances will any blame or legal responsibility be held against the publisher, or author, for any damages, reparation, or monetary loss due to the information contained within this book, either directly or indirectly.

Legal Notice:

This book is copyright protected. It is only for personal use. You cannot amend, distribute, sell, use, quote or paraphrase any part, or the content within this book, without the consent of the author or publisher.

Disclaimer Notice:

Please note the information contained within this document is for educational and entertainment purposes only. All effort has been executed to present accurate, up to date, reliable, complete information. No warranties of any kind are declared or implied. Readers acknowledge that the author is not engaged in the rendering of legal, financial, medical or professional advice. The content within this book has been derived from various sources. Please consult a licensed professional before attempting any techniques outlined in this book.

By reading this document, the reader agrees that under no circumstances is the author responsible for any losses, direct or indirect, that are incurred as a result of the use of the information contained within this document, including, but not limited to, errors, omissions, or inaccuracies.

© Copyright 2021 by Mark Davis- All rights reserved.

BOOK 1

FOREX
Trading For Beginners

Discover the Psychology of A Successful Trader. Learn How to Make Money By Investing in Forex. Start Creating Your Passive Income Today with Powerful Secret Strategies.

Written by **Mark Davis**

Table of Contents

Introduction 11

Chapter 1: Mentality of a Trader 13

Chapter 2: Emotions in Trading 23

Chapter 3: What You Need to Trade on Forex.........................29

Chapter 4: The Basics of Forex 37

Chapter 5: Macroeconomic Analysis...49

Chapter 6: Forex Correlations..59

Chapter 7: Technical Analysis of Forex.....................................67

Chapter 8: The Habits of a Successful Trader 87

Conclusion..97

Introduction

Welcome, I'm Mark Davis and I am a full-time professional trader, trade system developer, and trading coach with decades of experience.

I have taught hundreds of people how to make a living from trading. Investing in the foreign exchange (forex) market is an opportunity today that should not be missed. Forex is defined as the largest, most liquid, and most versatile financial market in the world.

Forex is like a video game; when you are inside, it takes over you and it becomes a huge passion, but unlike a video game, you get paid to play.

It is clearly not a real game, but it is serious business, and what I do is teach you how to become the best forex trading player.

Here's what you'll learn in this book:
- How to take advantage of the current big opportunity to invest in forex;
- The true strength of a forex trader;
- The importance of technical analysis;
- How to build winning trading strategies;
- Learn to manage the emotions that influence your trading; decisions (psychology of a trader);
- How to imitate the daily routine of successful people;
- And much, much more…

Even if you don't know anything about forex trading, don't worry; this book was written with the intent of giving you thorough knowledge on the topic, along with all the necessary means to start operating independently.

Before investing in something, you need to invest some time to understand it. After this brief introduction, I wish you a good read!

FOREX

Chapter 1: Mentality of a Trader

Some traders in the trading world believe that graphic patterns do not work. Others believe that the financial markets are manipulated by who knows who, but many investors do not understand the importance of trading psychology as they cannot bear the psychological load that each operation carries. The main psychological problems that a trader faces are the fact of knowing how to deal with losses and how to manage positive results.

In trading, it is very important to learn the right techniques but to be truly successful, it is not enough. There are quite a few traders who start in the simulated mode with very satisfying results, but when they start trading with real money, they can't achieve the same success.

What is the cause of this? It comes from the mentality!

It is said that in trading, as in other businesses, it is 90% psychology and only 10% technical. I can confirm this data, but I state that knowing the techniques is a fundamental and indispensable prerequisite for obtaining positive results. For example, if a person is successful in a certain field, with an excellent mentality, he cannot think of starting trading without technique, thanks to his mentality, but he must study and learn too. However, I have noticed that people with an excellent mentality are ready to learn and ready to make mistakes. A person with a winning mindset, along with the right techniques will be a 100% successful person in trading.

Three Characteristics of Man

In marketing, man is represented in three characteristics: he is a "sheep," he is selfish and emotional.

He is a "sheep" because he tends to copy the mass. Due to this characteristic, the average investor tends to enter a position late, when the markets have already made a move and are approaching a possible reversal point. This means that most of the small investors enter the market upwards at the end of a positive trend, so all those who could buy have already done so, and there can be no force capable of sustaining a further extension. The exact same thing happens when small investors go down.

As for the other two characteristics, selfishness and emotionality, they immediately liquidate the earning positions for the haste to monetize the positive outcome and not wait for the target price that was obtained following a careful analysis. Another mistake may be that of not closing loss-making operations in stop loss, not accepting the loss, and being convinced that sooner or later the investment will return profitable. With this attitude, the investor will find himself not closing an operation that is destined to get worse and worse, and to fuel the desire to recover lost money.

The Importance of Stop Loss

"Rule number one, never lose money. Rule number two, never forget rule number one." -Warren Buffet-

The stop loss serves to protect oneself from the risk of ruin, that is, from the risk of an irreversible erosion of capital, which makes it difficult to recover losses. The stop loss also serves to decrease the probability of loss in financial transactions.

Let's say that the stop loss is what distinguishes the novice investor from a professional investor.

Both can obtain results, but the first takes an indefinite risk and obtains unstable results, while the second has absolute control of his potions and manages to obtain stable and constant results over time.

Divide Position

Another excellent trading strategy presupposes an entry point, an initial stop loss and two exit points (the first more affordable, the second more ambitious).

In doing so, it is possible to liquidate half of the position and aim for a greater profit with the other half, obviously raising the stop loss at the breakeven point to avoid losing.

Mental Aspects in Trading

A question that many often ask is, "Why do two traders with the same financial instrument, with the same knowledge, open two different positions on an operation?"

The real answer is in the mind. Each trader has a different mind, with different opinions and expectations that are most likely conditioned by their daily life and their state of mind.

A mental aspect that I want to explain is the approach you have with money.

Let's say, in general, there are four types of approaches one has towards money:

1. People who like to spend money;
2. People inclined to save;
3. People who entrust the management of their money to third parties;
4. People who think that money is of no use

But why does a person have a certain type of approach towards money compared to another? Basically, they can be hereditary but largely derived from the paradigms that have been created by being conditioned by the relationship that the family of origin had towards money.

If the family has always represented money as a problem, it is likely that this can affect the economic choices made by the rest of the family members.

If, on the other hand, money has been seen as a means to achieve certain objectives, it will have a positive relationship with money.

If you have a negative relationship with money, you are not destined to have it all your life, but you just have to reprogram your brain in the direction in which you can evaluate money as a possibility to achieve certain goals, increasing your own style of life, helping the poorest

people, etc.

If, from an early age, the family describes rich people as selfish and greedy, it is clear that a negative prejudice will develop towards money. This will surely weigh on the will to become rich, because unconsciously you don't want to become like those "greedy and selfish" people, right?

So, if you were to realize that you have a negative association with money, you will have to work on re-programming your mind and change your mind about the personality of rich people. If a person is rich, it is because they have had some positive qualities and because they are probably better than the average person in that particular field. In fact, these people should be taken as points of reference, not denigrated. Then, of course, there are also people who are illegally rich, but we are not interested in that type of people.

Many think that when one person gets rich, another person gets impoverished. However, this is not the case, because if a person offers service and gets paid $1000, he earns $1000, but the other person earns value from the service offered. He wasn't robbed, but he paid what he felt was right for that particular service.

As for trading, there is a widespread belief that trading is pure speculation and that one's wealth derives from the subtraction of other people's wealth. But, this is absolutely not the case! The gain of an investor is not linked to the loss of another investor.

If an investor has sold a share and obtained a profit, there is certainly a counterparty who bought it, but the latter does not necessarily lose, because if the share price were to continue to rise, the latter investor would also gain. If instead, it was to fall, it will certainly not be the fault of the first investor, but of a wrong analysis by the second investor.

On the other hand, there are other people who trade, but with poor results, as they were not convinced that it was possible to make money with trading constantly. If this is the conviction you have, it will be impossible for such people to obtain positive and lasting results, because they will unconsciously adopt destructive operational strategies in order to be right.

Another mistake not to make is to consider a gain in trading as a win because it would be considered as a quick and easy gain. In doing so, you will believe that it is easy to make money and you will start investing unconsciously without making the right analyses. Unfortunately, you get to lose large sums of money!

The Best Conditions for Trading

A much underestimated factor in trading is the environment in which you work and the physical attitude you have.

During the trading sessions, it is very important to maintain a professional attitude, where you are aware that trading is a job where you can earn but also lose a lot.

Keep your back straight with your shoulders not hunched forward. There must be windows that provide good natural light and excellent ventilation for the work environment (it has been proven that oxygen-rich air and natural sunlight stimulate brain cells).

Another important thing is not to work if you are physically exhausted and mentally distracted because the trading activity will inevitably be affected in a negative way.

The work environment must resemble a trading room and if the workstation is located inside your home, it is preferable that it is in a room isolated from the rest of the house and furnished with a large desk and a PC with one or two screens.

Sit in a comfortable chair and have two notepads, one of which to write down any operational ideas that we will have to follow during the day and the other to take some notes that could be used later.

It must be made clear to family members that you are not playing and that you are working on something important!

Quality not Quantity

Very often, people think that starting to trade means maybe going to the Caribbean to sit on a beach and doing operations with their mobile phone or PC. I honestly do not recommend it. Associating trading with a moment of relaxation or a holiday makes you lose the right concentration and you will not take it as a serious profession but as a betting game.

There are going to be a few professional traders who operate while they are on the beach or on a ski slope, but certainly, for newbies I strongly advise against it. Since you are not yet prepared for the emotions of trading, you should concentrate as much as possible in a professional environment.

Another piece of advice I would like to give is to give yourself enough hours to work with trading, so as not to have the classic psychological stress of a trader. It is much easier to want to close the trading activity at a certain time of the day and not want to recover any losses at all costs with other trading hours that very often lead to mental, and portfolio, destruction. This does not mean that I will necessarily have to open or close positions in that time frame but that I will open or close them only if the conditions required me to carry out a specific operation that occurs in that period.

Obviously, if you work part time you cannot make the most of the opportunities on the financial markets, but this does not mean anything. It is not so much the number of operations that are done, but how they are done!

There will surely be days that you will spend analyzing everything but not opening positions! If after doing all the analysis, you think there is no entry point and you should wait, then wait! Don't think that by not opening any positions, you have not done anything! Yes you did–you avoided investing money that you would most likely lose!

FOREX

Rule Number 1: Never lose money!

I already mentioned this principle and you may be wondering, "What advice is it not to lose money? It's obvious, I already know that."

Exactly! The mistake of many traders is that they know that surely if you invest in trading it would be better not to lose, if not why should you invest? When I mean not to lose, I don't mean that all trades must go into profit, which is quite improbable. By not losing, I mean analyzing the market and always putting a target price and a stop loss. If you trade with your head, it may be that 60% of the trades go at a loss and 40% in profit, but that 40% brings you a greater profit than the 60% loss (this concept I will explain better later).

I'll give you an example.

Let's say you want to start trading, and after studying and investing in virtual money trading, you finally want to start trading with real money. You have $100,000 on hand. Let's say your trades bring you a 15% annual profit, so by the end of the year you will have earned $15,000 and your capital would be $115,000. A 15% profit in the following year would increase your capital no by $15,000 but by $17,250, and so on exponentially.

But what happens if you lose 50% of the capital in the first year? You get down to $50,000. If you get a 15% profit the following year, you would reach $57,500. The next year, you still have a 15% annual profit, up to $66,125.

Do you know what this means? To return to the starting capital you would have to make 100% profit immediately, to go from $50,000 to $100,000, which is very difficult to achieve. If you are a novice trader, you will have that feeling of wanting to recover all of the money at all costs, with the very high risk of losing the entire capital. But what if as soon as you hit $50,000 you want to go back to $100,000 with a 15% profit? How long would it take? 5 YEARS! (6 years since you started investing if you count that the first year $50,000 was lost.)

Well, you can understand why I consider this "trivial" principle very important. Recovering losses can be a long and exhausting job.

Trading is not a Game

In the world of trading, there are no employees. There are no customers, suppliers, or bosses who will force you to do certain things. This means that there are no interpersonal problems, and since there is no product to produce and sell, the energies required concern only the knowledge of the subject (through technical and fundamental analysis) and the psychological approach to it.

The entrepreneur or professional businessperson, after having done the work, has to wait months or years before making a profit, creating cash flow problems. However, in trading this is not the case. When you liquidate a financial instrument, its consideration is immediately credited.

Many start trading thinking of becoming millionaires in a short time, but this is the fault of the advertisements. Some brokers suggest the possibility that anyone without training in the field and without practice can earn a lot with trading. MISTAKEN! It may happen that an unprepared beginner makes an excellent operation and immediately makes a profit on the first try. I think this event is very negative because the trader in question will think that everything is easy. He will feel invincible, but rest assured that subsequent operations will go negative. By doing so, the trader in question will think that there is no profit from trading and will drop everything, saying that trading is a scam and it is all luck.

To be a good trader, you need a thorough study of the subject, observe the professionals who already carry out this work, and then, start trading. You start trading first with simulated trading and then with real trading.

You need to study technical analysis books, attend seminars, and have a great coach. The fact of being followed in the early stages of learning by a good coach has excellent advantages. Initially, the expert trading coach will explain the various types of orders to be entered into the machine and will introduce you to the broker's graphical platform. It may seem strange but it often happens that a different order is entered than the one desired, because the novice trader does not know all aspects of the work interface. Therefore, acquiring the automation of order entry is important and will avoid unnecessary errors.

After this phase, we move on to the phase known as "paper trading" or simulated trading. This phase constitutes a real training phase, where the theory learned previously is put into practice. You begin to face the first positive/negative emotions of trading (optimism and euphoria when you gain, and discouragement and fear when you lose).

In this phase, the emotions will only be perceived. It is in the next phase, the one with real trading, that the true emotions of trading will be felt, because this time the money is real, it is your money.

An absolute and very important advice I want to give is not to operate in real trading if, in simulated trading, you are unable to make a profit at the end of the month or at the end of the quarter. If you are losing out on simulated trading, it is very difficult to get positive results with real trading.

Nevertheless, as mentioned above, due to the emotions of trading, it can happen that you get very good results in simulated trading, but then have poor results in real trading. You already know the secret and it is in the mind!

Risk and Loss Aversion

Statistically, 90% of people who do financial trading find themselves, after a short time, with a capital lower than the starting amount. Those who started trading, thinking of making money quickly and easily, often find themselves having lost a part of the capital.

Trading often generates emotions that are present in everyone and can be an obstacle to achieving positive results. Suppose we invest in a $15,000 share because after careful analysis it suggests that prices could rise and get a 20% gain. After a certain period of time, prices that have risen by 10% temporarily interrupt their rise, suffering a settling pause, which does not change the bullish scenario, leaving intact the possibility that the stock can reach the identified target.

In this situation, most people feel satisfied and close the position, thus underestimating the analysis carried out previously and the fact that the price has all the credentials to reach the expected target. The investor is attracted by the possibility of collecting the $1,500 and prefers not to risk and thinks "better few, than risk losing," but does not take into account that when he opened the position he took a risk at the start risking losing part of the capital. This behavior is referred to as **"Risk Aversion."**

Still analyzing the previous example, let's assume another scenario. Suppose that after investing the $15,000, prices drop 10% in a short time and the investor finds himself in a $1,500 loss position. This decline has damaged the technical structure of the stock with the price, which, after having given up an important graphic support, could continue its descent.

How does an average investor behave at this point? Let's start by saying that many do not put a stop loss in place, or it is placed but not respected. The investor will do everything to prevent this loss from materializing (until the position is closed, the loss is to be considered only theoretical).

Faced with the possibility of losing this money, the investor will choose to remain in a position awaiting developments, thus developing the so-called

"Loss aversion." The average investor has this sense of loss aversion and therefore tries not to materialize it immediately by closing the position, hoping that the negative trend will reverse despite the analysis carried out on the stock.

But think about it; in the first example, the mind pushes us to make the profit of $1,500 despite the target being set at $3,000. In the second case, the investor does not accept a loss of $1,500 and induces the investor with the risk of suffering a larger loss.

How to make a total profit by having more trades at a loss than a profit?

Did you know that in trading on 100 operations you only need 40 correct ones to make sure that the final result is positive, despite the remaining 60 are at a loss? A successful trader is aware of the fact that losing positions can be the norm and not the exception, but the fact of having a final profit lies in knowing how to manage these losses.

How to do it

It is possible if the ratio "3:1" is respected. Based on this rule, only positions will be opened whose profit taking is three times greater than the loss that that operation could generate, i.e. the level where the stop loss would be entered.

For example: if a stock is worth $5 and, after a study, I estimate the hypothetical target at $8, to protect myself, I will position the stop loss at $4.

Doing so will change the approach to loss, and will be considered as part of the system and a technique, and not as a personal defeat.

If we return to the initial example, in which 60 out of 100 trades generated a loss, with prices that triggered the pre-established stop loss, we assume that the stop loss was 100 points, while the positions in profit produced a profit. Of 300 points, the final result will be:

- 60 losing trades x 100 points = 6000 losing points
- 40 trades in profit x 300 points = 12000 points in profit

So, if each point is worth $1, you would have a net profit of $6000.

By doing so, the trader is already psychologically prepared to have to manage losses. In this way, if the market does not behave as we hoped, the position will be closed in stop loss, aware of the fact that it is the best thing to protect us against further drops in prices and a further increase in the loss.

So, in summary, to do all this it is important to initially identify a financial instrument that has a technical-graphic structure that suggests a rise in prices. Then it is necessary to identify the potential target of a possible bullish movement by establishing adequate profit-taking.

I calculate the distance between the entry-level and profit-taking, divide it by 3, and subtract it from the entry-level to obtain a theoretical stop loss level.

Around the price level obtained, I will have to identify any graphic support and place the stop loss just below this level, thus avoiding the risk that prices will lean on this area and then start a technical rebound. Only a drop in prices below this support level will therefore trigger the stop loss.

In addition to the 3:1 ratio, in some cases, it can even reach a ratio of 2:1 but the important thing is not to have a 1:1 ratio or even with a stop loss higher than profit-taking.

A mistake may be to close a position early, before it reaches the predetermined target, for fear of losing the profit that is being realized. The trader who operates in this way does not respect the 3:1 ratio between profits and losses, with the consequence that the gains of his profit positions may not be sufficient to compensate and overcome the losses that will surely occur. The early exit does not respect the rules of money management and in the medium/long term can lead to a loss.

Chapter 2: Emotions in Trading

Often traders are influenced not only by knowledge, but they make decisions that are not always planned rationally but derive from the unconscious and its state of mind.

Usually, an inexperienced trader will create only one possible scenario, while a more experienced trader will identify two or more plausible scenarios. Having multiple scenarios is a positive factor because it allows you to focus on what will be considered most likely, based on knowledge of the financial markets, theoretical preparation on technical analysis, practical trading experience, your unconscious, and past results.

The most common trading emotions are happiness, calm, patience, euphoria, arrogance, anxiety, fear, immobility, sadness, loneliness, and despair.

Now we are going to analyze some of these emotions:

HAPPINESS.

Happiness is the emotion that should be the main element in a trader's mind. It must not only be a consequence of the positive results, but it is a factor that is born even before the positive results arrive. If a trader ties his happiness only to his positive results, he will fall into a spiral that, with the passage of time, will no longer make him appreciate his work.

In the situation where the 3:1 ratio is used, an inexperienced trader may be dissatisfied with the results obtained because he believes that he has not been able to correctly identify the subsequent price development too many times.

Successful traders, on the other hand, have a global view of the situation. They do not care about individual stop losses or a series of negative transactions but focus exclusively on achieving the final goal. The successful trader is happy before starting because he is confident of his means, his preparation, his psychological firmness, and is also happy with his work. Instead, many people approach the world of trading to earn a lot of money, and in a short time, without preparation and at the first obstacle, they give in to despair.

An attitude of discouragement will certainly not make you analyze the market in a calm and rational way.

CALM.

Calm is another emotion that a successful trader must have. An impatient and nervous trader is likely to carry out operations dictated exclusively by these emotions and not by the signals provided by the graphical analysis. The working mentality based on the assumption "the more you work, the more you earn," is not valid in trading.

The trader must have calm and coolness to try to identify and exploit only the most interesting situations–the most predictable ones. In this way, there will be days when perhaps no position should be opened. This does not mean that it has not worked.

Once the most favorable conditions have been identified, positions can be opened on the market.

From that moment, the trader enters a new emotional state and will be under pressure. What he has to do will be to stay calm and he will have to remember the targets and stop losses he had set. The position may only remain open for a few minutes but, in other cases, it may last for several days. In moments of waiting, the trader must not panic, but keep calm and wait for the prices to make the desired and hypothesized movement.

Remember that if the market is not in the best conditions to trade, the trader must remain on hold. You don't have to operate at all costs. The rule "the more you trade, the more you earn" does not apply, and the rule "the more time you spend trading, the more you earn" is not true either. Quality counts, not quantity!

Let's take an example. Once the signals have been obtained and after deciding how much to invest in a certain position, the target and its stop-loss are identified. At the end of this process, you can send the buy signal to your online broker. Subsequently, everything that has been theoretically analyzed, that is, suppose we have opened a purchase transaction and that the price, immediately after our purchase, rises quickly until it reaches our target price. During this climb, the trader's mood will be positive and serene. The climb, in fact, developed quickly and this prevented the creation of particular tensions. If the other positions also unfold in the same way, the trader could go from a happy situation to one of euphoria.

The trader begins to accuse the excess of security that could make him arrogant towards the market. The trader feels invincible and is full of energy. Right at this moment a negative operation usually arrives and the common sense that should be present in the trader's head is lost.

The mistake he usually makes in doing this is to presume to identify every single movement in the market. Although the market does not provide clear operational insights, new positions are opening up that depend on this feeling of omnipotence, combined with growing greed. It is believed that the more positions you open, the more you can earn. This attitude leads to the opening of various positions that, in all likelihood, will not be successful, especially because there were not the initial conditions necessary for the development of the movement that the trader had assumed. Only the excess of confidence prompted the trader to open those positions. Sometimes, the trader fails to enter the stop loss or does not respect it. When the price moves in the opposite direction to that hoped for a significant loss is produced.

In this situation, the trader in question considers himself infallible and, although the price has fallen below its stop loss level, he prefers not to respect it by remaining with the open position as he is convinced that the price will resume rising.

Subsequently, it is very likely that the price will continue to fall and by the time the trader finally closes the position, the loss may have taken on a size that cancels out all previously made profits.

Indeed, if the price, after falling below the stop loss level, were to rise and return the position to profit, there would be a dangerous strengthening in the trader's conviction of his invincibility and the futility of setting a stop loss.

In fact, it is inevitable that sooner or later an erroneous operation will occur, not protected by a stop loss, which will therefore produce a consistent and difficult to recover the loss.

Trading also generates strong emotional tensions. For example, after closing an upward trade in profit, you see that prices continue their rise, going beyond the identified target. There is no illusion that the market stops moving after reaching our target or that, after reaching it, prices reverse their course. If prices continue to rise, the greedy trader, despite having made a profit, will experience a feeling of unhappiness, created by the greed of not having earned even more. This feeling of discontent will be detrimental to subsequent operations. If you are not happy when you make a profit, you will not be happy when you suffer the inevitable stop losses, with the consequence that the trader's work can become a negative experience with negative emotions and influence the ability to analyze the market with the necessary serenity.

If the trader is always dissatisfied, or because he has not identified the maximum reached by prices during an uptrend, or because he has suffered a loss, the results and emotions arising from his operation cannot be positive.

For example, you have correctly positioned the target and the relative profit-taking of an upward position just below an important graphic resistance. If the target is reached, the position must be closed and the trader must be happy with it. If this resistance is subsequently overcome by prices, the trader will not have to regret having exited the market. Rather, it will be the technical analysis that will tell us if there are conditions to open a new upward position. You will have lost some profit points but it will have been earned safely.

IMMOBILITY.

This is another condition in which the trader could find himself, after opening a position that does not immediately go towards his target. The insecure trader is unable to do anything other than viewing his own operating position that does not go in the desired direction. He remains motionless in his chair, with his eyes fixed on the monitor, as if he wants to mentally push the price in the desired direction. He cannot devote himself to anything else, wearing so-called "negative glasses," in which his mind will only look for the negative aspects in trading. Unconsciously, the trader will select the positions that have a high probability of loss; will place orders on inaccurate levels or let the position run past the stop loss. The trader must get out of this state of immobility as soon as possible!

To get out of this condition, he must first act on his body, coming out of that position curled up on the chair, with his eyes fixed on the video, hoping that the operation changes direction.

If things did not go in the right direction and you suffer a stop loss, the trader must take note and in some cases, perhaps it would be better to unplug, turn off the computer, and go for a walk in the park. Physical activity is always useful because the body produces positive endorphins that cancel out the negative ones and, upon returning to work, you will have the opportunity to return with a new positive mentality. Another important advice is not to operate when the negativity originates from external situations (work tensions, family, etc.) because it would be done hoping to guess an operation capable of reviving the day. If you are not in optimal mental conditions, it is better to refrain from opening trading positions and wait for better moments, remembering that trading is a job of quality and not quantity.

SADNESS AND DEFORT.

This is a feeling that the trader perceives in a situation in which he obtains less than excellent results or suffers a consecutive series of losses or, by not respecting the stop loss, incurs a loss that cancels the profits obtained up to that moment. At some point, he may even think he is not suitable for the job, also affecting his social behavior. The trader will begin to materialize the losses by thinking about those assets and activities that, due to the money lost in trading, he had to deprive.

So how can a trader be able to manage and deal with all these deleterious emotions?

First, a good trader must have an excellent knowledge of technical analysis and must have carried out a long period in simulated trading, thus building a foundation of trust and self-esteem.

If this security of what you are doing is lacking, the results of the operations will be left to luck and chance.

Trading is a job, and only with a professional and positive mindset will you be able to deal with these negative emotions. Having a positive mentality means rejoicing in the positive results that have been achieved because it represents the right reward for the hard work done, both for having studied and for the experience that has accumulated with simulated trading. In order to mentally face a loss, the trader will have to consider it as a normal and completely physiological error within his trading strategy.

Another mistake to take into consideration is to perceive the profit obtained from trading as simple or unrelated to our abilities. Considering it as such, we will compare the profit to a lottery win and in this case, the trader is not ready to receive this money because it is not aligned with his "financial level" and as a result, such money could be squandered.

Other Factors Affecting the Choice of a Financial Instrument

In addition to the characteristics of price and graphic conformation, it often operates due to other external factors, including:

1. **Coherence:** All of our actions are inspired by the respect of some rules that must be coherent with our way of being. In fact, in trading it may happen that you do not buy certain shares because they would go against our principles. For example, if I am a vegetarian, I wouldn't feel like buying shares in companies that sell meat. If I did, I would risk losing my capital because my way of being would make me feel guilty.

2. **Authoritativeness:** An authoritative source, such as the bank, could push us to purchase a specific financial asset. In fact, banks play a fundamental role since they direct investors' savings with their indications, but they are not always advice in the interests of investors. This means that in order to invest your money in a conscious and profitable way, you need to know how the financial markets move, what their rules are, and what strategies they use.

3. **Reciprocity:** When we have made a profit in a given financial activity, the memory of both the profit achieved and the name of the financial instrument with which it is operated remains in our mind. So this principle of reciprocity is triggered according to which a title that has earned us in the past will also earn us in the future. Therefore, we are led to open positions not so much for the opportunities it presents, but for having obtained a profit in the past. In fact, our mind tries to make us stay within what can be defined as our comfort zone. By making decisions already successfully tested in the past, we try to minimize mental efforts and any unexpected events, neglecting the opportunities present on other financial instruments. It is not certain that if an action has made us money in the past, it must necessarily do so in the future as well, since the technical conditions may have changed in the meantime.

4. **Sympathy:** It can also happen that an investor decides to invest in a share only out of personal sympathy. Maybe a Juventus fan could invest in this club not because he has seen opportunities, but only because it is his favorite team.

Another thing to avoid is wanting to immediately recover the loss. This attitude often generates other losses, with the risk that the trader will zero his capital and enter an emotional state of frustration and pessimism. As already mentioned, a successful trader knows that his strategies can generate losses because he is aware that small losses are normal.

Chapter 3: What You Need to Trade on Forex

Definitions and characteristics of the forex market

Forex (Foreign Exchange Market) is the largest financial market in the world. To give you an idea of how big it is, I can tell you that every day governments, central banks, large banking institutions, speculators, and multinational companies operate in the Forex market.

What differentiates Forex from other markets?

1. Unlike other markets (stocks, futures, commodities), Forex does not have a physical location and is not subject to precise rules. It is defined as "Over the Counter" (OTC). All transactions take place online through authorized international intermediaries.
2. There is more liquidity in the Forex market. The transactions can reach a value of approximately $5 trillion per day. The advantage of this very high liquidity is that all trades can be executed immediately.

   Furthermore, it is almost impossible for the price to be manipulated. To move 10 pips (Percentage In Point: the smallest price movement that a change can have) the USD//EUR exchange rate must be made with about 1 billion euros!!
3. Forex is a global market that is open 24 hours a day, five days a week. This is due to the numerous world time zones, which allows for high volatility and liquidity.

The most liquid times are those where two sessions overlap; i.e., the London//New York overlap and the Sidney//Tokyo overlap.

Forex Trading in the Sydney and Tokyo Sessions

The volumes during these two sessions represent around 20% of the global daily total and the majority of trading is focused on pairs that include the yen: USD//JPY and EUR/JPY. The main financial centers are Wellington, Sydney, Tokyo, Hong Kong, and Singapore.

Forex Trading in the European Session

The volume in this session represents about 50% of the daily total. When it overlaps with that of NY, it reaches the maximum liquidity peaks. The pairs most traded during this Session are: EUR/USD, with 39% of the total volume; the "cable" that is the GBP/USD exchange rate, with 23%;

the American dollar/Japanese yen (USD//JPY), with 17%; the American dollar//Swiss franc (USD//CHT), with 6%; and the American dollar//Canadian dollar (USD//CAD), with 5%.

Forex Trading in the New York Session

In this session, the volume represents approximately 20% of the total. The busiest time, as mentioned above, is the one corresponding to the European session.

The Most Traded Currencies

With 86% of all trades, the US dollar is the most traded currency (with its various pairs). Immediately after is the euro (EUR) with 37% and the third is the yen (JPY), with 17%. This is considering only the single currency. If, on the other hand, we look at the various currency crosses, the most traded combination is EUR/USD (28%) while the second and third place are occupied by the USD//JPY (14%), and the GBP//USD (11%).

1	United States Dollar	USD ($)
2	Euro	EUR (€)
3	Japanese Yen	JPY (¥)
4	British Pound	GBP (£)
5	Swiss Franc	CHF (Fr)
6	Australian Dollar	AUD ($)
7	Canadian Dollar	CAD ($)
8-9	Swedish Krona	SEK (kr)
8-9	Honk Kong Dollar	HKD ($)
10	Norwegian Krone	NOK (kr)
11	New Zeland Dollar	NZD ($)
12	Mexican Peso	MXN ($)
13	Singapore Dollar	SGD ($)
14	South Korean Won	KRW (₩)

Why Trade On Forex?

At the beginning of the chapter, I mentioned what differentiates Forex from other markets. We will now go into more specifics of why you should consider trading in this market.

- Forex has the largest number of transactions worldwide. The very high liquidity allows brokers to accept any purchase and sale price, of any quantity. In the stock market for example, it may happen that there is no execution or that there is only partial implementation due to lack of significant volumes on the demand or supply side. This is an important thing you have to pay attention to, especially when you operate with large capital;
- High liquidity prevents a few strong hands from taking control of the market by manipulating it. Insider trading is therefore much more difficult to pull off. Insider trading is the trading of a public company's stock or other securities (such as bonds or stock options) based on material, nonpublic information about the company;

FOREX

- In Forex, the typical brokerage commissions envisaged for stock markets are not provided. The only cost is represented by the Bid/Ask spread (the difference between the first Bid price (Money) and the first Ask price (Letter) expressed in pips);

- There is the possibility of operating with reduced capital (although I always recommend starting with 5/10k). Thanks to the leverage effect, it is not necessary to deposit the total amount but only the required margin.

   Let me clarify with an example: If the broker offers a leverage of 100:1, you will need to deposit only $1,000 to trade with 100k. If the leverage offered is 50:1, you will have to deposit $2,000 instead. In this way, you have a multiplier effect of the possible gains, but also of the losses.

   For example, if you invest $1,000 with a leverage of 1:200, it means that the capital is moved 200 times, as if it were $200,000. This means that a gain of 1% is obtained not on 1,000 euros (therefore 10 euros), but on 200,000 ($2,000).

   It is a double-edged sword, but if handled well it can bring you a lot of satisfaction. The advice is to open a Forex account with at least $5,000/$10,000 available. This allows you to be more relaxed in the event that the first trades do not go in the expected direction and, at the same time, prevents the first losses from immediately burning the bill;

- You can build both Long and Short operations. You can then buy a cross-currency by expecting it to go up: in this case, the trade is called a 'long.' Or, you can sell a cross currency by expecting it to go down: in this case, the operation is called 'short.' You can have a graph that can also be analyzed on reduced time-frames, e.g. 1 minute, because the volume of transactions is very high, which often does not happen in stock markets with modest volumes, whose graphs have numerous holes and are therefore not easily analyzed with the classic tools of Technical Analysis;

- The Forex market is the one that is best suited to pure Technical Analysis, as there are reliable trends, repeating graphical figures, supports and resistances of good consistency respected, retracements attributable to the levels identified by Fibonacci, and movements that can be analyzed through normal indicators quantities.

That's Why Forex Is The Market With More Liquidity

Five main figures operate in Forex:

1. Central Banks: They generally intervene on Forex for monetary policy reasons;
2. The big business banks: They buy for hedging needs and their own speculation. About 75% of total trading profits come from Forex. In fact, these banks cover more than half of the volume of all world trade;
3. Large multinationals: They intervene on the Forex market to limit or cancel the exchange rate risk because also operating outside their own state, they buy or sell products in different currencies;
4. Investment funds: They are generally on Forex to diversify their investments;
5. Gi Hedge Fund: They make short-term operations with large capital and high financial levers. They trade in Forex for speculative reasons.

In addition to these Big 5, there are also private traders who cover about 10% of the trading volume and operate for speculative purposes.

What You Need to Trade On Forex

At this point, I think you understand the size and potential of this market and you are rightly asking yourself, "Okay, this is all very good. But what do I need to get started?"

I will try to explain it to you in the clearest and simplest way possible.

Today, trading on Forex is simple. Thanks to the internet, you can in fact get access to any data stream directly from your home PC. So, the first prerequisite is to have a PC. Initially, a large screen is also good so that you can monitor about six graphs but as soon as you get used to it you will need another screen to have coverage for twelve graphs. The goal is to follow the correlations between different markets to analyze price trends and their impact. Try to have a fast internet connection.

FOREX

Before starting to operate and signing a contract with a Broker, I recommend that you learn how to master technical analysis.

After this study phase, you must (yes, "you must" not "you can") start a period of paper trading. To do Paper Trading, you will need to open a demo account on a trading platform so you can begin to become familiar with it and implement your strategies using only virtual money. Getting positive trades during this period does not give the certainty of achieving the same results with real money.

When you start using real money, you will realize that emotions of Fear and Greed will come into play, which, if badly managed, do not lead you to have that peace of mind in the operation that you have with Paper Trading.

Initially, you can follow some companies that provide operational indications to begin to understand how the most experienced investors move. I recommend Tradermade or E-bull. In any case, a short internet search will suffice to find the right platform for you.

What must remain with you from this chapter is that becoming a trader takes time to study and understand the behavior of the markets. In the study and paper-trading phase, 2-3 hours a day must be dedicated to this new profession, which can be carried out simultaneously with your main one. If you really can't give even 1 hour, that's fine. Remember that the more time you spend on it, the faster you will improve.

The great traders carve out very specific moments of the day and certainly of longer duration.

Useful Definitions:

Before starting the next chapter, it is important to know the meanings of these terms:

Exchange rate: This is the relationship between two currencies. The first is called "certain" and is placed in the numerator, while the second is "uncertain" and is placed in the denominator. The buy/sell order refers to the currency placed in the numerator.

So, if you open a buy (long) position on the EUR/USD (euro/dollar) you think that the euro (EUR) will appreciate or that the US dollar (USD) will depreciate.

Conversely, if you open a short position, you think that the euro will depreciate or that the dollar will appreciate.

The EUR/USD ratio indicates how many units of USD are needed to buy or sell one unit of Eur.

The base currency (the one placed in the numerator) for most pairs is the US dollar, with the exception of EUR/USD, GBP/USD, NZD/USD and AUD/USD.

The euro, on the other hand, is the base currency for all the pairs with which it crosses, while the pound sterling (GBP) is the base for all the others except for the EUR.

Spot market: The spot Forex market is OTC (Over the Counter). It allows you to operate in leverage with margins whose value is established by your broker. The operations have a value of two days, after which the rollover comes into play, which postpones the value date after the payment/collection of interest.

If the position is not closed by 11:59 pm (GMT + 1), the interest rate differential of the two currencies will be credited or debited. This rollover operation takes place automatically on the account if the trading position is not closed on the day.

Interest rate: Each currency has one that varies over time. If the trader's foreign exchange position is held for more than two currency days (spot market), interest will be collected on the currency purchased and paid on the one sold.

Quotes and spreads: Indicative prices are provided by the main operators to info-provider circuits such as Bloomberg. Instead, operational prices are mainly provided by brokers. The main ones operating in the Forex market are EBS and Reuters dealing 2,000 and 3,000. These two telematic brokers have in fact supplanted the figure of the physical one who sends orders by telephone.

FOREX

Chapter 4: The Basics of Forex

THE ORDERS

Market Order	to buy or sell immediately
Limit Order	max/min price at which you are willing to buy/sell.
Stop Order/ Limit stop order	used to limit the loss.
Contingent Orders	- OCO (Order Cancel Order) - MIF (Market If Touched)

One of the first things a Forex trader needs to do to start trading is to place orders on the platform they are trading on. These are the main types of orders:
1. Market orders
2. Limit orders
3. Stop orders

Market Orders

When you open a market order, as the word says, you want to be filled by the current market price. This means that you are willing to buy at the Ask price or sell at the Bid price. The various prices are displayed by the broker you choose to trade with. Between the Bid and the Ask, there is a gap that is measured in pips and is called the Bid/Ask spread.

Everything will be clearer to you with an example:

On your trading platform, you will see: EUR/USD: Bid 1,336/Ask 1,338

- The Bid 1,336 is the price at which your broker is willing to buy the euro-dollar exchange rate, so it is the price at which you are willing to sell when you want to exit the market;
- The Ask 1,338 is the price at which your broker is willing to sell the

37

euro-dollar exchange rate, so it is the price you have to pay if you want to enter that exchange in the market.

In this case, if you want to *enter* with a market order, it means that you are willing to buy at 1.338 and if you want to *exit* with a market order, you are willing to sell at 1.336.

Keep in mind that you must be willing to pay a little extra to have the security of an instant execution. In situations with important macroeconomic data spread, the Bid/Ask spread can widen abnormally (4-8 pips), in these cases, it may happen that the selling price is very low and the purchase price very high.

Limit Orders

When you open the limit order, as the word implies, you are establishing a very specific entry or exit condition. Once you set your limit price, it cannot be higher, but equal or lower (in case of purchase) or lower, but equal or higher (in case of sale).

Look at this example:

With the EUR/USD exchange rate at 1.332, you can set up a limit order like this:

limit buy at 1,328/limit sell at 1,342

• In the case of a limit buy, the purchase will only trigger if the exchange rate drops to 1.328. Even if it drops from 1.332 to 1.219, the purchase will not start, but will only start if it touches 1.328 or less.

• In the second case, however, the sell order will be triggered only if the exchange rate manages to rise to 1.342.

[The difference existing between the price established for closing the position and the price at which it is actually executed is called "slippage." If the execution is at 1.3289, the slippage is only one pip; if the execution is at 1.3280, the slippage is instead of 10 pips.]

Stop Orders

When you set a stop order, you do it mainly to avoid losing too much money, or to enter short. Once the price level has been established, the stop order will go into action if and only if that level is touched.

For example, with the EUR/USD exchange rate at 1.336, if you enter a Sell EUR/USD at 1.327 stop order, you would go down on the euro-dollar exchange rate only if the latter were to go down until it touches the price 1,327. If you are already in the bull market, your stop order will not be executed as long as the trend is bullish. At least a trend inversion does not occur, and the price reaches 1.327 and at that point, the stop will be triggered to protect the position.

The orders just described can also be used together by combining them.

For example, you can open a limit stop order (limit order + stop order).

If you use this order, you want to open a position with well-defined price limits:

• **Stop order**: the price that triggers the order;

• **Limit order**: limit within which the price must be in order to be executed.

If, for example, you have noticed that 1.35 is a good place to enter, you can enter a limit stop order like this:

buy EUR/USD at 1.35 stop, limit 1.354

If the price touches 1.35 the order becomes a limit order with an execution limit at 1.354 and will therefore be executed within the range 1.35-1.354 and not beyond. Be careful because in periods of high volatility, the order may remain unexecuted if it is passed without being touched.

Other Orders

There are also other orders besides the three main ones I have described to you. I will talk about it more for cognitive purposes, but I will not go into too much detail because I believe that it is enough to know and study the three main types of orders to do well in Forex.

Remember, get to where you have complete knowledge of everything but specialize in that 20% of information that leads you to have 80% of the results.

Order Cancel Order (OCO)

This type of order involves the placing of two distinct orders, one for purchase and one for sale. As soon as one of the two is executed, the other is automatically canceled.

It can be used during congestion phases (trading range) to take advantage of the start of a directional movement.

Market If Touched (MIT)

These orders are similar to limit orders: Once the limit price is touched, the orders become market orders. (The execution, however, may be above or below the indicated price)

MARGINS AND FINANCIAL LEVERAGE

The operation on the Forex market requires that a position be taken on the market, such as to exploit the increase in the value of one currency with respect to another. The latter is called the "Exchange rate" and can be expressed in two ways:

1. How many units of the first currency are needed to buy or sell a unit of the second (Uncertain by Certain)?
2. How many units of the second currency are needed to buy or sell one unit of the first (Certain for Uncertain)?

Considering, for example, the euro/dollar exchange rate at January 2012 values: in case 1 there is an exchange rate of 0.7668; in case 2 of 1.304.

To avoid confusion, a convention has been chosen whereby the base currency (also known as "certain") is placed in the first place and the countervalue currency (also called "uncertain") in the second. The latter is the one that varies the value as the price changes. If the EUR/USD price is 1.304, it means that 1.304 dollars are needed to buy 1 euro.

In general:

The euro (EUR) is always a certain currency, therefore all the euro exchange rates against other currencies express the amount of these necessary to purchase 1 euro.

The pound sterling (GBP) is the equivalent currency against the euro but is a certain currency with respect to the others.

The US dollar (USD) is the equivalent currency against the euro and the pound, but it is a certain currency against the Japanese yen (JPY) and the Swiss franc (CHF).

When you operate on the currency market, you do not do it directly on just one, but on the exchange of one against the other. Available shifts are generally referred to as a "pair" or "cross."

On Forex, it is possible to take long or short positions on the cross as on any other financial instrument.

FOREX

Taking a long position on the EUR/USD cross means expecting an increase in the value of the euro against the dollar (a short position instead implies the opposite expectation).

The trading operations are carried out on quantities greater than a certain minimum quantity called "lot." Normally the quantity is considered as a lot 100,000, but for some time it has also been possible to operate with mini-lots of 10,000 or even lower (e.g. 5,000).

Let's assume that the Bid/Ask on the EUR/USD is:

Bid = 1.28160 Ask = 1.28180

If you want to take a long position on EUR/USD, you have to buy by placing a market order at 1.2818.

Assuming that the euro strengthens the Bid/Ask becomes:

Bid = 1.28930 Ask = 1.28950

If you want to close the position, you can do it by selling, again with a market order, at 1.2893.

If the trade was made with an amount of $100,000 (with reference to the counter currency, in this case, the dollar) you will get the following profit:

P&L = (1.28930-1.28180) * 100,000 = 0.00750 * 100,000 = 750 USD

Therefore, 75 pips of profit correspond to 750 USD of profit.

The pip is the minimum admissible variation for each exchange rate (the measure for which other financial instruments is called tick). In the example considered, one pip corresponds to 10 dollars.

It is possible to convert the amount obtained by aligning it with the currency of the account in euros. In this case, the calculation to be made is as follows: 750/1.2818 = 585 euros

If he had taken a short position by selling EUR/USD at 1.28160 and then closed it at 1.28950, there would have been a loss of -79 pips instead. In that case, if you chose to invest only one lot, as in the previous example, the loss would have been $790.

It has been said that the pip is the smallest movement to which a change can be subject and that it forms the basis for calculating the gains in Forex.

If you look at some changes, you can see that the price is almost always made up of five numbers: EUR/USD: 1.4234-; USD/JPY: 120.32.

In the first case, if the price rises from 1.4234 to 1.4284 it can be said that it has increased by 50 pips. If instead, it falls from 1.4234 to 1.4204, it has dropped by 30 pips.

FOREX

In this way, it is easy to calculate profits or losses: in a position of 100,000 EUR/USD, a variation of 50 pips equals 500$ of gain or loss (100,000 x 0.0050 = 500).

Before placing any order on the market, it is important to calculate the potential profits and losses that can be obtained in relation to the margin required by the broker. For example, if we assume to operate on the EUR/USD exchange rate, a lot of 100,000 euros moves.

In general:

a. the specified quantity (100,000) is the quantity in euros, i.e. the currency placed on the numerator, on which margins are calculated to operate

b. the profits or losses are instead expressed in dollars, or in the currency denominator

1 pip Value Tab:

CROSS	Minimal Variation	1 Pip Value
Eur/Usd	.0001	Eur 100.000 * .0001 = Usd 10
Gbp/Usd	.0001	Gbp 100.000 * .0001 = Usd 10
Eur/Ypy	.01	Eur 100.000 * .01 = Jpy 1000
Usd/Jpy	.01	Usd 100.000 * .01 = Jpy 1000
Eur/Chf	.0001	Eur 100.000 * .0001 = Chf 10
Eur/Gbp	.0001	Eur 100.000 * .0001 = Gbp 10

Contracts Value Tab:

CROSS	STANDARD CONTRACT		MINI CONTRACT	
	Value of a Contract	1 Pip Value	Value of a Contract	1 Pip Value
Eur/Usd	Eur 100.000	Usd 10	Eur 10.000	Usd 1
Gbp/Usd	Gbp 100.000	Usd 10	Gbp 10.000	Usd 1
Eur/Jpy	Eur 100.000	Jpy 1000	Eur 10.000	Jpy 100
Eur/Chf	Eur 100.000	Chf 10	Eur 10.000	Chf 1
Eur/Gbp	Eur 100.000	Gbp 10	Eur 10.000	Gbp 1
Usd/Jpy	Usd 100.000	Jpy 1000	Usd 10.000	Jpy 100
Usd/Chf	Usd 100.000	Chf 10	Usd 10.000	Chf 1
Usd/Cad	Usd 100.000	Cad 10	Usd 10.000	Cad 1

SPOT TRADING

The tools to operate on Forex are basically of two types:

1. "Spot" transactions

2. "Forward" transactions through swaps, futures, and options

When trading currencies, it is important to know all the costs associated with the operation as they can significantly affect the profitability of the operations. In particular, it is necessary to know and evaluate the three different types of costs:

- a) The spread
- b) Interests
- c) The margins

The Spread

There are two prices for each currency pair (The Bid/Bid price and the Ask/Ask price). The Bid/Ask spread is the difference between the immediately available price to sell (bid) and the immediately available price to buy (ask).

The trader must consider the spread very carefully, as its value constitutes the minimum movement that the market must make to bring his position into protection. The spread is measured in pips.

The Interests

Interest represents the cost of financing to carry forward your currency positions over the days (in this case, we speak of overnight positions).

If you are buying a currency with a higher interest rate than that offered by the secondary currency, you will receive an interest rate on your exposure equal to the differential between the rates on the two currencies.

If, on the other hand, you are selling a currency with a higher interest rate than the secondary currency, you will pay an interest rate on your exposure equal to the differential between the rates on the two currencies.

The Financial Leverage

One of the reasons why Forex has been widespread is related to the possibility of using financial leverage. Leverage gives you the opportunity to control very large sums by depositing only a small amount into your account. For example,

FOREX

with leverage of 1:100, you can open a standard lot (100,000 euros) with only 1,000 euros (1/100 of the nominal value). Or, you can trade a mini-lot (10,000 euros) having only 100 euros available.

With 1:1 leverage (which is equivalent to having no leverage) investing 1,000 euros, a 1% change would correspond to 10 euros.

With leverage of 1:100, investing 1,000 euros would control 100,000 euros, which represents the nominal value on which the variation is calculated. Assuming as in the previous case, that this is 1%, it will correspond to 1,000 euros.

Using financial leverage, you have the opportunity to increase the return on investment (ROI) exponentially: without leverage, if you invest 1,000 euros and get 10, the ROI is 1%; with leverage, by investing the same amount you get 1,000, thus doubling the capital (ROI = 1000).

Margin

The margin represents the share of capital that must be used as a guarantee to open a trade. It is related to leverage in an inversely proportional manner: the higher the leverage, the lower the margin required. Vice versa, the lower the leverage, the greater the required margin.

Here is the formula to calculate the percentage required by the broker for the margin:

Margin in% = 100/leverage ratio

The margin required for every single trade is given by:

Margin required per trade = Current price * Units traded * margin in%

Leverage				Margin
01:10	>	100/10	=	10%
01:50	>	100/50	=	2%
1:100	>	100/100	=	1%
1:200	>	100/200	=	0.5%
1:500	>	100/500	=	0.2%

Assume that you have an account of $2,000, operating with leverage of 100:1, and buying a mini-lot (nominal value 10,000 euros) on the EUR/ USD.

Margin in% = 100/100 = 1% = 0.01

Margin required per trade = 1.3030 * 10,000 * 0.01 = $130

Remember that this $130 cannot be used to open new positions because they are "blocked" as collateral to cover any losses.

Everything else, i.e. what remains in the account after calculating the profits and losses of the open positions, is called usable margin and as the word says, you can use it to open new positions.

Consequently, the more positions you open at the same time, the more the margin used goes up and the one you can use goes down. When the money you can use is zeroed, your broker will "margin call," where you will be asked to load more money into your account. If you don't load the money, the broker will automatically close all open positions. This is done to prevent you from losing more than you have on your account. So pay close attention to margin calls because it would be a shame if they close profitable positions you have opened.

Using leverage can be dangerous if you don't know it well. In fact, the risk is that of opening too many and/or too large positions with respect to one's own account, with the danger that losses can quickly eliminate one's liquidity.

Rollover

The "rollover" is an automatic procedure used by those who operate on Forex. Most people who invest in this market rarely want the physical delivery of the currency.

This mechanism ensures that the position at the end of the day is closed and immediately reopened, in order not to undergo physical delivery. It is a process in which you do not have to worry that it gives you the possibility to keep open positions for several days.

At the end of the day, if you don't close the position, the bank will rollover. The position you have opened is closed at the Bid or Ask price (respectively for long or short positions) and the relative daily profit or loss is debited/credited to the account. The reopening of the position occurs at the same time as closing, with the carrying price undergoing an adjustment proportional to the difference between the interest rates of the currencies making up the pair.

If you want to calculate the cargo price, this is the formula:

PC rett = Price rif * S

Price rif is the price of the cross obtained with the following criterion:

1. Bid price at 11:40 for open long positions
2. Ask price at 11:40 for open short positions

S is the coefficient for the calculation of the new carrying price.

The central bank issues an interest rate that is tied to each currency. The interest rate for the currency sold is referred to here as the short currency rate, while the interest rate for the purchased currency is called the long currency rate. To these two elements, a third must be added, relating to the share (2%) that the bank retains as a loan.

Forward Trading

The forward foreign exchange market includes all trading operations, both purchase and sale, with settlement currency other than the spot currency, with set deadlines and at a set exchange rate.

A forward transaction can be defined as a contract by which the parties agree to exchange, at a certain maturity and at a predefined price, one quantity of currency for another.

Forward transactions take place over the counter (OTC), i.e. outside a regulated market and with characteristics established by the contracting parties themselves.

Market makers guarantee liquidity by quoting the various maturities (3 6 12 months). You could use this type of transaction for foreign exchange risk hedging strategies.

It should be noted that, if the interest rate differential between the two currencies is positive, the forward price is lower than the spot price. Conversely, if the spread is negative, the forward price is greater than the spot price.

The variables that determine the forward price are:
- The spot price;
- The interest rates of the currencies involved in the transaction;
- Time.

If you want to calculate the premium or forward exchange discount, you can use this formula:

((Spot Price * (uncertain currency rate - certain currency rate) * days))/(36,000 + (certain currency rate * days)

The forward exchange rate is therefore determined by the sum of the spot exchange rate to which the premium/discount must be added/subtracted. The latter is determined by the interest rate differential that is recorded for the entire period of the transaction.

The Future

The future is a forward financial instrument with which a subject undertakes to buy/sell, on a specific future date, a currency at a predetermined price.

The technical structure of the currency future is standardized, with quarterly maturities (March-June-September-December).

For the euro/dollar exchange rate, for example, the main features are:

Contract value: 130,000 euros

Minimum price change (tick): 0.0001

Tick value: $14.5

Deadlines: March/June/September/December

The Options

An option is a contract that confers, upon payment of a premium, the right to buy (call) or sell (put) the underlying financial asset, at a certain price (strike price), at a certain date in the future, or by a certain future date.

The options on the euro/dollar futures are listed on the Chicago Mercantile Exchange (CME). These are of two types:

Call option: and the right to purchase euros, selling the equivalent value in USD, at the fixed strike price.

PUT option: this is the right to sell euros, buying the equivalent value in USD, at the set strike price.

The option price consists of the following elements:
- The spot change;
- The interest rate differential between the two currencies;
- Volatility;
- Duration;
- The strike price.

You can break the premium down into intrinsic value and time value.

When you buy, the intrinsic value is the difference between the market price and the strike price. It, therefore, expresses the profit that would be realized if the option were exercised at the same time as the contract is stipulated.

There are three different situations:
1. In the Money (ITM) is an option, which, if exercised immediately, allows you to buy the underlying at a better price than the market price.
2. At the Money (ATM) is instead, an option with a strike price equal to the market price of the underlying.
3. Out of the Money (OTM) is an option that the holder has no convenience to exercise immediately.

You can get the time value by subtracting the intrinsic value from the premium. It is made up of two elements: the volatility and the duration of the option.

The time value expresses the probability that the option can assume, by the expiry date, a positive intrinsic value or, if it already has one (i.e., In the Money), the probability that it increases.

Chapter 5: Macroeconomic Analysis

The price of a given product is determined by the match between supply and demand. The currency market also behaves in the same way, with the combination of some fundamental factors that significantly influence the exchange rate between different currencies. The demand for money comes mainly from importers who buy goods and services from a country with a certain currency, and from investors interested in holding securities denominated in that same currency. The request, however, also comes from central banks both for reasons of financial investment and for objectives linked to monetary policy choices.

There are fundamental factors that assume a relevant importance in determining the price; the economic, commercial, and financial conditions of a country are in fact decisive for evaluating the strength and solidity of a currency. For this reason, Forex operators, in order to understand the behavior of different exchange rates, focus on the performance of some macroeconomic variables, namely:

- Balance of payments;
- Labor market;
- Rate of inflation;
- Interest rates;
- Money supply;
- Productivity;
- The balance (debt/deficit) and income (GDP) of the state.

1. The balance of payments

If you operate on Forex, you must be very careful with the monthly figures relating to the balance of payments (it is an accounting document in which all transactions are recorded) as there are very close relationships between the trend of exchange rates and transactions in goods, services, and financial instruments that a country has with foreign countries. By impious, a country that imports more than it exports produces a deficit in its balance of payments account, which will necessarily have to be financed. On the contrary, the capitals arriving from abroad, in excess of those that flow out, generate a financial surplus for the country that receives them. The import/export of goods and services produces a financial deficit/surplus whose consistency significantly affects the monetary flows that leave/enter a country.

2. The labor market

The employment situation of each country (especially the unemployment rate) significantly affects the behavior of the currency. In general, a low unemployment rate signals a constantly expanding economy, with satisfactory annual GDP growth.

However, be careful because this situation could create inflationary tensions with a possible increase in rates by the central bank.

Conversely, a high unemployment rate indicates a problematic economic condition, with poor growth and a difficult financial state. When a country has a high unemployment rate, the central bank can intervene with a reduction in short-term rates in order to stimulate recovery.

3. The rate of inflation

A rising rate of domestic inflation makes goods destined for exports less competitive. A possible rebalancing can come from a depreciation of the currency, especially if exports are a fundamental element for the economic growth of the country in question. It could be the central bank itself that supports the weakening of the currency.

Inflationary pressures are a determining factor in central banks' monetary policy choices: the ECB, for example, has a primary objective of "maintaining price stability" through an inflation rate close to, but below, 2%. A consistent rise above this last level could force it to promptly increase short-term rates, with a consequent strengthening of the single currency.

4. The differential between interest rates

The increase in the differential between two currency areas usually produces an appreciation, both in the short and medium term, of the currency, which guarantees a higher return.

To give an example, over the last few years, the dollar has suffered a heavy devaluation against those currencies that offer higher interest rates (e.g., NZD, CAD). This is the phenomenon known as Carry Trade. Rising interest rates usually signal a positive trend in the economy, attracting direct investments that lead to an increase in the demand for currency in the country affected by the phenomenon.

However, the same interest rate differential can affect the country's growth expectations, as the persistence of high rates for a prolonged period can slow down the development of the economy, creating the conditions for a subsequent depreciation of the currency.

5. Growth-productivity differential

A country that can boast a solid industrial, financial, and technological structure naturally attracts capital for investments. This produces an appreciation of the country's currency, even in less positive phases. Good productivity values indicate a strong ability of the system to keep production costs low, containing internal inflationary pressures and allowing the central bank to implement an expansive monetary policy more easily.

6. Public accounts

Developments in public finances have a significant impact on exchange rate behavior. This is influenced by the reactions of the monetary authorities to any worsening of public finances (e.g., an increase in the annual deficit) to the rise in short-term policy rates, which also cause long-term rates on the bond markets to rise due to the decline in confidence of institutional investors' ability to repay their debt.

Such reactions, of both the monetary authorities and the bond markets, are justified by the consequences of a possible worsening of the financial situation. That is, expectations of higher inflation or taxation emerge. In both cases, the risk increases for the future of the country concerned, since, if the returns on real and financial assets do not rise, the exchange rate itself will offset the risk, with an inevitable depreciation.

MACROECONOMIC DATA

The macroeconomic data capable of influencing the behavior of different currencies can be divided into four categories.

1. Confidence indicators (concern both consumers and businesses)

- ZEW
- IFO
- CCI

2. Indicators of general economic activity referring to:

- real estate market
- labor market
- service sector
- manufacturing sector
- GDP/PIL

3. Central bank activity indicators:

- US Federal Reserve (Fed)
- ECB (European Central Bank)
- SNB (Swiss National Bank)
- BOE (Bank of England)
- BOJ (Bank of Japan)
- PBOC (People's Bank of China)

4. Indicators referring to inflation:

- CPI (consumer prices)
- PPI (producer prices)

Trust Indicators

In Europe, the most important confidence indicators are the ZEW and the IFO.

The ZEW expresses the confidence of 350 institutional investors in Germany with respect to the expectations of economic growth in the following six months. It is released monthly and covers both the German economic outlook and that of the entire euro area. This index is expressed in points and is the difference between the percentage of optimists and pessimists. The ZEW is much more volatile than the IFO.

The IFO index expresses the general situation of the German economy and is calculated on the basis of 100, as follows:

• If it is growing and is above 100, it indicates that the economy is expanding.

• If it is below 100, it signals that the economy is contracting.

It can be divided into two parts: the first refers to the current climate of confidence, the second to future expectations. It is calculated through surveys conducted on a sample of 7,000 German companies that are asked for an opinion on the current economic trend and future forecasts (usually for the next six months).

In America, the most important indicator relating to confidence is the Consumer Confidence Index (CCI), which is published monthly on the last Tuesday of each month and is the main tool for measuring the degree of US consumer confidence. The figure is mainly influenced by the expected purchasing power of buyers for the following semester.

The relationship that is created between this and the spending power is very strong:

- When the index assumes low values, consumption could suffer a decrease.
- When the index takes on high values, consumers will tend to increase their purchases.

Indicators Concerning General Economic Activity

As for the American manufacturing sector, the most important data are:

1. The Chicago Purchasing Managers Index (PMI)

PMI is a regional index that comes from a survey conducted with the purchasing managers of 200 companies in the manufacturing sector from the area, to test their opinions on the performance of their sector. It is published on the last day of each month.

A PMI value above 50 points indicates that the economy is expanding while a lower value signals a phase of economic contraction.

2. The manufacturing ISM (Institute for Supply Management)

ISM is a national report used to assess the health of the US manufacturing sector. It is based on a survey carried out among the purchasing managers of about 300 industrial companies in the country and is published monthly on the first working day of the month following the one to which it refers. It is the most important report for this sector in the US.

3. The Philadelphia Fed Index

This is published every third Thursday of the month. It is the first manufacturing data that is released relative to the month to which it refers (it is therefore an anticipator of the Purchasing Managers Index and of the manufacturing ISM).

It is able to promptly grasp the changes in the general conditions of the sector's activity and consequently in consumption expenses.

4. Orders for durable goods

This monthly statistic is very important because through the thirty-day variation of new orders from manufacturing, a good indication of the state of health of the industry can be obtained, as most of the industrial production is made to order.

The data are also collected net of the defense and transport sector (given the volatility of orders in these sectors) and the survey is conducted on 4,200 companies located in the United States grouped into 89 industrial categories, for each of which three different aspects are considered:

• new orders

• shipments

• back orders

When orders for durable goods are growing, it means that the economy is strengthening.

5. The GDP/PIL

This is the data that summarizes the general economic trend of a country (Gross Domestic Product).

It is made up of the sum of the value of goods and services produced within the country by companies (both domestic and foreign).

If the data is positive, it reflects the rate at which a country is growing. If it is negative, it reflects the rate at which a country is contracting.

Both quarterly and annual values are published. The main components of the GDP are:

- Investments;
- Private consumption;
- Public spending;
- The difference between exports and imports

6. The labor market

All data relating to the performance of the labor market are analyzed with the utmost attention by traders who operate on Forex. Jobless claims (unemployment benefits), non-farm payrolls (new jobs created), and the unemployment rate are very important.

• The unemployment rate

Published on the first Friday of each month and measures the ratio of unemployed to the workforce. From this data, we understand the current situation of the labor market and it is fundamental for understanding the future evolution of the national economy. Markets usually react positively to a reduction in the unemployment rate, as it anticipates greater consumption of goods and a general improvement in the economy.

• Jobless claims

Released weekly every Thursday. They are a forerunner of the labor market report, which is instead published monthly by the Bureau of Labor Statistics. This is a figure that measures the national number of new registrations for obtaining unemployment benefits provided by the state and is characterized by high volatility.

It is useful for analyzing potential changes in labor market conditions: an increase in subsidy requests signals an increase in layoffs and therefore a potential increase in the unemployment rate.

• Non-farm payrolls

Published by the Department of Labor on the first Friday of each month. This figure measures the new jobs created or lost monthly at the national level in companies not operating in the agricultural sector. It is at the center of the attention of operators, who prefer it to the unemployment rate, as it is characterized by a sectoral differentiation (construction, services, and manufacturing) which makes it very useful for understanding the trend in the various economic sectors.

An increase in the number of payslips is usually welcomed by the financial markets as it indicates an improvement in domestic economic activity. While a contraction in employment usually has a negative effect on the markets (causes both stock exchanges and the US dollar to drop), it indicates a slowdown in the American economy.

7. The real estate market

The most important data relating to this sector concern:

• **The sale of houses**. These are surveys that reflect the health of the construction sector. Generally, a growth in sales is welcomed by the financial markets while a contraction, especially if unexpected, can trigger a decline in equity indices.

• **Building permits**. They are released on the 16th of each month and, together with the data relating to the construction of new homes, indicates the possible evolution of the real estate sector. This is important data for interpreting future developments in the construction sector, as most of the permits obtained translate into the start of construction of private housing units in the following months.

8. Indicators related to inflation

The two most important macroeconomic data relating to inflation are producer and consumer prices.

Producer prices: The producer price index measures the variation, over time, of prices destined for producers in the various stages of the production process (raw products, intermediate goods, finished products). Specifically, changes in the prices of finished products are a useful indicator for analyzing the trend in commodity prices.

Those in the prices of semi-finished products and raw materials signal possible inflationary pressures. Operators look very carefully at the "core PPI" (the index calculated net of the food and energy components).

An increase in producer prices, especially if unexpected, is negatively welcomed by the stock market, as it can trigger a rise in the general price level.

The producer price index is the first indicator of inflation spread every month: through this data, it is therefore possible to anticipate any pressure on prices.

Consumer prices: The consumer price index (CPI) measures the trend in the cost of living, based on goods and services intended for consumers. Consumer prices are the best indicator of inflation.

As inflation rises, interest rates rise and vice versa. Equity markets typically weaken on a higher than expected figure as currency market participants react by buying domestic currency because they expect monetary authorities to raise the cost of money. The "core" data, concerning food and energy, is followed with greater attention as it represents the real change in prices.

The Activity of Central Banks

Central banks, in addition to directly influencing the currency markets with their monetary policy choices, affect the performance of the various currencies through the following:

Direct interventions on reference exchange rates: In this case, they buy or sell their own currency according to whether they aim at its strengthening or its weakening.

The publication of reference reports: The most important is the Beige Book published by the American Federal Reserve. It is published eight times a year, two weeks before each meeting of the Federal Open Market Committee, the executive committee of the Fed.

Communicate the health of the US economy through a comprehensive analysis of consumption, investments, and the labor market.

FOREX

Chapter 6: Forex Correlations

Markets are becoming more and more connected. In fact, the behavior of the four most important exchange rates (EUR/USD, GBP/USD, USD/JPY, EUR/JPY) has a direct impact on both bond and equity markets.

There are two primary situations in which we can find the financial markets:

A first condition defined as Risk on does not present particular tensions, and is characterized, as the word implies, by a certain propensity for risk, with investors looking for high returns. Liquidity shifts to more aggressive currencies that offer higher interest rates. At this stage, the New Zealand dollar, the Australian dollar, and the Canadian dollar usually tend to appreciate; they are very commodity currencies.

The second condition, defined as Risk off, is instead characterized by tensions and uncertainties. During this phase, the phenomenon of flight to quality occurs, which is a shift of liquidity towards assets with a low-risk profile such as the German bund or the Swiss franc.

These are the four most important changes.

EURO/DOLLAR

The euro/US dollar cross (EUR/USD) is responsible for approximately 30% of the volumes traded.

It is the most liquid pair in the world so daily volatility is usually very high. In some periods, the difference between the daily high and low has stood at around 130-150 pips.

The best times to trade on the EUR/USD

The time of day when the euro/dollar cross offers more trading opportunities is during the European session, so from 8.00 to 18.00 Europe time.

It is possible to draw guidelines but not every day is the same so don't rely on this information thinking it is foolproof or 100% safe.

a. From 3:00 am to 8:30 am (Washington) the market starts to take a direction. In particular, attention should be paid to the dissemination of macro data, especially the IFO index and the ZEW.

b. From 8:30 am to 10:00 am (Washington) market movements calm down for the lunch break in European markets.

c. From 10:00 am to 12:00 pm (Washington) trading is affected by the strong volatility caused by the opening of the American markets and by the macro affecting the United States.

d. From 12:00 pm to 1:30 pm (Washington) the most important movements usually occur before the European session ends.

e. From 1:30 pm to 6:00 pm (Washington) American traders usually operate which, in the wake of what is happening on the stock market, can trigger a physiological retracement from the main trend.

f. From 6:00 pm to 3:00 am (Washington) During the Asian session, the EUR/USD tends to consolidate in narrow trading ranges, which are usually broken at the opening of the European session.

Correlations

The euro tends to be positively correlated with financial assets, which are in turn negatively correlated with the dollar. In particular, a rising euro/dollar favors a rise in the stock markets while an excessive strengthening of the dollar usually triggers a decline in the stock markets.

In general, the euro/dollar exchange rate tends to be negatively correlated with the USD/CHF cross and positively correlated with the GBP/USD.

On a daily basis, the EUR/USD exchange rate tends to be more volatile on Wednesdays.

At the intraday level, the EUR/USD exchange rate tends to be more volatile during the European session.

STERLING/DOLLAR

The sterling/dollar exchange, known as the "cable," is one of the main pairs in the currency market due to the strong financial ties between the UK and the United States.

The cable is a volatile pair that statistically has a slow start to the week. On Monday, prices move much less than on other days, but on Tuesday there are important swings. Given this volatility, when trading on this pair, it is advisable to increase the stop loss, because the sudden fluctuations of a few dozen pips are the order of the day.

As London is the seat of the main world banks, there are the majority of the market makers and bank dealers, mainly responsible for transactions on GBP/USD. This implies that these institutional traders have a good view of their clients' positions and stop losses in their order book, and are famous for being true "stop-loss hunters." By this, I mean that it could manipulate the price by touching stop losses to get traders out of positions.

A crucial moment occurs at the opening in London, at 5:00 am Washington time, when very often the pound starts out in one direction, looking for stop losses, and then reverses course and generates the real directional movement of the day.

The best times to trade on the cable

Also for the cable, as well as for the EUR/USD exchange, it is possible to divide the day into different moments:

a. From 4:00 am to 6:00 am, Washington time, is the peak of volatility and are the crucial hours for the cable.

b. From 6:00 am to 7:00 am, Washington time, some important economic news for England can be released, with immediate repercussions on exchange rates.

c. From 7:00 am to 10:00 am, Washington time, the market calms down relatively.

d. From 10:00 am to 1:30 pm, Washington time, when the European session overlaps the American one, the market recovers.

Thereafter, the pound/dollar cross does not provide further operational indications.

Correlations

The pound is very sensitive to the prices of crude oil (i.e., natural products such as oil, diamond, etc.) of energy in general, because the production of the latter is responsible for about 10% of the British GDP. For this reason, an increase in the price of oil can cause a strengthening of the currency or, on the contrary, its decline can cause a weakening.

DOLLAR/YEN

Given the importance of the trade relations between the United States and Japan, the dollar/yen cross is very important because it is the reference pair for all crosses that include the yen.

The BOJ (Bank of Japan), in fact, intervenes on the exchange rate by buying yen and selling US dollars when the dollar/yen exchange rate falls below some critical thresholds (for example 76). Japan, in fact, being a major exporter, especially of technological products, has an interest in keeping its currency weak, making a competitive devaluation.

Volatility

The USD/JPY cross has an average range of about 100 pips and is therefore the least volatile of the exchange rates examined so far. It tends to take a very specific direction, overcoming resistance or yielding supports, in the hours in which the European session overlaps the American one. The most intense moments of trading are in fact the hours of the early European afternoon. However, although the volatility is lower, it is a pair that can still move significantly even when Europe is not operational, as it comprises two non-European currencies.

EURO/YEN

It is a more volatile pair than the USD/JPY, since it is characterized by an average daily range of about 200 pips.

Being active during the European session, the prices move constantly throughout the European day, but good movements are not excluded even when European traders are not in front of their screens.

In the European morning, the euro/yen exchange behaves regularly. In the afternoon, on the other hand, when the American markets open, there are frequent significant swings with wide trading ranges. Usually, however, it is from 15.30 until 18.00 European time that the change takes a very specific direction.

CORRELATIONS FOR TRADING

Correlation measures the relationship between two variables.

- A measure equal to +1 (the maximum) means that the two variables move in the same direction in 100% of cases;
- A correlation equal to -1 (the minimum) means that the movement between the two variables is identical in value, but occurs in the opposite direction in 100% of cases.

Correlations change over the course of days and months, although certain ratios have their own range within which they are. The EUR/USD and the USD/CHF, for example, boast a negative correlation that tends towards unity. This means that when the euro/dollar rises, the dollar/Swiss franc falls and vice versa.

Important: In the same way, simultaneously holding positions with correlation close to unity (for example EUR/USD and GBP/USD) does nothing but duplicate the risk to which the investor is exposed when operating on the market.

Operational Strategies Based On Correlations

The most important rule that the trader must respect to obtain positive results on Forex is the fact that both the entry and exit from the market must always have technical origins (for example, the breaking of a resistance or a support, a pattern of the candlestick analysis, the signal provided by an indicator).

The analysis of the correlations of the exchange rate on which it is intended to operate, however, can increase the probability of success of the operation. For example, there are exchange rates such as the euro/dollar and the dollar/Swiss franc that exhibit high negative correlations on each time frame analyzed.

This means that before going higher on the EUR/USD, you can look for a confirmation (downwards) on the USD/CHF chart. Similarly, you can decide to anticipate the exit from a position by identifying a weak situation on a cross that is positively correlated with the one on which you are working.

It is even more interesting to identify situations in which a change tends to anticipate the movements of another cross. The general rule is:

If the correlation is high (above 75) and positive, the crosses move in the same direction.

If the correlation is high (above 75) and negative, the crosses move in the opposite direction.

If the correlation is low (below 50) the crosses do not move in the same direction.

However, the existing combinations between the gearboxes are complex. Starting from the EUR/ USD (daily):

GBP/USD has an index of 32, which means that it does not move in the same direction as EUR/USD.

USD/CHF has an index of -85, which means that it moves in the opposite direction to EUR/ USD.

EUR/JPY has an index of 74.5, which means that it moves in the same direction as EUR/ USD.

In this way, after determining the trend of the EUR/USD, it is possible to construct operational strategies on the other crosses: for example, you can search for a sell operation on USD/CHF and/or a long operation on EUR/JPY.

In the Forex market, there are strong relationships between the various currency pairs. In these cases, we speak of "correlated pairs." For example, between EUR/USD and USD/CHF there is a negative correlation. When the EUR/USD goes up, the USD/CHF tends to go down and vice versa.

Very interesting are the positively correlated currencies; that is, the exchange rates that move more or less in parallel (e.g., the EUR/USD and the GBP/USD).

It should be remembered in this regard that currency pairs with CAD, AUD, and NZD tend to be positively correlated.

From an operational point of view, when correlated pairs lose correlation, it is only a matter of time before they find it again, according to a phenomenon called "mean reversion."

CURRENCIES AND RAW MATERIALS

The behavior of individual currencies is also conditioned by the trend in commodity prices.

In particular, the economic results of the countries that make up the largest producers and exporters depend, to a considerable extent, on their prices. The currencies of these intact countries tend to appreciate or depreciate following the positive or negative trend of the prices of the various commodities.

Knowing the correlations between commodities and various exchange rates, therefore, is fundamental to understanding the behavior of a certain currency. For example, if a bullish breakout occurs on gold, it generates an immediate strengthening of the Australian dollar, since Australia is one of the largest producers of gold.

1. Oil

The trend in oil directly affects the behavior of the Canadian dollar. Canada has the second largest crude oil reserves in the world and has one of the most accessible and liquid currencies. For this reason, its currency often gains towards the end of the month, usually starting on the 22nd, because that is when the oil export negotiations are concluded.

Another currency that reacts to oil trends is the Norwegian krone, also called "Nokkie," after its symbol, NOK. Although it does not have the same liquidity as the Canadian dollar, it remains the tenth most traded currency on the Forex market.

2. Natural gas and gold

The Canadian dollar is also linked to the trend of natural gas. In monetary terms, however, Canada exports an amount of natural gas equivalent to 50% of the amount of oil, so the incidence is lower. It should also be emphasized that the price of natural gas is notoriously very volatile: its daily movement is in fact double that of crude oil.

Regarding gold, it must be said that the market concerning it and the currency market have always been intertwined. In general, it can be observed that gold is:

- Positively correlated with the euro and negatively correlated with the US dollar;
- Positively correlated with the Australian dollar since Australia is one of the major exporting countries.

3. Copper and base metals

Nothing can anticipate the trend of the world economy better than copper and base metals. A substantial decline in the latter in particular signals a clear economic contraction that can also have repercussions on other raw materials. In general, it should be emphasized that yen crosses are particularly sensitive to the global economy, both because Japan is one of the main exporting countries and because of the Carry Trade operations built by financial operators. For this reason, AUD/JPY and NZD/JPY crosses usually follow the trend of copper and base metals.

In conclusion, all commodity/currency correlations fluctuate over time. In some periods, for example, the Canadian dollar goes up or down with oil. At other times, however, the Canadian dollar market itself focuses on different fundamental factors such as interest rates and national economic growth.

One of the most followed indicators to understand the general macro situation is the Baltic Dry Index (index of sea freight rates), released daily by the Baltic Stock Exchange in London. It records freight prices for the transport of raw materials at an international level and proves to be an excellent indicator to try to anticipate future economic activities. The rise in the index, in fact, signals an increase in the transport of goods, which is usually accompanied by an economic recovery.

A further element to consider, when trying to understand relationships between commodities and the US dollar is that all their prices are in US dollars. All other things being equal, a 1% decline in the value of the dollar will increase the prices of all raw materials by 1% and vice versa. This usually causes the trend in the commodity market to be opposite the trend in the US dollar.

Chapter 7 : Technical Analysis of Forex

The Basic Technical Analysis

Technical analysis is, quite simply, a careful and rigorous study of the movements made by prices on the various financial markets. It relies on past price movement data. In technical analysis, graphs and mathematical indicators are used to predict the future evolution of the prices themselves.

Unlike a fundamental analysis, those who use technical analysis do not believe that the market is a rational and efficient environment, but argue that the movement of prices reflects the psychology of man. In fundamental analysis, traders examine economic indicators such as GDP, inflation rates, interest rates, etc.

This is because, faced with similar situations, human beings tend to always act in the same way; during the positive phases, his greed and euphoria will condition the market, while in the negative phases, it will be fear and tension that takes over.

One of the objectives pursued by the technical analysis is to identify the levels of entry (buy) and exit (sell) from the market in order to identify, with extreme precision, the best market timing.

For years, there have been some fundamental rules handed down that constitute the central fulcrum of this type of analysis. I have listed some of the most important tips below:

1- The first rule is not to lose; the second is not to forget the first.
2- Do not panic due to market fluctuations; it is normal. This is the game and these are its rules.
3- Never follow the crowd; you can only get a higher return if you invest against the current. This does not mean doing the exact opposite of what you see on the graph, but it does mean studying, training, and forming your own ideas with your own strategies.
4- An investor who has all the answers does not understand the question.

5- Most investors tend to have the same view of things. The majority of people who invest in the stock market don't know what they are doing.

6- What happens in the market today has happened before and will happen again.

7- It is not wise to neglect the message that comes from the price trend, even if it conflicts with your opinion of the market and with your evaluation of supply and demand.

8- The point is not to buy at the lowest possible price or sell at the highest, but to buy and sell at the right time.

9- People think they are playing against the market, but the market doesn't care. It is actually playing against itself.

10- If you can't make money trading on the stock market, you probably aren't asking yourself the right questions.

Some people claim that successful traders use technical analysis as their only strategy, while others are in favor of the fundamental analysis approach. I believe that both the fundamental and technical strategies can perfectly integrate, as long as they are used with completely different time horizons.

Perhaps with this example, it will be clearer: when there are strong fluctuations/accelerations in the prices of a certain financial asset, fundamental analysts experience great difficulty, as they do not understand what caused the movement. This puts them in an unfavorable position compared to technical analysts because more time is needed to study the causes of the problem. Meanwhile, the technical analysts, who instead try to interpret the movement of prices, are completely disinterested in *why* it happens.

The main objective of this methodology is to identify the best time to enter and exit the market:

The signals are identified on the basis of some graphic situations, which tend to repeat themselves with a certain frequency, and which trigger predictable movements by prices.

Technical analysis is based on the assumption that the markets move within defined cycles and that the price action tends to reflect the reactions of investors to the dissemination of information relating to impactful events of an economic/monetary nature. This information is often repetitive over time and generates similar reactions.

We can say that the purpose of technical analysis is to study these behaviors from a graphic and quantitative point of view, with the aim of anticipating the future evolution of prices.

What Are the Cardine Principles of Technical Analysis?

Technical analysis is based on three fundamental principles:

1) History repeats itself. The movement of prices reflects the psychology and behavior of man. The future itself could be a repetition of the past. One piece of advice I can give you is to study the past to better understand the future.
2) Prices move by trends. An uptrend is characterized by increasing minimums and maximums. On the contrary, a downtrend is distinguished by decreasing minimums and maximums.
3) Any available information is already reflected in the market price itself.

The Dow Theory: One Of The First Theories Of Technical Analysis

At the basis of this theory is the close relationship between prices and the time axis, where prices move according to a very specific direction: up, down, or sideways. This direction can be identified through one or more trendlines.

According to Dow, therefore, the market is not so unpredictable; but it follows trends that can be identified with a good chance of success.

There are a series of theorems that can be summarized by four rules:

Rule No. 1

The market is made up of three trends: Primary, Secondary, and Minor.

The **primary trend** can be bullish or bearish, with a duration of more than one year: it is in an up phase if the market shows rising highs and lows; on the other hand, it is in the down phase if the minimums and maximums are decreasing.

Secondary trends are intermediate corrective phases of the primary trend. These reactions usually last from one to three months and are one third/two thirds of the previous secondary trend.

Minor trends are very short-term movements with a length ranging from a few days up to a maximum of three weeks.

The primary trend has three phases:

a) The first phase, accumulation, develops with the purchases of the most astute and informed investors. It usually occurs when all the negative news has already been discounted by the market.

b) In the second phase, there are trend followers who take a position. At this stage, as you can guess, prices begin to rise rapidly and economic news signals a continuing improvement in the fundamentals of the economy.

c) The third phase begins as corporate news becomes increasingly positive. Most small investors enter the market causing exponential growth in both stock prices and speculative volume.

d) During this last phase, in which no one seems willing to sell, more informed investors begin to distribute the stocks they had accumulated when no one seemed interested in buying.

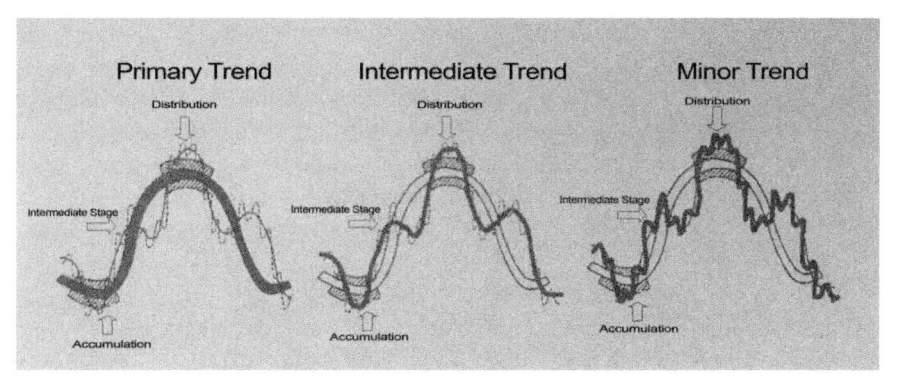

[This figure shows the three trends identified. As shown, both medium-term (secondary) and short-term (minor) movements interact within the primary trend.]

Rule No. 2

The market trend deletes the information available to all operators, i.e., all that there is to know is already reflected in the markets through prices, which therefore represent the global sum of all the hopes, fears, and expectations of market participants.

Rule No. 3

Dow, referring to the industrial index (Dow Jones Industrial) and the railway index (now called Dow Jones Transportations, then Railways Index), argued that no substantial change in the primary trend could have occurred if both indices had not given the same indication. As long as the two indices are moving in the same direction, the primary trend is still considered strong.

Rule No. 4

Volumes must confirm the trend, expanding in the direction of the primary trend: if this is up, the volume should increase when prices rise and decrease when they fall; if it is on the downside, it should rise when prices fall and decrease when prices rise.

It can therefore be concluded that Dow's theory consists of a series of tips and principles that can assist investors in their market studies. Its purpose is to identify the underlying trend and participate in the most important market movements.

HOW TO IDENTIFY THE TREND: THE TRENDLINE

Since an uptrend is defined by a series of increasing highs and lows, to have a negative reversal, prices must draw a lower high and low than the previous ones. On the contrary, we have a positive trend reversal when prices draw a high and low higher than those already touched.

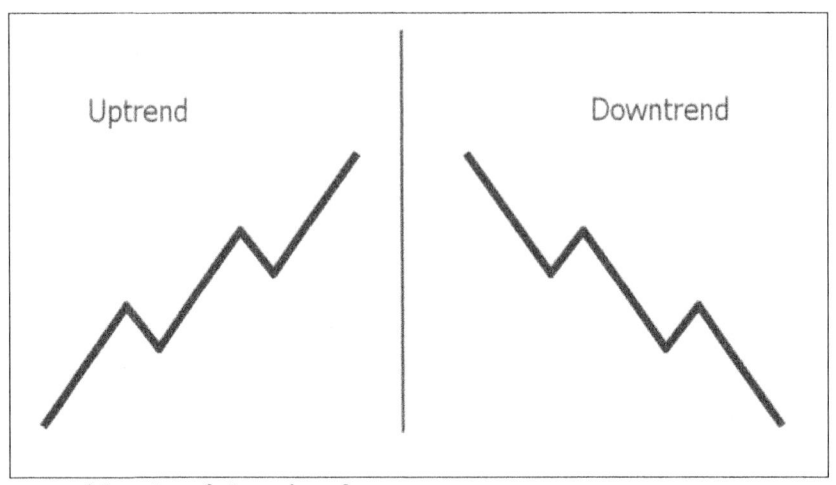

From a graphic point of view, therefore:

- an uptrend is highlighted by joining two or more rising lows through a line called a trendline.

-a bearish trend is instead detected by combining two or more decreasing highs.

The more a trendline lasts over time and has numerous points of contact, the stronger it means.

Until a trend provides clear signs of exhaustion or reversal, then it must continue to be considered intact. The breaking of the trendline is the clearest. When the bullish trendline identifies ever-higher support levels, or when the bearish trendline identifies ever-lower resistance levels, they are called "dynamic" supports and resistances.

FOREX

[The first graph shows a typical bearish trendline that combines the decreasing highs drawn by prices and therefore constitutes a dynamic resistance. The second graph shows instead shows a classic uptrend line, which combines the rising lows drawn by prices and constitutes a dynamic support.]

Bearish Trendline Indicator

Bullish Trendline Indicator

Important: The breaking of a trendline, while either marking the end or pausing the current trend, does not automatically imply its inversion.

After a trend, whether bullish or bearish, a lateral consolidation phase could begin intact, usually characterized by low volumes.

When tracing the trendline, it is also advisable to draw its parallel called "channel line," because a channel is formed that is useful to contain the movement of prices. This line represents dynamic resistance in an uptrend and dynamic support in a downtrend. In the event that the graph was to break it, there would be an acceleration signal of the dominant trend.

A channel represents a strong and sustainable trend when it has a good slope and is wide enough. While strongly inclined and very narrow, channels generally represent accelerations destined to run out in a short time with violent and sudden corrections.

Example of an Uptrend Channel:

It is very important to understand whether the market is in a trend phase, either bullish or bearish, or is in a lateral phase.

If the market is in a positive trend, the best strategy you can adopt is to ride the bullish trend with long positions. When you are riding a trend, every day is an opportunity to increase your positions.

If, on the other hand, the market is in a phase of lateral congestion, that is, it is devoid of directionality, the most appropriate strategy is to buy when prices fall towards the low part, and then liquidate the positions when they go towards the high part.

THE MAIN FEATURES OF TRENDLINE

For a better understanding of what a trendline is, its main features are listed below:

-A trendline is a line, positively or negatively inclined, which joins two or more relevant points identifiable on a graph.

- Upward trends are identified by a trendline that is drawn by combining two or more rising lows, which also represent important support levels. Descending trends are instead defined by a trendline that joins two or more decreasing peaks that constitute important resistance levels.

-One of the basic principles of technical analysis tells us that once a trend has formed (two or more highs/lows touched by a trendline), it will remain so until the trendline is broken. You can stay on the upside until the uptrend line that supports an uptrend is broken.

-From an operational point of view, trendlines allow you to follow the main trend and remain in position until there is a clear signal of reversal. In an uptrend, for example, you will hold your long position until prices fall below the trendline that joins the rising lows drawn during the rise.

SUPPORTS AND RESISTANCES

The supports and resistances identify the areas where there is a balance between the strength of demand and that of supply.

FOREX

The breakout of a certain level of resistance is caused by a strengthening of the demand line and signals that a large number of buyers are willing to buy at higher prices.

Many technical analysis tools try to quantify the strength of supply and demand, and price charts provide the best possible view of these two forces.

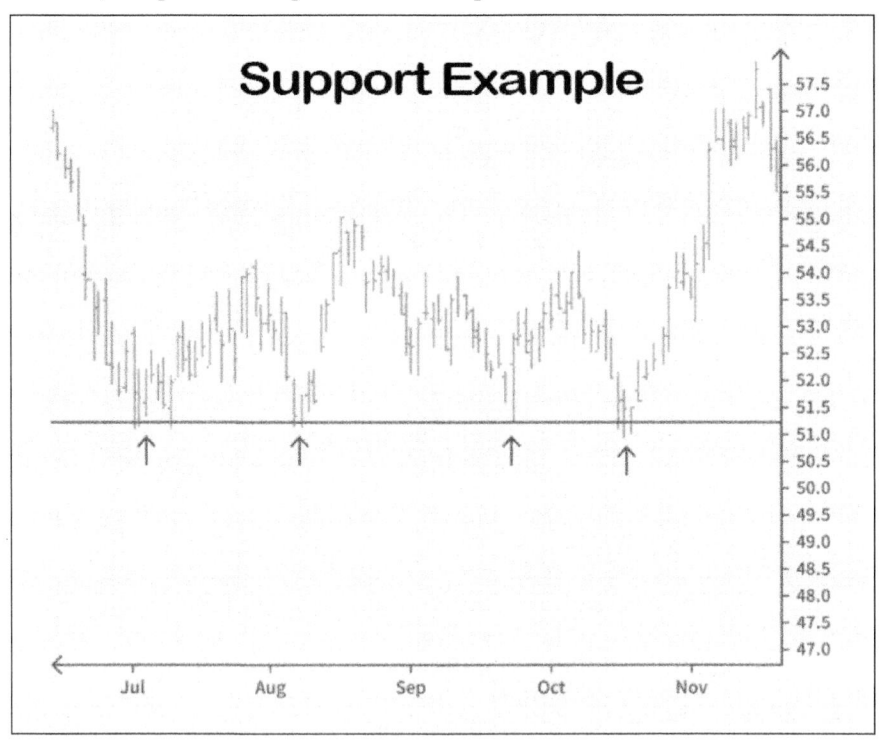

Support Example

[The graph shows the solid static support. As you can see, the quotes have tested this level several times before making a major technical rebound.]

Here are the rules you must follow when drawing resistance and support lines, both static and dynamic:

- -The more lows/highs are joined by the trendline, the greater the importance of support or resistance.
- -A support level is reliable when it shows good resilience to repeated sellers' attacks and a resistance level is all the stronger when it resists repeated attempts by buyers to break.

- -A historical low or high represents a level of strategic support or resistance.
- -If a support level is broken, it turns into a resistance level and vice versa. This is because sellers and buyers usually place their sell and buy orders at important technical levels.

THE GRAPHIC CONFIGURATIONS

Particular attention is to be given to the graphic configurations that are formed on the price chart. It is important to consider them because they are useful to try to predict the trend and to build valid operational strategies.

The graphic configurations can be of two types:

- **Reversal patterns**: they test a change in trend, from positive to negative or vice versa.
- **Continuation patterns**: they constitute a pause in the main trend before it resumes its original direction.

The continuation pattern

Typically, with the formation of these graphic configurations, there is a decrease in the volumes traded and, above all, a much lower level of volatility than that detected during the trend phase.

Below I have reported the main continuation figures:

a) Triangles (symmetrical, ascending, descending);
b) Rectangles;
c) Flags (flags) and pennants (flagpoles)

The triangles

The triangle figure is used to anticipate the continuation of the main trend. The ranges in which prices fluctuate tend to narrow as the breakout time approaches, creating a squeeze of volatility.

Triangles can appear in three different structures:

1. **Symmetrical triangle**. This figure is formed due to a constant reduction of the maximums and a constant increase of the

minimums that make prices move in a range that gradually becomes narrower with the passing of the sessions. A symmetrical structure is created, which makes it difficult to interpret: any hypotheses on the direction of the future breakout must necessarily be based on the main market trend.

2. **Ascending triangle.** The range within which prices move is reduced. This happens thanks to an increase in the lows, with the highs remaining unchanged. This behavior makes evident the greater pressure of buyers compared to sellers and gives this figure a bullish value.

3. **Descending triangle.** This is the opposite of the ascending triangle, as it is characterized by a constant reduction of the maximums, with the minimums remaining unchanged. In this case, the figure assumes a bearish value.

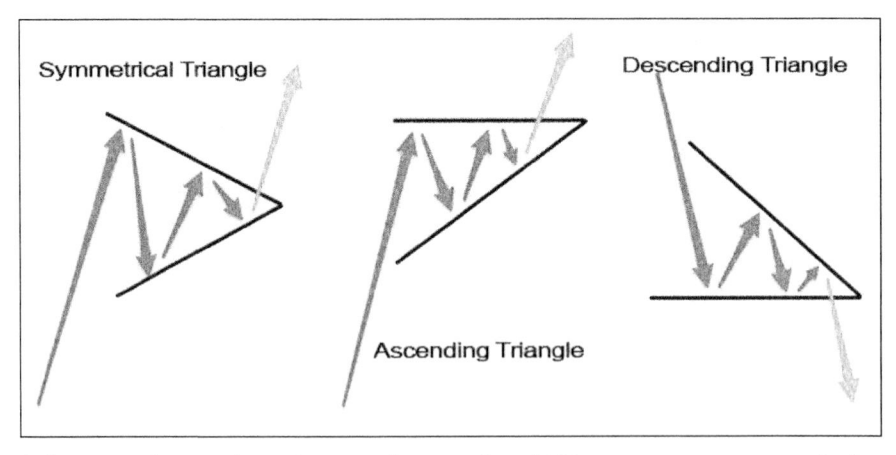

[The graph in this figure shows the different structures of the triangles.]

It is possible to establish the level that prices should reach in the phase following the breakout by projecting, from the breaking point, the base of the triangle, i.e. the maximum amplitude that the figure recorded during its formation.

The rectangles

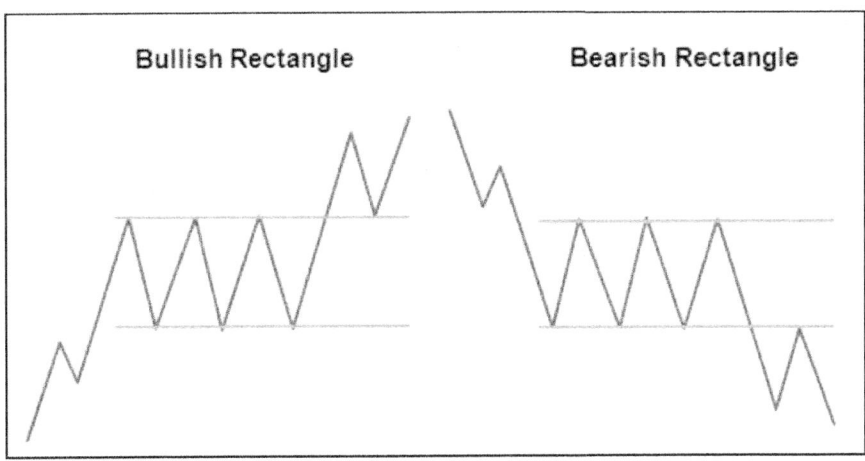

When we notice that there is a price fluctuation graphically contained by two parallel lines, it is the rectangle formation. The upper line represents a classic "level of static resistance," and the lower line represents a "level of static support."

The volumes traded, within the figure that is formed, will certainly be lower than during the dominant phases of the trend, even if the reduction is less evident than in other continuation figures.

Once you have identified a formation of this type, you should proceed to purchases near the lower part of the rectangle (static support) or sales near the upper part (static resistance); with very low stop losses to protect operations than putting a few ticks* (which is the smallest price change that a financial asset can record) outside the identified rectangle.

The possible break (up or down) of a figure of this type, especially if accompanied by consistent volumes, usually represents a very reliable operational signal, to be followed without hesitation by taking a position in the direction of the break itself. Remember that it is always very important to set an adequate stop loss level.

The length of a rectangle is given by the time duration of the congestion phase and its width is given by the thickness of the congestion phase. The larger and more extensive these two variables are, the stronger the movement that will follow. The minimum price target can be identified by projecting, up or down, the height of the rectangle starting from the breakpoint identified.

There can be two operational ideas that the rectangle can provide:

1- The first requires waiting for prices to exit the identified congestion zone, which must necessarily be classified as a breakout and, therefore, be characterized by an increase in volumes and volatility.
2- The second instead derives from the possibility of exploiting the lateral movement of prices to buy close to the identified support and sell when the values approach the top of the figure again.

FLAG AND PENNANT

Flags and pennants are part of the continuation figures. They identify a moment of slowdown in the current trend, which is then destined to resume and frequently occur within a very strong movement, therefore with high volatility and volumes.

The flags are due to a phase of congestion that generally assumes an opposite inclination with respect to the movement within which it is inserted; therefore, during the formation of this figure, the volumes remain low and then record a sharp increase at the breakout.

Pennants, on the other hand, represent a phase of contraction that does not necessarily have an opposite inclination compared to the basic trend. Again, volumes remain low, and then rise sharply when the breakout occurs.

When identifying these figures, you can identify your potential target in these ways:

The first is determined by projecting the width of the base from the breakout point but assumes less importance due to the small size of the figure.

The second can be obtained by projecting, from the breakout point, a distance equivalent to that covered by the movement that preceded the formation of the pennant.

They usually occur around the middle of the main movement. This information can be exploited at an operational level as the temporary phase of price weakness can be used to enter the market or to increase a position already taken previously.

Reversal pattern

These are figures that herald an inversion of the current trend. The greater the time required for their formation and completion, the greater their validity and the more important the inversion will be.

Remember that if a reversal figure is not confirmed, it is a sign of continuation of the current trend.

The main reversal figures are:
- a) The bearish head and shoulder top;
- b) Double and triple top/double and triple bottom;
- c) The diamond.

The bearish head and shoulder top

This inversion figure consists of three phases:

1. The first is upside (A), characterized by strong volumes, followed by a rapid downward correction (B) accompanied by reduced volumes. This is where the "left shoulder" is drawn.
2. Second, up again, with the previous highs exceeded in terms of price (C), but with lower volumes than the previous bullish impulse, followed also in this case by a corrective phase (D) usually near the base of the left shoulder. This is where the "head" is drawn.
3. Third, and last, still rising (E) characterized by lower values both in terms of price (therefore with the maximums that cannot exceed those reached during the formation of the head) and of volumes. A new decline will also follow this last phase (F). This is where the "right shoulder" is drawn.

Once the formation of the two shoulders and the head has been identified, what is called the "neckline" should be traced. To trace it, simply join the point where the left shoulder begins with the point where the right shoulder begins to form.

If the decline causes the neckline to break, with a significant increase in volumes, the head and shoulders figure will be completed and prices will accelerate violently to the downside (G).

Usually, the real downside starts after a small bullish reaction from prices, which are brought back near the neckline to "test" its validity. It is a movement called pull-back.

From an operational point of view, the pull-back represents the last chance to exit the market: the neckline transformed into resistance, in fact, will reject any bullish attempt by giving way to a bearish impulse that is accompanied by very high volumes.

From an operational point of view, the movement after the breaking of the neckline will be of an extension equal to the distance between this and the maximum of the head projected from the breaking point of the neckline itself.

This allows you to build a short trading operation, with an entry-level that corresponds to the break of the neckline and a profit target coinciding with the one reached by the projection of the head height.

If you spot a potential head and shoulder top, do not make the mistake of anticipating the opening of the short position before breaking the neckline. Only the break of the neckline causes the bearish reversal of the trend.

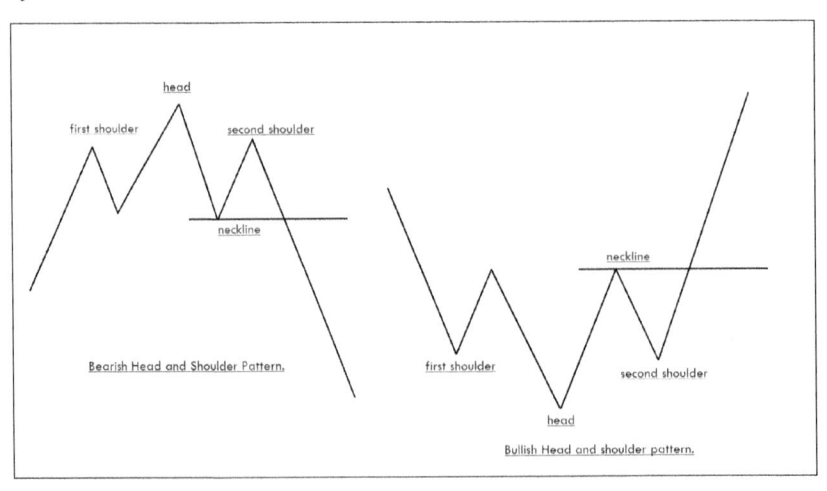

Bearish Head and Shoulder Pattern.

Bullish Head and shoulder pattern.

FOREX

THE REAL CHART VERSION:

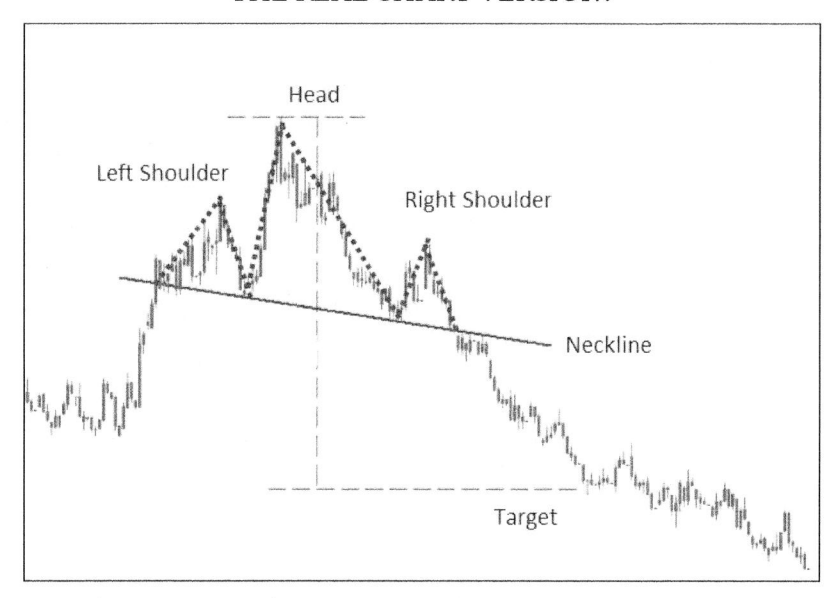

There is also an opposite figure to the head and shoulder top, namely the head and shoulder bottom, which occurs at the end of a bearish trend and causes a bullish reversal of the trend. Again, in this case, three distinct phases can be identified:

1. The first is decline characterized by strong volumes and followed by a rapid rebound accompanied, however, by reduced volumes. This is where the "left shoulder" is drawn.
2. Second, down again, with the previous lows exceeding in terms of price, but accompanied by lower volumes compared to the previous bearish impulse, followed by a recovery phase that ends near the base of the left shoulder. This is where the "head" is drawn.
3. Third, and last, still even lower, characterized by lower values both in terms of price (therefore with the minimums that do not fall below those recorded during the formation of the head) and volumes. This last phase will be followed by a new correction. This is when the "right shoulder" is drawn.

To obtain the neckline, just draw a line that joins the point from which the left shoulder begins to where the right shoulder begins to form. The breakout, accompanied by a sharp increase in volumes, of the neckline thus traced will refine the head and shoulder bottom figure, triggering a sharp rise in prices.

Double and triple top and double and triple bottom

These reversal figures are among those most noticeable in operational reality and can be both bearish and bullish.

1. The double and triple top: This is formed when the analyzed financial activity reaches two or three times a certain price without ever being able to exceed it, and then falls back towards the base of the movement, breaking it down with strong volumes. In an attempt to break this resistance, the latter will draw, in the case of the figure of the double top, an M configuration. In the case of a triple top, on the other hand, a lateral zigzag is drawn.

The volumes that develop at the second or third highs are lower than the first and signal that the bullish pressure is contracting.

From a graphic point of view, it will be necessary to break the base of the figure to be able to speak correctly about the formation of double or triple maximum.

From an operational point of view, we can identify our potential target by projecting down the distance between the intermediate minimum included and the two maximums.

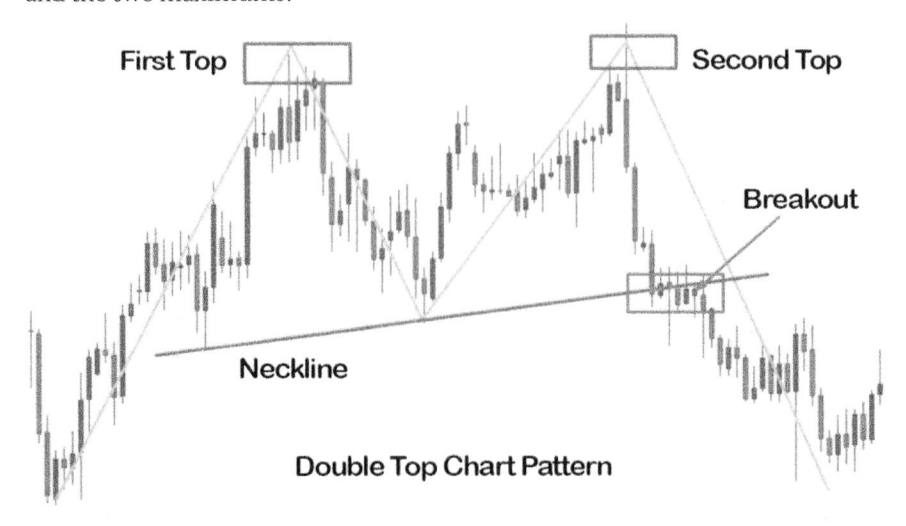

2. **The double and triple bottom** occurs when, following a clear bearish trend, prices test a price threshold two or three times without, however, being able to sell it decisively. This situation may signal the exhaustion of a bearish trend. In this case, it will only be the exceeding of the intermediate maximum between the two or three minimums to cause the upward reversal of the trend.

The diamond

It is a configuration that is not very frequent and not easy to detect, but I will tell you about it anyway. Unlike what happens for other reversal figures, the diamond can also occur during simple pauses in the trend and take on the characteristics of a continuation figure.

A diamond can occur in two different circumstances:
1. At the end of an uptrend, taking the name "diamond top."
2. At the end of a bearish trend, taking the name "diamond bottom."

From a graphic point of view, the diamond formation consists of two parts: a broadening top (left) and a triangle (right).

Remember that the figure does not always develop symmetrically: it frequently happens that the second part extends over time, more than the first did.

There are four fundamental elements to identify its formation:
1) An initial phase of price expansion;
2) A maximum followed by;
3) A minimum (for the diamond top);
4) A phase of price contraction.

Even the diamond is only completed when the breakout occurs.

To calculate the target price, it is sufficient to project the maximum width of the figure starting from the point where the breakout occurred. If instead it becomes a continuation figure, it is also possible to derive a second target, projecting, from the final breakout point, the amplitude of the movement that preceded the beginning of the diamond.

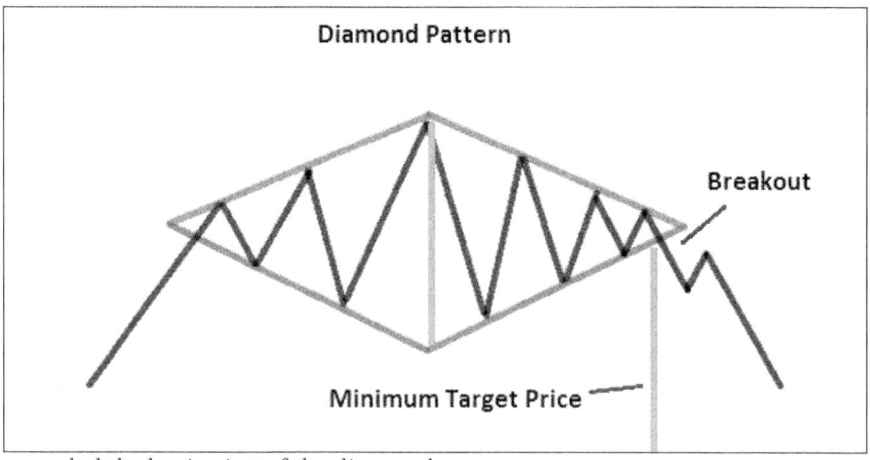

[The graph shows an example of a diamond.]

Chapter 8: The Habits of a Successful Trader

I'll start by saying that there is no magic formula for success; there is no single action or single habit. Success is a habit that is built day after day, month after month, year after year.

It is the set of multiple habits protracted over time that will make you become a successful person in trading, and in everything you want. Perseverance and the desire to commit to achieving that goal will finally make that dream come true.

In this chapter, in fact, we will see the habits that a successful person must have in order to achieve their goals. I have used it myself for trading, as have many other successful people in other fields, and I can assure you that adopting these habits will differentiate you from those who do not achieve goals.

Before starting with the actual habits, I'll start by explaining the reasons for building a successful routine that will allow you to more easily reach your goals, allow more time for yourself and your family, and regain control:

1- You will increase your ability to think long term.

"Plan your future, because that is where you are going to live."

We know that today, people want everything and they want it immediately; we are not satisfied with waiting.

We want the new iPhone model, we want fast shipping from Amazon, and we don't want to wait even a minute in line at the supermarket.

It is important to know how to manage your time, but it is even more important to be able to think long-term, imagine your future, and choose your direction.

It is not enough to dream big; it is not enough to visualize. You have to divide everything into micro-objectives from the short to the long-term. Think step-by-step to make this dream concrete. It doesn't matter how long the journey is, but it matters that you take the first step. Gradually, your goal will get closer and closer, but if you don't think long-term, and don't plan every step you take, it will seem like you aren't moving at all and you will most likely give up.

An African proverb: "The best way to eat an elephant in your path, is to cut it up into little pieces."

There are precise rules to divide our dream into micro-steps and formulate smart goals, which I will explain to you later.

2- You will fully be the master of your life and your destiny.

Have you ever felt like you have no control over your time, risking living a life not yours?

We all have 24 hours a day available to us. Jeff Bezos, Richard Branson, and Warren Buffett are all successful people who have the same number of hours as you have. Why does it seem like you don't have enough time to be able to do the things you want to do? It's because you don't have a successful routine.

How many times have you happened to take time away from your family, friends, and hobbies because you think you don't have time? Maybe you too can reach your goals, but you feel like you have a stressful and super busy life keeping you from being successful. A morning routine, the single tool that the world's brightest and most successful entrepreneurs use every morning, will be a good option for you. You will finally be the master of your life and your destiny.

3- You will be more focused, therefore more satisfied and more productive.

When we run out of time to work towards our goals, we understand that we have to change our strategy. However, to achieve more we don't have to work harder, but in a different and more focused way, allowing us to multiply the hours at our disposal by offering ourselves two advantages:

- **It saves you energy**: if you are focused, you can reach the goals you have set in a more relaxed and calm way.

- **It makes you more effective:** if you are focused, you take the right time to carry out activities consistent with your vision, freeing up time that you can dedicate to other things such as family, your social life, and your passions.

Working without focus is very dangerous. The cost of switching is likely to make us work harder, with fewer results and less satisfaction.

How many times do you look at your Facebook feed, Instagram, or Exchange messages every 5 minutes? Did you know that every time you get distracted, it takes 25 minutes to get back to focusing on what you were doing?

According to a study at the University of California, on average, those who work in an office are interrupted every 11 minutes, but it takes 25 minutes to get back to being fully focused on their task.

The cost of switching is paid mainly on a personal level - in terms of time and state of mind.

In a distraction-free environment, people complete their tasks earlier, with less stress, less frustration, less pressure, and less effort.

On average, each distraction costs us 15 minutes: try to count all the distractions you indulge during the eight hours you plan to work, and imagine how much earlier you would be able to finish your work if you just stayed focused. Now that you've realized it, do you still think that you don't have much time available?

4- You will increase your energy, strengthening your body and mind

Do you know that not all energy is the same?

There is empowering energy that brings you success capable of changing the world, while changing you too. I call this energy "energy rich" which is contrasted with that sluggish energy you experience when you try to engage in jobs in which you do not have the slightest passion and without enthusiasm–that I call "energy poor."

Think for a moment about the people around you. Many will be able to give you incredible energy, capable of stimulating your ideas and encouraging you to give your best. When these people are with you, they put you in a good mood, rarely complain, and look at everything with extreme positivity. Together with these people, you will certainly increase that "energy rich."

On the other hand, however, there are those people who spend time complaining and focusing on their problems without ever thinking about the solutions they almost never find.

If you try to share an idea with them, they don't listen to you and try to make you stay where you are by listing all the possible problems for which it would not be worth the risk.

Very often, these people are the ones you love most of all, but before listening to a judgment and an opinion of a person you need to understand if that person is truly an expert in his field and if he has achieved success in that field.

If someone who has never traded ever tells you not to trade for various reasons, do not listen to her as she will most likely be listing problems that she only says by hearsay, without any experience.

If no one had ever risked, had never persevered, and had never brought forward an idea just because other people didn't support it, by now most likely the internet wouldn't exist. You also couldn't make a phone call, drive your own car, take a plane trip, turn your lights on or off, etc.

With a good, successful routine, you will be able to increase your "energy rich."

5- You will increase your attitude to be successful

How you start your day determines your mental attitude for the rest of the day, which is why so many of the richest and most successful people in the world wake up early in the morning to dedicate the first hours of the day to themselves.

For them, waking up at dawn (or just before dawn) is essential to maintaining a balance between a high level of productivity and personal space to be dedicated to the important things: family, body, spirit, and mind.

Ninety percent of top managers wake up before 6am on weekdays.

Why?

To take control of the day before it begins, gaining precious time to enjoy a hearty breakfast with wife/husband and children, meditate, exercise, focus on personal growth by reading or taking a course, reflect on one's priorities or vision, and to organize their agenda.

Each of the people I met with this habit has consolidated their own routine over time.

SUCCESSFUL HABITS

Let's start by saying that it would take a whole book to talk about just this topic. What I will discuss are tips, which come from my experience and the experience of other successful people.

In the United States, an academic discipline has recently been born that studies self-determination for success. The University of Rochester fosters it with the research group founded by Richard Ryan and Edward Deci and led by Dr. Shannon Robertson Hoefen. The fact that the pursuit of success has entered university classrooms is yet another proof that different skills are needed to enhance one's career path fully. It is almost never just about skills learned at school.

The 2016 biopic, *The Founder,* is dedicated to McDonald's founder Ray Kroc. In this biographical movie, he says, "Nothing in the world can take the place of persistence. Talent will not; nothing is more common than unsuccessful men with talent. Genius will not; unrewarded genius is almost a proverb. Education will not; the world is full of educated derelicts. Persistence and determination alone are omnipotent."

So, what are the potential habits to develop for success?

These are the morning habits that have enabled me and other people to become successful.

1- Get Up Early

Before the rest of the world starts running, it's good to have done something quietly.

I admit that I didn't agree with this at all, until a year ago. I came to realize what it means. It is a matter of habit. At first, anticipating the alarm clock takes effort, then you can't do without it.

Waking up early means being in absolute tranquility; in the streets, there is silence (almost always), no one calls you for work commitments, no responsibility. You are you with yourself and you disconnect from the world to dedicate time to yourself.

Waking up early in the morning is a great way to save time in productivity and energy.

However, waking up early in the morning and staring at the wall isn't enough to be successful; you need to use those extra hours well. A few ideas for making good use of your time follow.

2- Meditate

Stop and take a moment with just your mind. Meditation is one of the best-known morning practices and many successful people practice it routinely. It takes 10-20 minutes to make a difference. You can sit in a quiet corner of the house or go out into the fresh air. The key thing is to start the day with a moment of mental serenity.

For years, I thought that meditating was a waste of time, boring, or useless. Then one day I wanted to try it. After all, if 90% of Silicon Valley CEOs meditate, there must be a reason!

It wasn't easy to get started and I still don't think I've become a "professional meditator."

At first, my mind wandered constantly. I was bored and the practice seemed useless, but with some practice, anyone can become good at it and begin to benefit from it.

If I had to summarize meditation in a single motivation, it would be serenity: meditating has made a difference in my life. I really feel in control of what happens to me.

Then there are the physical advantages: the insula and the prefrontal cortex (the areas of the brain responsible for coordinating memory and complex actions) show an increased volume, probably due to the strengthening of the neural connections involved.

The amygdala (involved in the processing of fear-related emotions) is of decreased thickness.

Meditation increases the ability to control basic physiological responses, such as inflammation and stress hormone levels in the blood. Meditating makes you feel good and helps you start the day stress-free, more serene, and focused. You can stay focused longer than before. When you focus on something, you can isolate yourself from everything else with greater ease and much more. Try it and you too will have great satisfaction!

3- Visualize

I already know what you are thinking: visualization is an Indian shaman or guru practice. However, that's not true.

Neuroscience has shown that thanks to mirror neurons, a vividly imagined action is processed by our brain as a truly lived action.

This explains the power of visualization.

Not to mention that visualization is now a practice that has also come into use among professional athletes.

How many times before a ski race have you seen athletes go through the movements as if they were already in the race? In their minds, they were.

Visualize what you want to become, where you want to go, and whom you will be with. Close your eyes and visualize your perfect future. You will trigger such emotions and behaviors to be able to achieve that goal.

4- Read

All of the successful people I know read. Constantly learning must be a prerogative of the human being.

You could read before going to bed to relax and sleep peacefully, or if you are someone who just touches the bed and cannot stay awake, you could spend thirty minutes in the morning reading business books, trading, and anything else related to the growth of skills to improve your business and your mindset.

Thirty minutes a day means at least two books a month.

Two books a month means twenty-four books a year. Do you think that reading twenty-four books a year that you will not change for the better, and that you will not have learned many new things?

I say YES!

You are lucky because audiobooks are readily available today and if you are not a reading enthusiast, you could very well listen to a narrated book.

Listening will make concepts come into your head better.

It is nice to read because it gives you that feeling of total silence, where you are yourself creating that little voice that narrates. It's up to you to figure out what is best for your needs and tastes.

5- Write The Things You Are Grateful For

Gratitude is known to be one of the healthiest habits. Saying thank you for what we have each day should be the first thought in the morning. It only takes a few minutes to make a difference in our attitude. Keep a diary in which you put the date and the three things you are grateful for: people met, emotions experienced, opportunities grasped, moments, places visited, etc.

Gratitude will put you in the role of positive people–those people with "energy rich" who always want to improve, who help others, and who will always give a touch of creativity in everything they do.

Expressing gratitude is one of the most important skills of an entrepreneur.

Attention demonstrating gratitude does not mean being satisfied, but living in a positive way without negative thoughts that will make you perceive your days and life as something happy.

6- Do Physical Activity

FOREX

Exercise allows you to increase your energy levels during the day, to develop your character, and to acquire those fundamental characteristics for your work (resilience, responsiveness, self-esteem, discipline, etc...).

There is no need to train for an hour but even twenty minutes may be enough.

You could run for half an hour, you could do some stretching, or you could do some tabata exercises.

Training in the morning will give you the right energy to face the day in the best possible way.

7- Take A Frozen Shower

This is the habit that is often seen as "strange" or "difficult," but it is not.

There are tons of studies that show how an ice shower has beneficial effects on energy, mood, the immune system, and the whole body.

The sensations at the end of the icy shower are priceless: muscles like new, energy skyrocketing, a clear mind, and feeling of being able to do more or less anything.

It takes twenty to thirty seconds to get so many benefits.

To make it less traumatic, you could first put on hot water and gradually switch to ice water.

I know you must be saying, "Are you out of your mind? I have to get out of the duvet and instead of taking a nice hot shower, I have to take it ice cold?"

That's right; the hot shower will only decrease your energy and make you relax. After a hot shower, you will most likely want to get back under the covers and that's not what we want if we want to be successful, right?

Don't worry. Once you start, and you have established the habit, you won't be able to do without it.

8- Schedule And Plan

After working out and then clearing your mind with a nice ice cold shower, it's time to think about things to do.

The agenda does not have to be daily: do not allow the chaos of urgencies to dictate the course of your day.

Every day you have to spend at least fifteen minutes identifying the three most important things of the day.

In this way, no urgency or interruption can make you forget what is really important.

It is useless to have an infinite to-do list in which the most important things are camouflaged with the less important ones.

As far as planning is concerned, we speak of corporate strategic planning (it is defined corporate because it is usually used by companies, but it can very well be used by people).

With strategic planning, it is necessary to define the mission and the objectives to be achieved in a given period of time, generally medium-long and to list all the activities to be undertaken to achieve what has been planned.

In strategic planning, all possible future scenarios in which it will operate must be described, as well as the investments necessary to finance each action that is planned to achieve the indicated objectives.

We remind you that the objectives must always be measurable and verifiable to understand the progress of the plan clearly.

So how do you plan?

First, identify the long-term goal (5 years).

After you have identified your long-term goal, divide this into smaller micro-goals (1-year and 3-year goals), until you get to even smaller goals (month to month, and week to week).

Once you have identified the goals, divide the things you need to do to achieve that particular goal.

Example: You want to earn 1 million dollars within five years. This means that you have to make $200,000 a year. That is $16,666 per month, or $4166 per week, or $595 per day.

You have to be able to divide your commitments.

Remember, the bigger the goal, the more commitments you have to make to achieve it.

One trick I teach is to tell someone where you want to go.

This principle is called commitment-consistency. That is, you will be challenged to succeed based on the consistency of what is promised to the particular person you care about achieving that goal/commitment at any cost.

To be as focused as possible during the day, build 45-minute power blocks, where you focus as much as possible without getting distracted.

After 45 minutes, you can rest for 15 minutes and so on.

If you work this way for 8 hours, that is 8 power blocks of 45 minutes, for a total of 6 hours of maximum concentration work. I assure you that in one day you will achieve what I normally think you would do in almost three days of work where you get distracted continually with social media and other distractions.

Once you get used to the 45-minute power blocks, you may want to upgrade to four 1.5-hour power blocks, followed by a 30-minute break.

Many large companies already use these techniques for their employees.

Remember that it will take at least 30 days for a habit to become part of the normality of your life.

That's all for this chapter. It is clear that explaining time management, strategic goal planning, and successful daily routines requires a longer argument, but I hope these little tricks can help you begin to find success.

Conclusion

"The mind that opens up to a new idea never returns to its original size." – Albert Einstein

We have come to the end of this book.

There is no such thing as a "Get Rich, Quick" scheme, no matter what people say. People that are trying to convince you of this are lying to you. This book has the basic information you need to get started on a new journey in your life, and although it is still a daunting concept, it is one that is very attractive.

The stock exchange and trading platforms are not for the faint-of-heart, and is a very stressful environment, even for the most experienced of traders. The basics in this book are enough for you to get started, but this is only the beginning of your learning journey.

You don't have to go on this journey alone. You know what type of individual you are and many brokers will suit your type of personality and will help you build your skills and techniques to become a successful trader. However, don't forget that if you do prefer the prospect of working alone, then you have to make sure that you have educated yourself enough to make educated strategy plans and have the knowledge and techniques to work by yourself.

Always seek advice from people that are more experienced than you are. Learning does not necessarily have to come from books and a computer screen. Some traders and brokers can give you the advice needed to become a successful trader. Other brokers will charge you to teach you and if you can afford it, this is a worthwhile choice.

Gaining knowledge and advice from someone that you can discuss problems is a much-needed boost for the new trader. If you can't afford the fees of private brokers there are always other options. Many online sources offer you the same advice at no cost.

Sites like Investopedia, and even YouTube, are filled with experienced and successful traders who are offering free advice.

Do your market research and look for trends. Watch what certain prices do during certain periods. You need to learn to predict the probability of how currencies prices will fluctuate. This is not a skill that can be learned overnight, and even the most experienced traders make mistakes with this type of predictive skill.

FOREX

Forex trading is a tough endeavor to undertake, but there's no reason to complicate it needlessly. By following a structured approach, you too can realize the immense potential it has to improve your life.

Indeed skills are very important, but without the right mindset and adaptation to the psychology of the successful trader, you will never be successful in this field.

Many people do not see the results that they're hoping to get because they don't apply the tips and tricks provided to them and they don't operate with the right mindset. It is essential for you to exercise everything you learn, as that is how you will succeed in your future endeavors. Make mistakes and learn. No pain, no gain!

Nonetheless, the topics we talked about will help you to not only become good at forex investing but to take you to the next level. Even though this book has been geared toward beginner investors, advanced people can still reap the benefits of this book. Making money on forex doesn't have to be a big mystery. It doesn't have to be a gamble. By being clear on what your needs are as well as the trading strategies available to you, you can put together a plan of action that will help you mix successful trades, not just once in a while, but every single time. Trading takes many forms, and it is dynamic as well. Times change, and with change, markets and operational methods also change. With the advent of computers, it was logical that trading would become better and faster.

This came to pass, and traders now can trade on the go and use programs that make trading easier. It all boils down to the learning curve and you have to stick to this learning curve. You have to learn what you need to learn and take the necessary risks until you get the hang of it. Put another way, if it were very easy, then everybody would be millionaires.

Alas, that's not the case.

You have to stick to it, and you need to put in the time to become skilled at what you need to learn to develop enough expertise to at least trade profitably consistently. Trading does not mean speculating and earning just enough to buy a pair of shoes; you have to use the right techniques and you will see that there will be no escape for anyone. Whether it's a dollar or hundreds of thousands of dollars, it's up to you.

The financial markets are full of abundance and all you have to do is work to achieve all of it! I wish you the best of luck and success in trading.

FOREX

BOOK 2

OPTIONS
Trading
Crash Course

Discover the Secrets of a Successful Trader and Make Money by Investing in Options. Start Creating your Passive Income Today with Powerful Strategies for Beginners

Written by **Mark Davis**

Table of Contents

Introduction 103

Chapter 1: How to Get Started in Options Trading 105

Chapter 2: Mindset and Secrets of a Trader 109

Chapter 3: Learn the Purpose of Options and When to Use Them . 117

Chapter 4: Advantages and Disadvantages of Options Trading 121

Chapter 5: Overview of Options 127

Chapter 6: Simplified Examples of Options Trades 133

Chapter 7: Myths About Options Trading 139

Chapter 8: Puts and Calls 143

Chapter 9: Technical Analysis 149

Chapter 10: Chart Reading 157

Chapter 11: Candlestick Common Patterns 163

Chapter 12: Wave Analysis: Elliott Wave Decomposition 177

Chapter 13: Tools and Indicators for Options Trading 183

Chapter 14: Strategies for Options Trading 193

Chapter 15: Money Management 209

Chapter 16: Risk Management 217

Chapter 17: The Market Environment 223

Chapter 18: Options to Pursue If Your Options Aren't Working 229

Chapter 19: Creating an Options Trading Plan 233

Conclusion 239

Introduction

In this volume, I'm going to introduce this fantastic and interesting world for you. Options trading sounds complicated, but the reality is pretty simple. You just need a serious person to explain it to you.

I'll start by explaining the basics of options trading and how Options are used to make gains. Of course, like in all kinds of investments, there are risks. Even in this.

But against others, options require relatively small amounts of capital to start. This means that you can experience some losses without losing huge amount of money.

And most of the time, you can avoid losses if you are well prepared. The key is understanding when to get in and out of trades and what strategies should be used to minimize losses and increase profits.

I will cover this kind of information using understandable and clear explanations so that you can get started trading as soon as possible.

I Can't assure you won't lose money. It's part of the process, but if you follow my advises, you can develop a solid trading plan with options and it will be relatively easy to protect your investment account.

To prepare you better, I will also explain some of the big reasons people lose money following this path.

Options trading isn't for everyone. It does require active involvement in the market, and you're going to have to follow the market reasonably carefully to survive and make profits. So, let me state upfront that if you are the kind of investor who wants to set it and forget it, options probably aren't going to be of interest. They have a limited lifetime, and they can gain or lose value very quickly, and so it requires a lot of diligence and keeping up with what's going on with the markets to be successful.

With that being said options aren't nearly as complicated as people imagine. So, if you're a little bit cautious about becoming actively involved in your trading, let me suggest you give it a chance and read the book before deciding whether options trading is something that you can include as part of your investment plans. If you are brand-new to options, you need to understand that options trading is done to make profits over the short term. Options trading is not about long-term investing or even something like swing trading over months.

Chapter 1: How to Get Started in Options Trading

Walking you through the learning curve of options trading will always start with the most basic move you'll need to make: setting yourself up in a position actually to be able to trade.

To do that, you're going to need an options account. For now, you must know your starting point –and just how easy it is to reach it.

One thing to know before you pick your firm: times have changed considerably over the last couple of decades when it comes to options trading. Back before the internet became such a constant part of our lives, your brokerage firm – or, at least, your representative at the firm – would make your options trades on your behalf and you paid a hefty price for their services. Nowadays, however, you'll be doing most of your trades yourself.

Commission for your representative is thus a whole lot lower than it used to be, which means it won't cost you an arm and both legs to rely on your rep in the early days of your experience. While you are learning, feel free to make use of your firm's services to place and confirm your trades, if it helps you feel more comfortable getting to know the process.

With this in mind, there are going to be certain things to look for when you select your firm:

- Compare commission prices to make sure you're getting a great deal.

- Make sure the firm has up-to-date software and is capable of setting up trades quickly and reliably to make sure you get those trades you want at the best prices.

- Check out the hours of service to ensure they are compatible with your needs. In these days of online firms, you could be dealing with a firm that's across the ocean from the markets you have an interest in, or you might find that a firm only makes its reps available for the length of the working day, which might not suit your timing.

- Speak personally with the reps at the firm, as these are the people who are going to help you during the process of setting up your strategy. You want someone personable and knowledgeable – and, most importantly, who speaks in terms that you find easy to comprehend.

- Take a look at the additional services the firm supplies. Many will offer learning materials, guides, and even classes or webinars to help you hone your strategies. Even if you feel that you know all you need to know already, there's no harm in a refresher course or a little nugget of inspiration every once in a while.

Once you select a firm, you'll then need to consider signing a "margin agreement" with that firm. This agreement allows you to borrow money from the firm to purchase your stocks, which is known as "buying on margin."

Understandably, your brokerage firm is not going to allow you to do that if you don't have the financial status to pay them back. They will, therefore, run a credit check on you and ask you for information about your resources and knowledge.

A margin account is not a necessity for options trading – you don't use margin to purchase an option because it must be paid for in full. However, it can be useful as you graduate to more advanced strategies – in some cases, it will be obligatory. If you opt to sign a margin agreement, talk it through thoroughly with the firm as there are certain restrictions on the type of money you can use that may apply to you.

Next, you'll need to sign an "options agreement" – and, this time, it's an obligatory step. This agreement is designed to figure out how much you know about options and how much experience you have of trading them. It also aims to ensure that you are aware of the risks you take by trading and make sure that you are financially able to handle those risks.

By ascertaining these things, your firm can determine what level of options trading you should be aiming for. It will, therefore, approve your "trading level," of which there are five:

- **Level 1**: You may sell covered calls.

- **Level 2**: You may buy calls and puts and also buy strangles, straddles, and collars. You may also sell puts that are covered by cash and by options on exchange-traded funds and indexes.

- **Level 3**: You may utilize credit and debit spreads.

- **Level 4**: You may sell "naked puts," straddles, and strangles.

- **Level 5**: You may sell "naked indexes" and "index spreads."

Don't worry if you're not sure yet what each of these things means – you will be by the time you finish reading this book. For now, all you need to be aware of is that your firm will determine for you which level you should be at. As a beginner, don't be surprised if you only reach the first two levels.

Once you've signed the agreement, you'll be handed a booklet that contains a mine of information about risks and rewards within options trading. Right now, if you were to read that booklet, it would seem to be in a foreign language. By the time you finish this crash course, it will be a lot more decipherable – and it's very important for your success that you do read it.

Finally, your firm will present you with a "standardized option contract." It's the same for every trader, which means you stand the same chance of success as every other person out there in the options market.

By trading an option, you are entering into a legal agreement that is insured by the Options Clearing Corporation, which guarantees the contract will be honored in full. Make sure you read that contract to be aware of not only the rights you have as a trader but also the obligations you must follow in the same role.

Congratulations, you have an options account. This is the conduit through which you will create and implement your strategies and begin your adventure in options trading.

OPTIONS

Chapter 2: Mindset and Secrets of a Trader

Options Trader Mindset

Options trading is most suitable for a certain personality type and mindset. But if you are intrigued by the concept of options, but simply have not had a chance to develop the correct mindset before, there are a few tips that we can rely on to get in the right frame of mind.

You Can Weather the Storm

Options prices can move a lot throughout short periods. So, someone who likes to see their money protected and not lose any is not going to be suitable for options trading. Now, we all want to come out ahead, so I am not saying that you have to be happy about losing money to be an options trader.

What you have to be willing to do is calmly observe your options losing money, and then be ready to stick it out to see gains return in the future. This is akin to riding a real roller coaster, but it is a financial roller coaster. Options do not slowly appreciate the way a Warren Buffett investor would hope to see. Options move big on a percentage basis, and they move fast.

If you are trading multiple contracts at once, you might see yourself losing $500 and then earning $500 over a matter of a few hours. In this sense, although most options traders are not "day traders" technically speaking, you will be better off if you have a little bit of a day trading mindset.

You Don't Make Emotional Decisions

Since options are, by their nature, volatile, and very volatile for many stocks, coming to options trading and being emotional about it is not a good way to approach your trading. If you are emotional, you are going to exit your trades at the wrong time in 75% of cases. You don't want to make any sudden moves when it comes to trading options. As we have said, you should have a trading plan with rules on exiting your positions, stick to those rules and you should be fine.

Be a Little Bit Math-Oriented

To understand options trading and be successful, you cannot be shy about numbers. Options trading is a numbers game. That doesn't mean you have to drive over to the nearest university and get a statistics degree.

But if you do understand probability and statistics, you are going to be a better options trader. Frankly, it's hard to see how you can be a good options trader without having a mind for numbers. Some math is at the core of options trading and you cannot get around it.

You Are Market-Focused

You don't have to set up a day trading office with ten computer screens so you can be tracking everything by the moment, but if you are hoping to set up a trade and lazily come back to check it three days earlier, that isn't going to work with options trading. You do need to be checking your trades a few times a day. You also need to be keeping up with the latest financial and economic news, and you need to keep up with any news directly related to the companies you invest in or any news that could impact those companies. If the news does come out, you are going to need to make decisions if it's news that isn't going to be favorable to your positions. Also, you need to be checking the charts periodically, so you have an idea of where things are heading for now.

Focus on a Trading Style

As you can see, there are many different ways that you can trade options. In my opinion, sticking to one or two strategies is the best way to approach options trading. I started off buying call options, but now,

I focus on selling put credit spreads and iron condors. You should pick what you like best and also something that aligns with your goals. I moved into selling put credit spreads and iron condors because I became interested in the idea of making a living from options trading with regular income payments, rather than continuing to buy calls and hoping that the share price would go up.

There is no right or wrong answer, pick the trading style that is best suited to your style and needs.

Keep Detailed Trading Journals

It's easy to fool yourself when trading options, especially if you are a beginner. I hate to make the analogy, but this is kind of like going to the casino. If you have friends that gamble at casinos, then you are going to notice that they tend to remember the wins, and they will forget all the times that they gambled and lost. I had a cousin that won a boat, and she was always bragging about how she won a boat at the casino. I remember telling her that, yes, she might have won a boat, but she paid $65,000 more than the boat was worth to the casino over the years. You don't want to get in the same situation with your options trading. It can be an emotional experience because trading options are active and fast-paced. When you have a profitable trade, it will be exciting. But you need to keep a journal to record all of your trades to know exactly what the real situation is. That doesn't mean you quit if you look at your journal and find out you have a losing record, what you do is figure out why your trades aren't profitable and then make adjustments.

Options Traders Are Flexible

I have said this before, but one thing you need to remember about options trading is you can make money no matter what happens to the stock.

So, you need to avoid falling into the trap of only trading options to make money one way. Most frequently, people do what they have been brainwashed to do and they will trade call options hoping to profit from rising share prices. If you are in that mindset now, you need to challenge yourself and begin trading in different ways, so you can experience making money from declining stock prices, or in the case of iron condors, stock prices that don't even change at all. You need to be able to adapt to changing market conditions to profit as an options trader. So don't entrap yourself by only using one method. Earlier, I said to use one or two styles, but you should be ready to branch out when market conditions change. Remember this – market conditions always change eventually. As I am writing, we are in the midst of a long-term bull market, but it won't last forever.

Take a Disciplined Approach

Don't just buy options for a certain stock because it feels good. You need to research your stocks. That will include doing fundamental analysis. This is going to mean paying attention to the history of a stock, knowing what the typical ranges are for, what the stock in recent history is, and also reading through the company's financial statements and prospectus. Remember, I suggest picking three companies to trade options on for a year and also two index funds.

The index funds require less research, but for the three companies that you pick, you should get to know those companies inside and out. Stick with them for a year, at the end of each year, evaluate each company.

Then decide if you want to keep them and bring them forward into the following year's trades. If one company is not working out for you, then move on and try a different company.

Making it in the trading market does not require you to be highly educated with a college degree. A successful trader also doesn't need to spend all their day working to achieve it in the market. What makes a trader successful in their state of mind? In trade, you need to combine a great strategy with an excellent state of mind will help a trader gain confidence in all their transactions. Mindset is how your emotions and thoughts make you respond to issues. We generally react to problems due to how our mind is set up, and that's why it is essential to have the right mindset to be able to make significant decisions. That is why to achieve anything, all we truly need is the right mindset that will encourage us to push on despite the many challenges we are likely to encounter along the way. The right state of mind gives calmness that earlier results in a trader being able to make decisions that are free of any emotions. Without emotions, a trader can look at the market at all angles without being forced to fall on one side. You appreciate the wins and all the profits you get as a trader you are aware you earned it by putting your hard work into it. You also take the losses positively to be a lesson for you so that you know what to do and what not to do in the future. Therefore, as a trader, you can take responsibility for all the decisions you make.

Successful traders understand why it is essential to keep away their emotions from trading.

Trading can be taught, and anyone can make it in the market, but who stays in the market is determined by their ability to separate the two. Being an emotionless trader means that not only do you make stable decisions, but you are also very accountable as a trader. You will never place blame on anyone or anything for your mistakes because you know you did your best it's only the circumstances that weren't favorable.

When the trader has the right mindset, it also means that they make the right realistic goals. A trader does not become too over-ambitious, making rational decisions that will not yield any results. Having set realistic goals means that your strategies as a trader are practical; therefore, there will be no time wasted trying to figure out the market. You already know what to expect from the market, and the market is also ready for you to make you a successful trader. Your expectations as a trader are also very realistic. You only take risks that you are aware of as a trader you can handle. A person who is not in their right state of mind will take risks that are way beyond him and then lose his mind when things don't work out.

The "Secrets" That Make a Profitable Trader

I decided to call them secrets because I noticed that they are characteristics that every successful trader has. Learn these skills too, and you will see that everything will seem easier.

Here are the 7 secrets on how to be a profitable trader:

1. **Learn to lose**: fear and greed heavily affect the activity of each trader, do not be pervaded by the fear of losing money and not even by the desire to earn more and more.

2. **Simplify your life**: the essential task of a trader is to simplify life, and therefore, simplify the analysis. Do not mask the insecurity behind an infinite number of indicators. You have to opt for clean graphs, using the bare minimum at a technical level (very often indicators are in contrast, some indicate you buy and others short... so use simple strategies and with a clean graph. The task will be to recognize the moment.)

3. **Always be informed**: those who want to start trading must have some basis and must study. Trading is not a game of chance but a job, read industry blogs, read business magazines, read trading books (in fact I am proud of you, who are reading this book).

4. **Have a trading plan and patience**: a trading plan and behavioral discipline will help you get to the top. In trading, it doesn't matter to cross the finish line first. Discipline and patience must be gained. Choose a broker that's right for you.

5. **Create a strategy that is suitable for you**: evaluate the time you can, devote to trading, and create a strategy. Creating your strategy will help you succeed in trading. Each trader must have a strategy that will make them stand out.

6. **Trading on opportunities**: the trader's skill is not measured by the number of investments he opens on the market. The important thing is that the investments you make are of quality, find the right opportunity (rule 20 / 80..20% of the actions bring 80% of the results). Return risk ratio at least 1 to 3. Always learn to grab opportunities because this will be your guide towards success.

7. **If you stop, you forget**: it is normal to lose, you need to know how to manage risk, maybe before reinvesting use trading simulators. Always remember that if you stop, you lose the opportunity to take the risk and step into success.

Top Trader Mistakes to Avoid

Options have always been a great trading tool that can be exercised in all types of market conditions. You can use options for generating income, making profits, or also for risk hedging. But most of the new traders in the world of options trading tend to make certain common mistakes as they start with trading. If not used in the proper way, options come along with the capability of emptying an account very quickly. In the worst-case scenario, options might even result in creating margin calls. So, let's have a look at some of the most common mistakes that are made by beginner traders.

No Proper Plan of Exit

One of the greatest mistakes that are made by beginners is that they pay less attention to the exit plan. As you opt for trading, you will be expecting to earn some amount of money. But how much is it? How will you determine that the generated amount of profit is the perfect one? If the option in hand is going to expire unexercised, will it be better to sell that option before the date of expiry? Will it help in reducing your losses? Will you stick to a particular option until it reaches the expiry date?

Before you get indulged in any form of trade, you will need to address all of these questions. You are required to make a proper exit plan with the perfect strategy. You will also require finding out the ways by which you can reduce the overall risk.

Make sure that you are having a clear idea when to exit a position if it is going to fail.

Not Paying Attention to Written Options

You can generate a great amount of profit by writing options. You will be receiving the profit amount upfront at the time of selling such options. If the option tends to expire unexercised, you will be able to keep the total amount that you received.

The option premium is the maximum profit amount that you can generate.

If the price of the underlying assets makes a move against you, you will be incurring huge losses. But, what mistake will result in the loss? The writer of an option fails to lock in a part of the premium amount when they have the chance to do so. If you are trading options thinking of it like gambling, you are making a huge mistake. When you have the notion, "I hope the option expires unexercised, and I can have the entire premium" is wrong. You are required to be actively involved in the trades. You are required to have a proper idea about the changing conditions. If you are 100% sure that an option will expire unexercised, then you can just sit back and relax. However, when the outcome of the option is not clear to you, it would be better to close your position before the date of expiry. For example, when you sell output options for $2, and you have the chance of exiting the position when the premium is $0.40, just exit the trade.

When you do this, you will still have the chance to have 80% of the initial premium that has been received by you. You will have the chance to keep $1.60 x the total number of shares on which you have written an option. It is better to have 80% of the premium than losing all if the scenario turns against you. So, it would be wise of you if you can keep track of the scenario and you will be able to save everything that you have. It would be better for you to remove the mentality of gambling when you want to generate consistent income.

Not Being Concerned About the Small Gains for the Big Profit

Every trader loves the feeling of generating a huge profit in their trades. You might think that it is an easy task to look out for the trades of a home run. But, in actuality, it is not much easy as it seems. The majority of time stocks do show any kind of action. It is very hard to determine when any such stocks are going to make a big explosion. The percentage points of the markets keep on changing daily. So, you can say that it would be much easier to generate small gains in a continuous stream without waiting for the big return. Although generating about 2% every week in comparison to generating 20% every week might not seem much attractive. But it is always better and safer to store in 2% for various weeks rather than giving in your all for the home run. Always note that as you start generating small gains consistently, you are decking your capital at a slow pace. This way, you will be able to generate compound returns.

Chapter 3: Learn the Purpose of Options and When to Use Them

How to Determine the Value of an Option

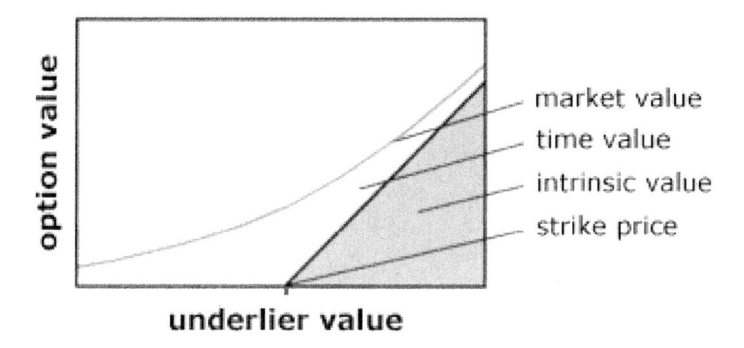

[Figure: Graph with "option value" on y-axis and "underlier value" on x-axis, showing market value, time value, intrinsic value, and strike price.]

Always bear in mind that when you are paying a premium for a stock option, you are betting on the future value of the underlying stock to generate profit from the sale of the stock. This is why you need to understand and know all the factors that determine the value of a particular option.

The pricing model used in determining the value of an option varies. But of all the ones being used, Black Scholes Model seems to be the most popular. The following are the key factors that determine the value of a stock option:

1. Current Stock Price
2. Market Volatility
3. Time of Expiration/Time Value
4. The Intrinsic Value
5. Interest Rates
6. Cash Dividends Paid

Current Stock Price

The current stock price is usually obvious as it is being displayed by the stock exchange. The most important thing, however, is the changes or fluctuations in the stock price over time, tending to affect the price of the underlying option.

The higher the movement of the stock price, the higher the call option will rise, and the lower the put option will fall. However, if the stock price moves down, the price of the call option will go down and the price of the put option will go up. It is, therefore, imperative that you always start with analyzing the trading price of the underlying stock in the market before making any option's trading decision.

Market Volatility

The current stock's price is affected by fluctuations in the marketplace, also known as volatility. A great price swing of an underlying stock will be caused by an increase in its volatility which will lead to higher premiums. Volatility affects the price of a stock, and the price of the stock affects the underlying stock option.

To make predictions about a particular stock option, it is very important to analyze the historical volatility of the stock. This is the reason why options trading has also been linked with volatility in the stock market. Highly volatile stocks like Amazon provides more avenues for speculation, as well as increasing the premium for the stock option.

Time of Expiration

While volatility affects the price of a stock, time value affects the probability of a stock option to generate profit. Your chosen stock can be volatile and have a great price swing in the marketplace, but if it is the time value that makes the stock option profitable.

Usually, the closer the time value, the lower the premium will be, and the higher the probability of the underlying stock option not getting "in the money." Therefore, when you are considering selecting a stock option in the market, endeavor to monitor the time value of the stock.

Only about 10% of options written are exercised, 60% are traded (closed) out while the remaining 30% expire worthlessly. To avoid being in the number of people whose stock options get worthless, you need to ensure that consider the time value of the stock against the fluctuations in the financial market.

Intrinsic Value

The intrinsic value of an option is the "in the money" amount of the options contract.

If you bought an options contract that is already "in the money," that options contract will be said to have an intrinsic value and thus profitable. The intrinsic value is usually, the amount of money above the strike price of the stock option.

Generally, stock options that are already "in the money" at the time of the contract have a higher premium. The options writer considers the additional time as an added benefit to the stock option buyer/holder, reducing risk, and making the entire transaction profitable.

It is also important to note that options trading that is "at the money" or "out of the money" has no intrinsic option value. Oftentimes, these are the type of options that creates losses for the buyers and wins for the sellers, unless they have a long-term value.

However, in real life stocks are usually traded slightly above the intrinsic value to nullify the fact the probability for an event to occur is zero or negative. In that case, the long-term value of the stock will provide the added time for the value of the stock. The premium paid is calculated from the intrinsic value of the stock plus the related time value.

Interest Rates

One of the most important factors that many option analysis tools skip is the effect of apparent interest rates on the price of options in the market.

This is because many of those tools use the simple Black Scholes Model. Even though interest rates and dividends are not primary determinants of the price of stock options, you need to put an eye on them.

When interest rates are relatively high, a call option buyer, for instance, will look towards buying more call option premiums than 100 shares of stock since it will be much cheaper to do so. Therefore, when interest rates increase, it tends to drive up call premiums and therefore causes put premiums to decrease in price. It is always to look at the interest rates before exercising any right for a call or put option.

Dividends

When cash dividends are paid to shareholders of a company, it plays a critical role in affecting the price of an option. This is the reason option prices are determined days or weeks after cash dividends have been dished out to the appropriate investors. Cash dividends affect the underlying stock price, which goes to affect the price of options.

When cash dividends are high, it will simply lower call premiums and higher put premiums. It is, therefore, prudent to check the ex-dividend date before evaluating and analyzing the price of an option. To capture cash dividends, in the money option holders will have to exercise the right on time. This makes perfect sense if you want to get access to the cash dividends to be paid by the company.

Chapter 4: Advantages and Disadvantages of Options Trading

Advantages of Option Trading

Although options trading began a long time ago, it has a huge reputation as a risky investment that only experts can understand.

However, for individual investors, options trading can be useful in various aspects. In this section, I will expound on the key advantages options offer and how valuable it is to add them to your portfolio.

Recently, options trading has received wide recognition. At the same time, many investors try to stay away from it because they believe it is sophisticated and hard to understand.

Others, who have given it a try, have had a bad experience because of their poor background in trading. This situation has led to major problems with many discouraging others from taking part in trading.

Furthermore, terms like "dangerous" or "risky" have been attached incorrectly to options trading by various financial media and public figures in the financial market.

Notwithstanding, it is vital for investors not to conclude based on this bad experience without getting the other side of the story. This will be impartial and inappropriate to conclude that options trading is risky and dangerous suddenly.

In this book, you will understand four key advantages you will benefit as an investor trading options. With these advantages, you will understand why many people have considered it risky and dangerous.

Cost Efficiency

Trading options gives you great leverage. Because of this, an investor can get an option position that is similar to a stock position but which offers a better cost-saving opportunity. For instance, you buy 100 shares of a $40 stock, which must result in a payout of $4,000. Nevertheless, if the investor decides to buy two $10 calls (remember each contract is equivalent to 100 shares), the total cost will be $2,000 (2 contracts x 100 shares x $10). The $10 is the market price. From this, the investor has an additional $2,000 to use for whatever purpose.

Although it is not as easy as you see it because the investor must select the right call to buy to make such profit.

For clarity, let us use another example. Assuming you want to buy Apple's share because you anticipate it will rise within several months. So, you bought 150 shares of Apple while it is trading at $120; the total cost would be $18,000.

Rather than spending so much more, you would decide to select the option imitating the stock closely and purchase the August call option with a predetermined price of $60, for $16. To get a position as the same as the 150 shares aforementioned, you have to buy two contracts. This will bring your investment to $32,000 (2 contracts x 100 shares x 16 current market price), which opposes the $18,000 you could have invested.

Less Risky

In options trading, you will find situations where buying the options is riskier than you owning equities. Nevertheless, sometimes, you will find when options can help you reduce your risk.

However, this depends on how you choose to use them. Options trading is less risky for traders because they don't require much financial commitment when compared to equities.

Options are safer than stocks because they are the most reliable aspect of hedging. If an investor buys a stock, he has to place a stop-loss order regularly to protect this position.

The purpose of putting the stop order is to stop losses when it reaches its predetermined price set by the investor. Even if this looks good, the issue is that it depends on the nature of the order.

For instance, you decide to buy a stock at $150 but don't want to lose anything below 15% of your investment.

So you decide to place a stop order at $145. This order will be activated once the order sells at or below $145. Peradventure, you woke up the next morning after seeing the stock closed at $151 the previous day and heard that the CEO of the company wasn't truthful concerning the earning reports.

Furthermore, there were rumors of embezzlement in the company with the expectation that the stock will open around $120. Once this happens, $120 will be your first trade below the stop order you placed at $145. Immediately, the stock opens, it will first sell at $120. The stop-loss order you activated wasn't there to "save" your investment when you need it.

Peradventure, you trigger the put option to protect your investment, it couldn't have affected you. Options are different in the sense that they don't shut down even when the market closes.

They provide insurance every day of the week. Stop orders cannot do this for you. This is the reason why options are a more reliable aspect of hedging.

Additionally, instead of buying the stock, you could have used the stock replacement strategy, which allows you to buy an "in the money" call option rather than buying the stock.

With certain stock options, you can mimic an equivalent of 75% of the stock performance; however, this cost one-quarter of the stock price.

If you had bought the $145 predetermined price call rather than the stock, your loss would have been limited to the amount you spent. If the option cost you only $6, your loss would have been only $6 rather than the $31.

Higher Profitability

There is no need to use a calculator to find out if you are making the same profit as you are losing money because options trading comes with higher returns. The example below will clarify that.

We will make a comprehension of the percentage returns when you bought the stock at $50 and $6, respectively.

Let's assume the option has a delta of 70. This means the price of the option will change 70% of the stock's price change. Peradventure, the stock rose to $5; the position of your stock would return a 10% increase.

Strategic Alternatives

The last benefit to options trading is the alternative investment opportunity it offers. Options trading offers a flexible tool and allows investors to recreate their options in many ways.

These positions are called synthetics and offer investors with different means of achieving the same investment goals for their trading.

Even though synthetic positions are regarded as advanced in options trading, they offer various strategic alternatives for investors.

For instance, most investors use brokers who charge a margin when the investor decides to short a stock. However, some investor doesn't use brokers that offer a margin.

Using options in your trading as an investor allows you to trade the "three dimensions" of the market if you like.

Disadvantages of Option Trading

You may be thinking, are there any disadvantages to options trading? Well, anyone who tells you no is only deceiving you.

Options trading is a short-term investment, and there are bound to be some disadvantages. For instance, if you mistakenly make a wrong prediction on a particular trade, within the next couple of months, you will lose money instead of waiting for years.

Another disadvantage is taxes. You think because you trade online, you won't pay tax. You got that wrong because everything you do on the options trading market requires you to pay tax.

However, in certain rare cases, you may not pay. Therefore, include that in our business plan and ensure to fill your IRA form before you start investing. Additionally, you won't have any certificate of deposit when you trade options, unlike shares. The only thing you get when trading options is your paid rights, and this doesn't prove ownership of the option.

Besides this, the issue of uncertainty is a turnoff for most investors. It is scary to invest in something you do not know about. Because of this, most investors take the time to understand everything about the market and investing. With that knowledge, they can easily turn a loss into a profit. The important thing is to know the strategy you want to use. Endeavor to start small; take only trade you can afford to lose. Options' trading is like learning how to drive.

At first, everything looks scary and impossible. However, with time behind the wheel, you begin to perfect your driving skills. Over time, you start using a single hand to turn the steering; options trading works similarly. To be at the top, you have to practice, learn, and unlearn what you have learned.

Why Consider Options Trading?

"Never rely on a single source of income." This gives you the idea of why you should consider options trading because it enables you to diversify your investment while improving your general investment portfolio. This may come as a surprise to you. Still, most big corporations throughout the world use options trading as a hedging tactic to defend themselves against losing money when there is a heavy fluctuation of stock prices. To cut the story short, with options trading, you have the advantage when trading and the opportunity to have a larger payout if you decide on selling the stock. The most interesting aspect is risk management.

Just know that as a new investor, you have nothing to worry about your portfolio going bad because it can only get better with options trading.

The primary motive behind most people venturing into options trading is to make money. There are various reasons to support their quest because options trading offers numerous advantages when compared to other financial instruments. However, options trading may not be suitable for everyone, but if you are ready, you can make good money.

The following are some reasons why many consider options trading as another source of income.

- **Risk management**: When you trigger the put options, it offers you the opportunity to hedge against a likely fall in the share value you are holding.

- **Speculation**: The flexibility of trading inside and outside of options positions affords you the chance of trading options without any intention of putting them to action.

If you anticipate a rise in the market, you may choose to buy the call options. However, you can also trigger the put options if you expect the price to fall.

- **Time to decide**: When you trigger the call option, you lock the share to the buying price. This gives the buyer adequate time to decide if to exercise the call option and purchase the shares.

- **Leverage**: This gives you the control to collect high returns from a smaller initial amount instead of investing directly. Nevertheless, leverage comes with its own risk when compared to direct investment.

In general, trading options allow you to benefit from a price change without paying the full share price.

Where to Trade Options

This question is a crucial one in the mind of many beginners, looking forward to trading options. While it is quite easy to trade options on various options exchanges in the world, you still need the services of a reliable broker because you cannot make your transaction. There are various options brokers to select, and they come in different types. One of the key decisions facing most beginners is their inability to find the best broker to use for their options trading.

Chapter 5: Overview of Options

What Are Options?

	Call	Put
Buyer	Has the **right** to buy stock at a certain price.	Has the **right** to sell stock at a certain price.
Seller	Has the **obligation** to sell stock at a certain price.	Has the **obligation** to buy stock at a certain price.

An option is a contract that provides the buyer the right, but not the obligation, to buy or sell an asset subject to a specific price no later than a specified date. An option, such as stock or bond, is a type of security. It is also a contract that comes with strictly defined terms and properties.

After all, a contract for stock options can take two forms: call options and orders. In both cases, you have the right, but not the obligation, to buy or sell the shares subject to a predetermined price. The default price is also called the strike price.

An important feature of options, both put and call, is the expiration date, when the option is no longer valuable.

Before that, investors give another person the option to make a profit during the month. However, due to decreased time, the option's value will decrease while the expiration date is set.

Let's say on June 1, 2021, ABC traded at $10 per share. You can buy a call option that allows you to buy 100 shares at any time (for example, August 22, 2021) for $12 per share.

You can act in this way (buy the option and wait) If you think the ABC Company is underestimated.

45 days have passed and now ABC Company trades at $ 15 a share. You could exercise your stock purchase option to $ 12 and gain a significant profit. If ABC Company is trading below $ 12, it will not exercise your option and will be useless. Remember that in options, the first price is the option contract's price. It changes continuously depending on market conditions and the underlying security.

The first is the intrinsic value (the amount of the option is in cash) + the time value (the more extended time remains until the expiration date, usually the higher). When you sell your option, you must subtract the amount of premium from the profit.

Buying and Selling Options

You can be the buyer or seller of the option in options trading.

If you buy a call option, you acquire the right to purchase the underlying shares at the strike price. Not later than the expiration date.

If you buy a put option, you have the right to sell the shares at the strike price no later than the expiration date.

You can sell the option to another buyer or drop it as well.

When selling or writing options? You are required to abide by the option contract terms if the buyer wishes to apply it.

If you sell a call option, you have to sell the underlying assets at the strike cost to the buyer. And in the position of a put option, you have to buy the stock at the strike price.

If you write options, you must know that it is up to the buyer to decide whether to exercise the contract or not. Nevertheless, it is possible to get out of the deal by buying another contract to offset your obligation.

Types of Options

TYPES OF OPTIONS

Options are of two types –
- Calls and Puts.
- Calls give the buyer the right but not the obligation to buy a given quantity of the underlying asset, at a given price on or before a future given date.
- Puts gives the buyer the right, but not obligation to sell a given quantity of the underlying asset at a given price on or before a given date.

Luckily, there are just two kinds of a standard option: a call and a put. A call option contract gives the owner the privilege to buy 100 portions of predetermined security at a predefined cost within a predefined time. A put option contract gives the owner the privilege to sell 100 portions of predetermined security at a predefined within a predetermined time allotment.

Basic Terms Used in Options Trading and Their Explanation

Call Option

A Call Option is a security that gives the proprietor the privilege to buy 100 portions of a stock or a record at a specific cost by a specific date. That "specific cost" is known as the strike cost, and that "specific date" is known as the termination date. The accompanying four attributes characterize a call option:

- There is an underlying stock or record

- There is a lapse date of the option
- There is a strike cost of the option
- The option is the privilege to BUY the underlying stock or file.

Benefits of Options Trading

There are numerous reasons options trading can be an excellent supplement to your current contributing procedure.

They incorporate the accompanying:

Options give you influence in your contribution. An options contract can give you a cheaper introduction to a stock than buying shares out and out, increasing the profits and losses if the stock value moves.

Options can also decrease the chance in your general portfolio. For example, you can consolidate buying put options to sell stock at a predefined cost with responsibility for offers themselves. That exchange, known as a defensive put, gives you the advantage if the stock value rises but protects you from a part of the losses if the stock value falls.

Options can offer a source of portfolio pay. Selling options as opposed to getting them, you're the one to get the installment for that particular option. Regardless of whether the options are not exercised, you get the opportunity to keep that installment as pay for having expected the commitment for the agreement.

Options Trading Risks

Balancing these advantages is some genuine danger for options. Above all, options frequently terminate uselessly, bringing about a total loss of whatever the buyer paid for the option. For those used to seeing a stock movement of 5% to 10% as a huge arrangement, the unpredictability of options can come as a gigantic stun.

Second, there's an expectation to absorb information associated with options trading. Numerous financier organizations offer options trading, yet you'll need to meet some additional administrative needs before your merchant gives you a chance to exchange options. For example, you'll need to read some informative material about the options showcase to find out how your merchant handles tolerating option orders. And, you'll have to recognize what you need to do to advise your facility that you need to practice an option. This also happens if you choose to sell an option, and the buyer chooses to practice it against you.

Finally, few options systems possibly function admirably when you perform several trades at the same time. Options markets aren't generally as fluid as the financial exchange, those concurrent trades don't generally work flawlessly — and that can present the risk that your procedure won't work how you proposed or trusted.

How to Pick a Good Broker

If you need to trade options at a point, picking a decent dealer is vital. This is what to search for:

- Considerable research: Exceptional instruments for assessing options can be helpful; however, not all business organizations offer them.

- Low commissions: Merchants regularly have distinctive commission rates for options than they have for stocks. Because a specialist offers shabby stock exchanges doesn't imply that the commissions on those options will be aggressive.

- Extraordinary client support: Dealers of options are bound to need to speak with client administration specialists to complete their exchanges how they need, particularly for progressively complex procedures. Nothing's more disappointing than having a merchant's client administration delegates not by any stretch of the imagination understand what you're attempting to do with your options trading.

How to Go About Opening an Option Savings Account

Before you can even begin, you need to clear a couple of obstacles. Due to the measure of capital required and the mixed nature of anticipating numerous moving parts, brokers need to discover more about a potential investor before granting them an authorization slip to begin trading options. Financier firms screen potential options brokers to survey their trading background, their understanding of the dangers in options, and their budgetary readiness.

You'll have to give a planned agent:

- Investment targets, for example, salary, development, capital safeguarding or theory;
- Trading background, including your insight into contributing, to what extent you've been trading stocks or options, what number of exchanges you make every year and the size of your exchanges;
- Individual budgetary data, including total fluid assets (or investments effectively sold for money), yearly pay, all-out total assets, and business data;
- The kinds of options you need to exchange.

In light of your answers, the representative relegates you an underlying trading level (regularly 1 to 4; however, a fifth level is winding up progressively normal) which is your vital aspect for putting particular kinds of options exchanges. Screening ought to go two different ways. The specialist you exchange options with is your most significant contributing accomplice. Finding the handle that offers the devices, research, direction, and bolster you need is particularly significant for investors who are new to options trading.

Core Elements in an Option Trade

Whenever you take out an option, you're getting consent to buy or sell a stock, for the most part, 100 segments of the stock per contract, at a pre-arranged expense at a particular date.

To put the trade, you should choose three fundamental options:

- Pick which course you think the stock is going to move;
- Anticipate how high or low the stock cost will move from its present expense;
- Choose the time length during which the stock is most likely going to move;

Chapter 6: Simplified Examples of Options Trades

It is sometimes difficult for a beginner to understand options trading and the various associated terms without viewing them in the context of an actual trade.

Therefore, in this section, you will get to read about two different trades involving a cattle breeder and cattle traders—trades that will help you understand the connection between options trading and physical trading in the real world. The first trade is an analogy of a typical call option trade while the second example is an analogy of a put option trade. Once you read through these examples, you will be able to understand how call options and put options work easily. These examples should also make it easy for you to comprehend the various terms used in trading.

Trade 1: Bob's Call Option Trade

Jacob is a farmer and a cattle breeder who owns several dairy cows. Bob, who is an acquaintance of Jacob, is a trader of farm animals.

One day, Bob gets a tip from a friend that the town's main dairy was negotiating a deal with a large international chocolate manufacturing company. If the deal were to materialize, the chocolate company would triple the quantity of milk they purchase from the dairy every day.

To meet this increase in demand, the dairy would also have to increase milk production, and for increasing production, they would have to purchase a large number of dairy cows at short notice – a move that could result in a substantial increase in cow prices locally.

Bob realized he could make some excellent profits if he bought some cows from Jacob and then sold them after the prices went up. However, Bob wasn't completely certain about this tip and did not want to buy cows upfront at the full price of $2,000 (which was the market price for a dairy cow at that time) and later sell out for a loss if the price did not rise as expected.

Therefore, Bob approaches Jacob and makes him a unique offer.

Bob tells Jacob that he will pay the latter a sum of $50 upfront for the right to buy one of his cows at the prevailing market price of $2,000, for the next 30 days. Also, Jacob would be under no obligation to return that amount if Bob no longer wanted to exercise his right (if cow prices dropped below $2,000).

Jacob saw no reason for cow prices rising anytime soon and was therefore glad to sign a contract to receive $50 from trader Bob in exchange for giving Bob the right to buy a cow at $2,000 for the next 30 days.

However, Jacob puts forth a condition that the proposed contract should cover 5 cows and not just 1 cow and that meant Bob, would have to pay a total of $250 for the right to purchase 5 cows for 30 days.

Bob agrees to Jacob's condition and therefore, Jacob pockets Bob's $250 and then signs the contract—the contract that gave Bob the right (but not the obligation) to buy 5 of Jacob's cows at the price of $2,000 for the next 30 days.

Bob knew that in the next 30 days, the market price of cows would either rise (as per his expectations), or continue to stay the same, or perhaps even fall (in the worst-case scenario).

If the market price for cows stayed the same at $2,000 or fell below that value in the next 30 days, Bob would have to simply forfeit the $250 he paid Jacob to get the agreement in place. Bob was under no obligation to buy cows at a lower price and hence his losses will be curtailed to $250 only – the money he paid Jacob to sign the contract.

On the other hand, if the market price for cows did go up within the next 30 days, Bob would approach Jacob to get 5 cows at $2,000 each and Jacob would be contractually obliged to sell the cows at $2,000, irrespective of how much more the cows were worth at that time.

Bob waits.

Three weeks after the contract was put in place, the town dairy signed a deal with the chocolate company to increase its daily supply of milk to the chocolate company by almost 4 times. To meet that demand the dairy started purchasing a large number of dairy cows at increasingly higher rates that resulted in the prices of dairy cows surging by almost 25% in the locality.

Following this price surge, Bob goes to Jacob and exercises his right to buy the 5 cows at $2,000 each. Bob then goes ahead and sells these cows to the dairy at $2,500 each.

Bob, thereby, makes a total profit of $2,250 for these 5 cows ($500 times 5 less the $250 for the contract amount he paid Jacob).

The trade that took place between Bob and Jacob is representative of how an options trade works and if we apply stock market terms into the aforementioned scenario then:

- A single cow represents one particular underlying share/stock.
- Bob is the buyer of the contract and Jacob is the seller. Since this contract gives the buyer the right to buy – this contract is a call option.
- $2,000 represents the market price of the share of the given company (at the time the agreement was put in place).
- $2,000 also represents the strike-price (SP) or the pre-determined price at which the proposed trade would take place between the buyer (Bob) and the seller (Jacob) – remember that Jacob paid $50 to purchase a cow at a fixed price of $2,000.
- The $50 paid against each cow is called the premium.
- The number 5 indicates the lot size of the contract – it is the fixed number of shares that an individual options contract covers.
- Lastly, the 30 days in this scenario denotes the time to expiry of the options contract.

I hope you have perfectly understood how a call option works now.

If you are a little unclear on this still, try reading this entire section one more time and try correlating the various terms with what they represented in the Bob-Jacob trade and you should understand the concept of a call option trade without any further difficulty.

Note: In this example, Bob had the right to exercise his option at the time during the 30 days – this is representative of American-style options. Had this trade followed the European style, Bob would have had to wait till the end of the 30 days to exercise his option.

Now that you understood how a call option works, the logic behind the working of a put option should come to you much easier.

Trade 2: Jacob's Put Option Trade

After being forced to sell 5 of his cows at a price lesser than the market price due to his contractual obligation, a rather disappointed Jacob starts thinking.

From his experience, Jacob has seen that in situations where livestock prices increase sharply due to some change in the environment, the prices eventually come down marginally before reaching stability.

However, Jacob wasn't certain if cow prices had hit the ceiling yet – if he sold off his cows right away and prices continued to rise, he would miss a chance for selling at even better prices. The market price for a cow was currently at $2,500 and Jacob wanted to wait for a couple of weeks and see if it went up any further. If the prices were already at a high and if they dropped sharply, Jacob wanted to ensure that he could sell a few cows for at least $2,400.

Considering his predicament, Jacob decides to get into a contract similar to the one he had earlier signed with Bob. However, this time, he would be the 'buyer' of the right – the right to sell cows at a fixed price (unlike the right to buy that Bob purchased from him).

For this purpose, Jacob approaches Chad, a livestock trader in the local market, and offers him a deal. The deal was that, for the next 60 days, Jacob would have a right to sell Chad 10 cows at $2,400 each. And to own that right, Jacob would pay $30 per cow - a total of $300 for 10 cows.

Chad agrees and signs up for the deal and pockets the $300 since he didn't expect prices to fall from $2,500, let alone fall below $2,400. As long as cow prices stayed above $2,400 for the next 2 months (which Chad thought was very likely), he had nothing to lose.

A month and a half later, Jacob's prediction turned out to be right and cow prices dropped down to $2,250.

Therefore, Jacob goes to Chad and exercises his right to sell the cows at $2,400.

Since Chad was contractually obliged to buy the cows at $2,400, he has no choice but to buy the cows at the fixed price despite the cows being worth $150 less in the market. Jacob thereby profits by $1200 ($150 x 10 less the $300 paid for the contract) off his trade.

Like we did last time, let's apply the various stock market terms to this trade too:

- A single cow represents one particular underlying share/stock.
- Jacob is the buyer of the contract while Chad is the seller. Since this contract gives the buyer the right to sell – this contract is a put option.
- $2,500 - the price of the cow, represents the market price of a share (at the time the agreement was put in place).
- $2,400 represents the strike-price (SP) or the pre-determined price at which the proposed trade would take place between the buyer (Jacob) and the seller (Chad).
- The $30 paid against each cow is the premium.
- The number 10 indicates the size of the contract.
- Lastly, the 60 days in this scenario denotes the time to expiry of the options contract.

OPTIONS

Chapter 7: Myths About Options Trading

A popular misconception is that trading in options is quite risky when compared to other forms of investments. Well, there is a certain degree of risk involved with everything you do in life, and the same stands true for options trading as well. You cannot earn a profit if you are unwilling to assume a little risk. However, the level of risk you expose yourself to is entirely up to you. In this section, let us bust the most popular myths about options trading.

Losing and Winning

It is a myth that trading in options is a zero-sum game. Options can very well be used as insurance policies. There is a great way to mitigate risk and not just to be used as a vehicle of trade. For instance, if you purchase a call option and earn a profit when you sell it at a higher price, there is no reason to believe that the seller incurred a loss because of your gain. The seller might have hedged his options and might have earned a greater profit than you did. So, when it comes to hedging transactions based on options, it is not a zero-sum game. It isn't necessarily true that one person has to lose for the other to win when it comes to trading in options.

Easy Money

The concept of easy money does not exist. You are required to put in a little effort if you want to own some profit.

The same stands true for trading as well. You must not only learn how to trade but must also work on using this knowledge to invest successfully. So, trading in options requires a willingness to learn, dedication, patience, and focus. There is a learning curve associated with it, and you must ever stop learning.

Only Buying Calls or Puts

Another popular misconception is that a trader can stay profitable only if he purchases calls or puts. Yes, this is a profitable strategy, but it isn't the only way to be profitable. When you're purchasing calls or puts, there are three things you must be right about—the direction of the price movement, the size of the movement, and the time at which the move of course. If you get any of these things wrong, then you stand to lose if you only concentrate on purchasing also puts.

Only for Speculation

Well, when it comes to trading in options, there is a lot of speculation involved. They cannot only be used for speculative purposes. Still, they can also be used as an insurance policy, to earn an income, and also for hedging or to cushion any losses. For instance, an investor who feels that the market will be trading in a specific range can trade in the options market by using income-producing strategies like calendars or condors.

Naked Options Are Risky

A lot of people seem to believe that selling naked options is quite risky.

However, the profit or loss profile of selling a naked put is quite similar to that of selling a covered call. Writing naked puts is certainly a conservative approach. Still, the risk involved is quite low when you are buying or selling stocks using this strategy.

Only for Options Sellers

Another popular misconception is that the only people who stand to make money are the ones who sell options. If the seller were the only ones who made money, then there would be no buyers in the market. If there are no buyers, then the market will cease to exist. The option seller certainly has a slight edge over the bios, but this isn't necessarily true. It isn't possible to determine whether it is more profitable to sell or buy options. It merely means that there is more than one way to reach your financial goals.

Worthless on Expiration

Only a small portion of options are ever exercised—that is only certain traders use their right to buy or sell the underlying asset. A significant portion of positions related to options is always closed before the expiration date. Only one-third of options tend to be worthless upon expiration. If an option expires worthless, it doesn't say anything about the profitability of the strategy that might have been used. There are several strategies where it is profitable if the option is worthless upon expiration. Now that you're aware of all the myths and the corresponding facts keep them in mind whenever you are trading in options.

OPTIONS

Chapter 8: Puts and Calls

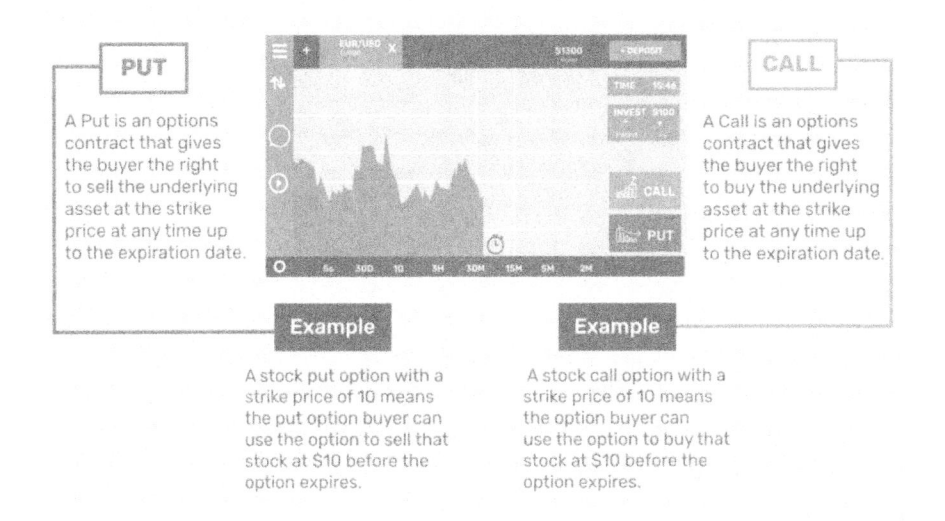

PUT

A Put is an options contract that gives the buyer the right to sell the underlying asset at the strike price at any time up to the expiration date.

Example

A stock put option with a strike price of 10 means the put option buyer can use the option to sell that stock at $10 before the option expires.

CALL

A Call is an options contract that gives the buyer the right to buy the underlying asset at the strike price at any time up to the expiration date.

Example

A stock call option with a strike price of 10 means the option buyer can use the option to buy that stock at $10 before the option expires.

The Put and call options price movements as a derivative investment are based on a different financial product.

With options, you won't have the ownership of the shares, but you make smart bets on a stock's price and its value in the future.

What makes options a good subject is that you can choose whether you want to exercise them or not. You can let the options expire If your bet is wrong. Although it still wouldn't compare had you paid for the stock's full price if the options' original cost is lost.

Call options are purchased when the trader thinks the price goes up within a particular time range.

Put options are purchased when the trader thinks the price goes down within a particular time range.

A call is an options contract that gives the buyer the right to buy an underlying asset at a previously set price at any time up to the maturity date.

Being a buyer, you can choose to exercise the option to purchase the underlying. Only on the set expiration date.

The price previously determined at which the call buyer has the choice to purchase the underlying asset is called strike price.

Let me explain it to you with an example: a buyer of a call option on a stock with an exercise price of $ 10 may choose to buy that stock at the same price before the option's expiration date.

This expiration can be short or long-term. It can be worth it for call buyers to exercise the option, which consists of asking the call's writer or seller to sell the shares at the set strike price, only if the current price is more than the strike price.

Here is an example: if a stock trades at $ 10 on the stock market, it's not profitable for the call option buyer to buy the stock at $ 11 as you could get the same at a lower price on the market.

The right to sell stocks at the strike price in a specific time range is reserved to put buyers.

The volatility the stock market goes through can be both exciting and nerve-wracking. When you operate with your money, it's a complete different game. Anxiety and fear are two insidious emotions.

But don't worry, with well-planned strategies and costance you can be successful in this field. And Options might be perfect to start cause you avoid the risk of directly selling stocks or buying them.

Using options strategically allows very low-risk whit huge profit potentials.

All of these benefits of trading in options got you excited, right? After all, options have lower risk and are much cheaper.

You need to know that there are two significant disadvantages: – the limited-time aspect and the reality that you don't own the stock until you choose to exercise your options..

Call Options

Talking about the call options, you pay for the 'rights to buy' certain shares at a set price and are covered by a specific time frame. In May, let's assume that stock ABC is selling for $90 per share.

If you think that the stock's price will go up in a few months, you can purchase a three-month option to buy 100 shares of ABC by August for $100.

You would be paying $200 (with the option cost per share $2). Remember that you are only allowed to buy in increments of 100 shares in options.

This allows you to buy 100 shares of ABC anytime within the three-month range. The $ 200 investment is significantly less than the $ 9,000 you would have had to shell out if you had bought 1k shares outright.

If you bet on July 15, ABC shares hit the market at $ 115, you can exercise the call option and you would have earned $ 1,300 (i.e. 100 shares multiplied by the $ 15 profit you earned per share and deducted from your original investment of $ 200).

If you can't buy the shares, you can also make a profit if you re-sell the option to another investor or via the open market.

The gain will be more or less similar to this option. If you are wrong and the ABC stock price drops to $ 80 and never reaches $ 100 within three months, you can let the option reach its maturity. This saves you money (if you bought the stock outright, your original $ 9,000 investment has now dropped to a value of just $ 8,000, so you've lost $ 1000).

This means you've only lost $200. Your investment for the call option.

Risks Involved in Call Options

I will never tire of saying it. Like any other form of investing, options have their own risks.

Let's consider a second scenario where you bet wrong and stock ABC never got to $100 during the three months, you would have lost the entire $200 of your investment, right? In terms of loss percentage, that's a complete loss of 100%.

Anyone playing the stock market would tell you that it's very rare for an investor to lose 100%. This scenario can only occur if ABC suddenly fails, causing its stock price to reset. If you look at it from the point of view of percentages, options can cause huge losses. Let's elaborate on this point.

If the ABC stock price has risen to $ 99 and it is the last day to exercise the option, buying the stock will mean losing one dollar per share.

What if you invest $ 9,000 in the stock and own 100 shares? In three months (the time frame of the example), you would have earned 10% off your original investment ($ 99 from $ 90). Comparing both, you would have earned 10% if you had bought the shares outright and lost 100% if you had chosen the option but not exercised it.

This is an example that makes you understand how risky options can be. However, the opposite can happen if stock ABC reaches a price higher than $100.

If you bought the option, your gain would have been higher than buying the stocks outright.

If the stock reached $ 110, you would have earned 400% ($ 10 gain versus $ 2 per equity investment) if you opted for the option and only earned 22% ($ 20 gain versus $ 90 per equity investment) if I had bought the shares.

Lastly, when you have ownership of the stock, you are free to make your decisions. Nothing can force you to sell. This means that if the ABC stock price falls, you can hold on to it if you feel it still has the potential to bounce back and even increase in value from the original.

If the price goes up, you'll make significant gains and you didn't incur losses. However, the expiration of the options investment method would have forced you to suffer a 100% loss after the set range. There will be no option to hold on to the stock even if you believe it will go up in value soon.

You need to be aware of all the pros and cons before you step into the arena of options trading.

Put Options

"put' gives you the option to sell at a set price within a specific range of time. Investors usually purchase put options to protect the price of a stock in case it drops down.

With put options, you can always sell the shares and your investment portfolio is protected from unexpected market swings. So Put options are a way to hedge your portfolio or lower its risk.

Let's explain this with an example. You invested in ABC stock for 100 shares, which you bought for $ 50 per share. As of May 31, the price per share has reached a market high of $ 70. You would like to maintain this position in your stock and at the same time protect your profits made if the price of this stock falls. Then you can buy a put option with a three-month maturity and a strike price of $ 70 per share.

If the ABC stock price drops dramatically over the next couple of months, hitting a low per-share price of just $ 60, you'll still be protected. By exercising your put option, you will still be able to sell the shares at $ 70 each even though the ABC stock is now trading at a lower value. If you are confident that ABC can still bounce back in the future, you can hold the stock and simply resell the put option. The price of this put option will be increased due to the underwater shares taken by ABC.

On the other hand, if the value of the ABC stock continues to rise, let the put option expire and you will still profit from the increase in the share price.

Even though you lost your investment in the put option, you still have the underlying stock with you. This is why you can view the put option as a kind of insurance policy for your investment. Just like you would in a call option, you can purchase put options even if you don't own the underlying stock. You are not required to own the stock itself.

Risks Involved in Put Options

Like call options, put options carry the same risks. Here too, there is a 100% loss potential when the underlying stock price goes up and a huge gain when the price goes down because you can resell the option at a higher price.

OPTIONS

Chapter 9: Technical Analysis

History

Technical analysis has been used over the years in trades. The technical analysis methods have been used for over a hundred years to come up with deductions regarding the market.

In Asia, the use of technical analysis led to the development of candlestick techniques, and it forms the main charting technique. Over time, more tools and techniques have come up to help traders predict the prices in various markets. There are many indicators that you can use to determine the market's direction, but only a few are valuable to your course. Let us look at the various indicators and how to use them.

What Is Technical Analysis?

Technical analysis uses charts and other recording methods to analyze various data in options trading. Using these visual instruments, you have the chance to determine the direction of the market because they give you a trend. This method focuses on studying the supply and demand of a market. The price will be seen to arise when the investor realizes the market is undervalued, and this leads to buying. If they think that the market is overvalued, the prices will start falling, and this is deemed the perfect time to sell.

You need to understand the movement of the various indicators to make the perfect decision. This method works on the premise that history usually repeats itself – a huge change in the prices affects the investors in any situation.

When operating with technical analysis, you have to remember that it functions because of the belief that the way the price of a trade has moved in the past will be a reliable metric for determining what it's likely to do again in the future.

Regardless of which market you choose to focus on, you won't be sifting through the data all on your own, and you'll have numerous technical tools, including trends, charts, and indicators to help you push your success rates to new levels.

Understand core assumptions: Technical analysis is all about measuring the relative value of a particular trade or underlying asset by using available tools to find otherwise invisible patterns that, ideally, few other people have currently noticed. When it comes to using technical analysis properly, you will always need to assume three things are true. First and foremost, the market ultimately discounts everything; second, trends will always be an adequate predictor of price and third, history is bound to repeat itself when given enough time to do so.

Technical analysis believes that the current price of the underlying asset in question is the only metric that matters when it comes to looking into the current state of things outside of the market, specifically because everything else is already automatically factored in when the current price is set as it is. As such, to accurately use this type of analysis all you need to know is the current price of the potential trade-in question as well as the greater economic climate as a whole.

When it comes to technical analysis, asking 'how' is always going to be more important than 'why.' That is, the fact that the price moved in a specific way is far more important to a technical analyst then why it made that particular movement. Supply and demand should always be consulted, but beyond that, there are likely too many variables to make it worthwhile to consider all of them as opposed to their results.

Chart Patterns to Be Aware Of Flags and Pennants

Both flags and pennants show retracement, that is, deviations that will be visible in the short term with the primary trend. Retracement results in no breakout occurring from either the resistance or support levels, but this won't matter as the security will also not be following the dominant trend. The lack of breakout means this trend will be relatively short-term. The resistance and support lines of the pennant occur within a larger trend and converge so precisely that they practically form a point. A flag is essentially the same except that the resistance and support lines from the flag will be essentially parallel instead.

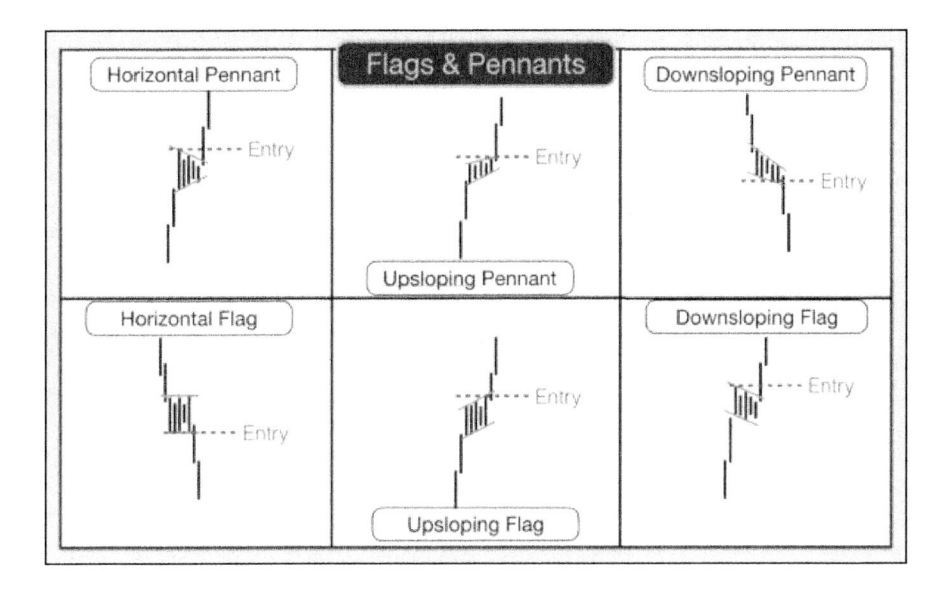

If you are looking for them, both flags and pennants are more likely to be found in the mid-section of the primary phase of the trend. They can last up to two weeks before being absorbed back into the primary trend line. They are typically associated with falling volume, which means that if you notice a flag or a pennant and the volume is not falling, then you are more likely seeing a reversal, which is a changing trend instead of a simple retracement.

Head Above Shoulders Formation

If you are looking for indicators of how long any one particular trend is likely to continue, then looking for a grouping of three peaks in a price chart, known as the head above shoulders formation, can indicate a bearish pattern moving forward. The peaks to the left and the right of the primary peak, also known as the shoulders, should be somewhat smaller than the head peak and also connect at a specific price. This price is known as the neckline and when it reaches the right shoulder the price will likely then plunge noticeably.

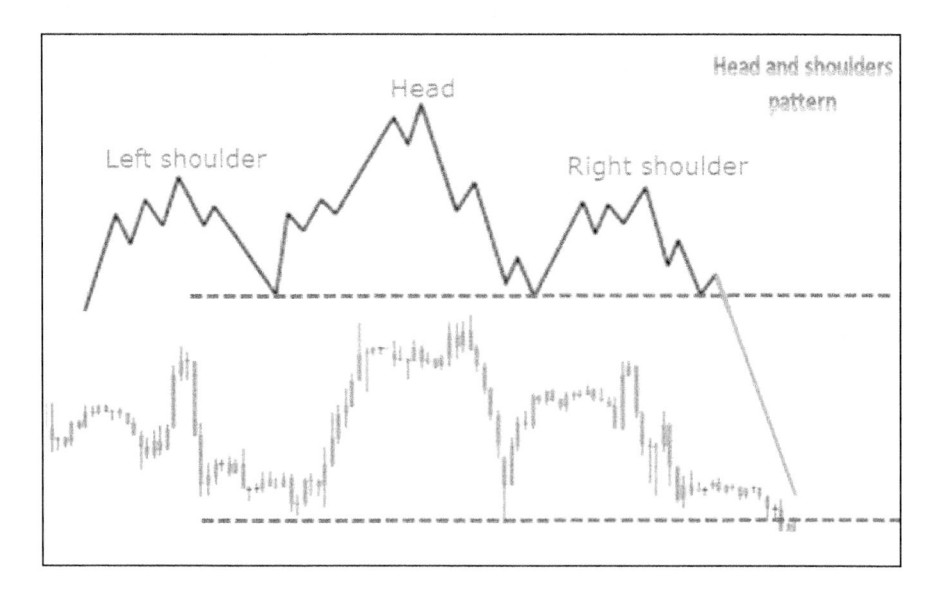

Head and shoulders pattern

The inverse head and shoulders (or head and shoulders bottom) is a sign that the price of the security in question is about to rise in the face of an existing downward trend. It typically forms at the lowest overall price of the trend.

Based on the analysis of the peak-and-trough pattern from the Dow Theory, an upward trend is then seen as indicative of a series of successive rising troughs and peaks. Meanwhile, a downward trend is indicative of a series of lower peaks and deeper troughs. If this is the case, then the head and shoulders pattern represents a weakening of an existing trend as the troughs and peaks deteriorate.

The head and shoulders top forms at the peaks of an upwards trend and signals that a reversal is often forthcoming through a process of four steps. The first of these starts with the creation of the far-left shoulder, which can be formed when the cryptocurrency reaches a new high before dropping to a new low. This is then followed by the formation of the head, which occurs when the security reaches an even higher high before retracing back to the low found in the left shoulder. Finally, the right shoulder is formed from a high that is lower than the high found in the head, countered by a retracement back to the low of the left shoulder. The pattern is then completed when the price drops back below the neckline.

In both instances, the price dipping below the neckline signals the true reversal of the trend in question, which means the security will now be moving in the opposite direction. This breakout point is often the ideal point to go either short or long. It is important to keep in mind, however, that the security is unlikely to continue smoothly in the direction the pattern suggests. As such, you will want to keep an eye out for what is called a throwback move.

Since all times exist on the same line, the Gann angle can then also be used to predict resistance, support, and direction strength as well as the timing on bottoms and tops as well. Gann angles are typically used to determine likely points of support and resistance and it is easy to get started with as it only requires the trade to determine the proper scale for the chart before drawing in the relevant Gann angles from the primary bottoms to the tops.

Essentially, this means that they make it less complicated for the trader to properly frame the market and thus makes it easier for them to predict the way the market is likely to move in the future based on the way it is currently moving in the predetermined framework. Angles that indicate a positive trend determine support and angles that show a downward trend outline resistance. This means that by understanding the accurate angle of a chart, the trader can more easily determine the best time to buy or sell far more simply than what could otherwise be the case. When utilizing Gann angles, you must keep in mind all the different things that can potentially cause the market to change between specific angles.

Cup and Handle Formation

The cup and handle formation most commonly appear if given security reaches a peak price before dropping off significantly for a prolonged amount of time. Sooner than later, however, the security will rebound, which is the perfect time to buy.

This is an indicator of a trend that is rapidly rising, which means you are going to want to take advantage of it as soon as possible before you miss out.

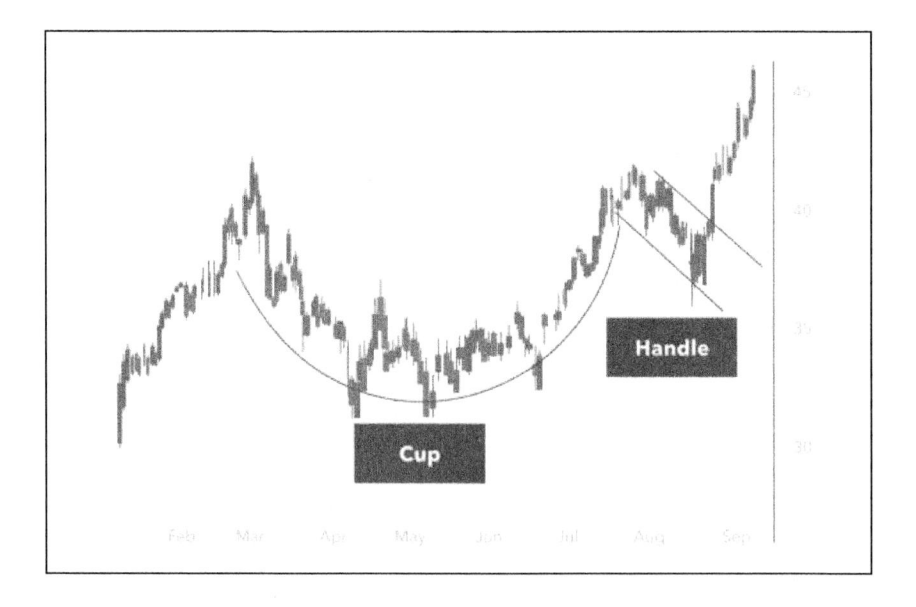

The handle will form on the cup when those who purchased the security at the previous high-water mark couldn't wait any longer begin to sell which makes new investors interested who then begin to buy as well. This type of formation does not typically form quickly, and indeed, has been known to take a year or more to become visible. Ideally, you will then be able to take advantage of this trend as soon as the handle starts to form. If you see the cup and handle forming, you will still want to consider any other day to day patterns that may be interfering with the overall trend as they are going to go a long way when it comes to determining the actual effectiveness of buying in at a specific point.

Trend Lines

Trend lines represent the typical direction that a given underlying asset is likely to move in and, thus, can be very beneficial for traders to highlight before trading. This is easier said than done, due to the high degree of volatility those assets of all types experience regularly. As such, you will find it much more useful to consider only the highs and lows that the underlying asset experiences as this will make it far easier to determine a workable pattern. Once you have determined the highs and the lows for the underlying

OPTIONS

asset it then becomes much easier to determine if the highs are increasing while the lows are decreasing or vice versa. You will also want to remain alert to the possibility of sidewise trends, where the price doesn't move much of anywhere, as this is a sign that you should avoid trading for the time being. When watching the trend lines, you will likely notice that the price movement of a given underlying asset tends to bounce off the same high and low points time after time. These are what are known as resistance and support levels and identifying them makes it easier for you to determine the supply and demand of the coin in question. The support level is the level that the price is unlikely to drop below because there are always going to be traders who are willing to buy at that point, driving demand back up. Once the price reaches the point where traders feel the price is unlikely to go any higher, they start to sell, and a level of resistance is created.

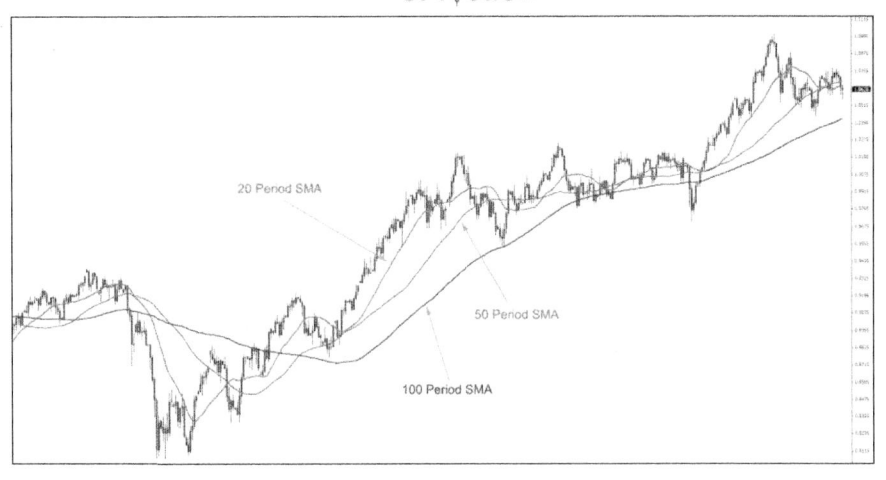

Moving Averages

The most commonly used confirmation tool is one that is referred to as the moving average convergence divergence or MACD for short. This tool measures the amount of difference that there is between two averages that have been smoothed to minimize ancillary noise. The difference between the two results is then further smoothed by the process before being matched against the moving average that it relates to as well. If the resulting smoothed average is still greater than the existing moving average, then you can be sure that the positive trend you were chasing exists. Meanwhile, if the smoothed average ends up below the existing moving average than any negative trends will be confirmed instead. The MACD chart is typically based on a combination of several EMAs. These averages can be based on any timeframe, though the most common is the 12-26-9 chart. This chart is typically broken into multiple parts, the first of which is the 26-day and 12-day charts. Mixing up the EMAs will allow you to more accurately gauge the level of momentum that the trend you are tracking is experiencing.

If the 12-day EMA ends up above the 26-day EMA, then you can assume the underlying stock in on an uptrend and the reverse indicates a downtrend. If the 12-day EMA increases more quickly than the 26-day EMA then the uptrend is going to be even well-pronounced. However, if the 12-day EMA moves closer to the 26-day EMA then you can safely assume that it is starting to slow and the momentum is waning, which means it is going to take the trend with it.

Chapter 10: Chart Reading

Broadly speaking, markets tend to move in one of two ways: either in trends or within ranges. Trends refer to movement in a particular direction, either down or up. Ranges refer to sideways movements where there's no real progress on either side. How are trends and ranges formed? You might be wondering.

Well, it all comes back to the order flow. Remember how buyers and sellers are constantly negotiating over prices? If the demand for a particular stock being to exceed the supply, the price is going to rise, in other words, buying pressure and volume is higher than the supply or sell side. The opposite happens in case of a downward move. You need to see trends as a result of this interaction instead of just geometric shapes. Understand where those shapes come from, and you'll unlock a lot of the markets' mysteries.

Trends

This shows what a trend in the market usually looks like.

An Uptrend

As you can see the overall movement of the price is upwards when viewed from left to right, but look at the gyrations in the order flow price undergoes before it gets there. In fact, before that last push-up on the right, it looked as if the price was ready to give up on the uptrend and turn downwards.

This is why directionally trading the markets is so hard. Markets are not clean. Price never goes up in a straight 45-degree angle or decline the same way. It moves up and down while going up or down if that makes sense. If you look at trends as a simple geometric thing where you apply the logic that if the right-hand side is higher than the left-hand side, then it is a trend, well, you'll end up donating all of your capital to other traders in the market.

When viewed from an order flow perspective, things become a lot clearer. Notice how there are bullish and bearish bars in this trend? Well, this is because bulls and bears exist. One side is trying to push prices up, and the other is trying to push prices down. The struggle between the two sides is the only constant in the market. The degree to which one side has supremacy over the other determines the angle of the trend and the cleanliness of it.

Think of it this way. All the orders in the market constitute 100% of the order flow. What proportion is controlled by bulls and what by bears?

In the uptrend given above how many times the bears keep coming in and stopping the bulls, it's safe to say that it is a significant percentage. Yet the bulls keep pushing the price up so they're in the majority.

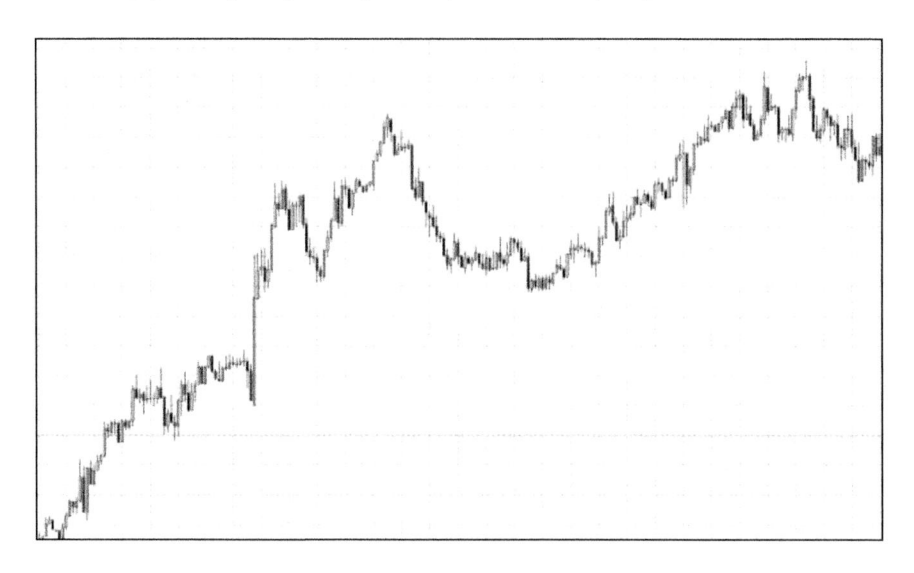

Another Uptrend

What is the respective proportion here? The bulls control a far larger percentage of overall order flow here as compared to the first uptrend. However, notice that the proportion seems to change. The left half of the trend is very different from the right half of the trend. Visually we can see this, but are there some concrete pointers we can develop to nail down how to determine to order flow dominance percentages? Well, I'm glad you asked!

Briefly, here they are:

1. Size of the with trend versus counter-trend bars;
2. Frequency of with trend versus counter-trend bars;
3. The angle with which price moves in a trend;

4. How far back into the trend do counter-trend reactions go;
5. How much progress do with trend bars make.

Looking at the left of the second uptrend, we see that bullish bars are bigger and far more frequent. The price moves at a steep angle and counter-trend reactions are pretty small and are easily overcome by the bulls to make constantly new highs. Contrast this with the right-hand side of the second uptrend and note the differences. You'll see that as price moves higher and higher, the counter-trend reactions grow from small to pretty big until, around the middle of the figure, it manages to undo the entirety of the previous push upwards. Price eventually bounces from a level and moves upwards at a far shallower angle than previously with bearish bars becoming more frequent. All market action follows this pattern. At first, one side is dominant and the other is weak. Eventually, over time, the other side begins asserting more dominance, and what was once the weak side becomes dominant again. The place where this change of power takes place is within a range.

Ranges

Ranges occur in two places: Either at the end of a trend or within them as small sideways movements as the trend takes a breather. The order flow characteristics of both types of ranges are very different, let's examine them in more detail.

First, the ranges that occur within trends can be seen as continuation ranges. In other words, with trend traders are taking a small break from their dominance before pushing higher. You can think of it as a high-powered sports car accelerating at top speed that needs to refuel every twenty minutes because it drains itself.

Of course, as trends move one, these ranges get bigger, but even these bigger ranges are indicators of trend continuation. Only when the trend reaches a situation where the order flow is far more evenly balanced, it becomes indicative of a change in direction in the trend. This is the situation that is happening in the first uptrend. Notice how strong the counter-trend traders are in there. Price is probably heading into a range where the order flow, balance is going to be 50/50.

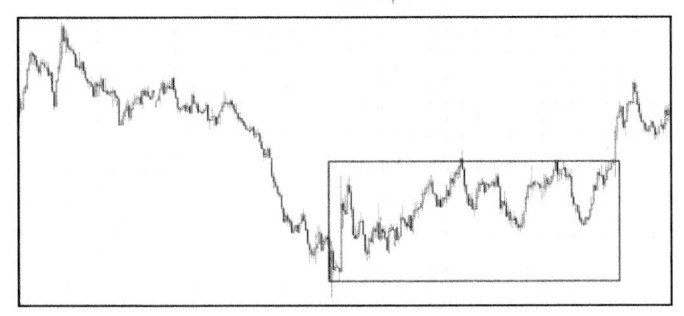

These 50/50 ranges are called accumulative or distributive ranges and occur at the end of trends. Accumulative ranges are where ownership of the stock is transferred from bearish traders to bullish ones. The bulls are 'accumulating' stock to push it higher into a bull trend (reversing the bear trend). A distributive range occurs at the top of a bull trend where sellers are absorbing the buyers and are getting ready to push prices downwards into a bear trend. Such ranges tend to be quite big and often take up large spaces on the chart. They're tough to spot at first since, being so huge; it's difficult to pinpoint the moment when they begin. This illustrates a classic accumulation range.

A range

The range in the illustration occurs after the bearish trend. Notice how it has an upward tilt to it before it finally breaks out upwards. This is the thing about such ranges. They don't go perfectly sideways, and you need to view them in the big-picture context to understand what is going on.

Support and Resistance

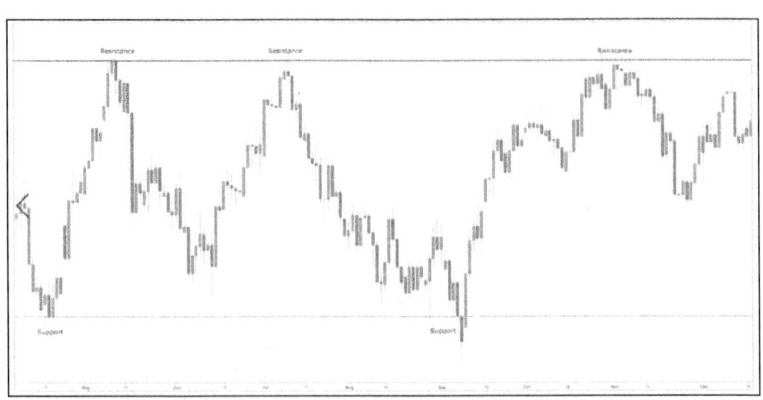

One major part of analyzing the big picture is to understand how support and resistance works. There is a lot of literature on the topic, but unfortunately, almost all of them seem to treat it the wrong way. Before I get into that though, let us ask ourselves first what is support and resistance (s/r).

As we've seen so far, the market is full of traders constantly negotiating on price, which makes up the order flow.

There happen to be some places on a chart which are significant and affect the supply and demand of the stock. Taking the example of a physical market, let's say you set up a stall to sell Christmas trees in the middle of summer, it's unlikely you're going to have a lot of demand (unless you're in the southern hemisphere).

However, during December, you will likely do great business. The seasonality of the Christmas tree market directly affects the supply and demand and the prices as a consequence. Similar phenomena take place on the price chart, except instead of seasons of time affecting price, it is prior price levels. When the current price reaches these important levels, traders become conscious of them, and supply/demand dynamics change.

All of this is a fancy way of saying that there are places on a chart where price bounces (support) and halts at (resistance). You can figure out these levels in advance, and as price approaches them, you can draw conclusions about its behavior and thus place profitable trades.

At this point, beginners usually rush out to draw every single s/r level on their charts and end up with more lines than clarity on them. Let's first look at what s/r levels look like.

Types of S/R Levels

There are three categories of s/r you should look out for and pay attention to:
1. Prior levels where price bounced or reacted from previously;
2. Swing points;
3. Higher time frame levels.

Let's look at the third point first. This refers to levels which are important in the higher time frames but don't necessarily show up on the lower ones. For example, if the price is approaching a level it previously bounced massively from, and if this bounce and level show up quite clearly on the daily, you can bet that this price level is going to be important even at the lower time frames. The graph below illustrates this phenomenon.

H4 Chart Reaction

The graph is the four-hour chart of an instrument. Looking at just this chart, if we were to look at just the push into the two horizontal lines at the top of the chart towards the right-hand side, it seems inexplicable as to why the price would suddenly turn downwards, after all the push into the two lines was quite strong, as evidenced by the strong bullish bars heading into the level. Well, the answer can be found on the higher time frame, the daily chart. This is shown in the graph below:

Daily Chart

In the daily chart above, the final move into the two horizontal lines is the one we were looking at in the H4 chart reaction. You can see that there are two prior reactions and that the two lines indicate a good s/r level on the daily chart.

Notice how despite the strong push into the level on the H4, the price still respected the daily time frame's s/r level and turned downwards.

The illustration of the daily chart is a good example of the first type of s/r level from the list above. Places or levels where price has reacted from previously have a good possibility of creating a reaction once more as price approaches the same levels, the greater the number of previous hits and the greater the reaction from that level in the past, the better. From the daily chart, we can see that the level held twice previously and therefore, as price approached it a third time, it held once again.

In the future, if price approaches it for the fourth time, this is a great place to short once again since it is likely that price will react at this level and move downwards. When does it finally breakthrough? Well, we can't know this. However, as traders, we will short this level until price breaks through.

Chapter 11: Candlestick Common Patterns

Reversal Pattern

Bullish Engulfing Candlestick Reversal Pattern

This formation comprises two primary candlesticks. The first is a small bearish candlestick supporting short wicks and tails. The second candlestick is a very large bullish one that completely engulfs the size of the first one. The following diagram displays the key features of the Bullish Engulfing pattern.

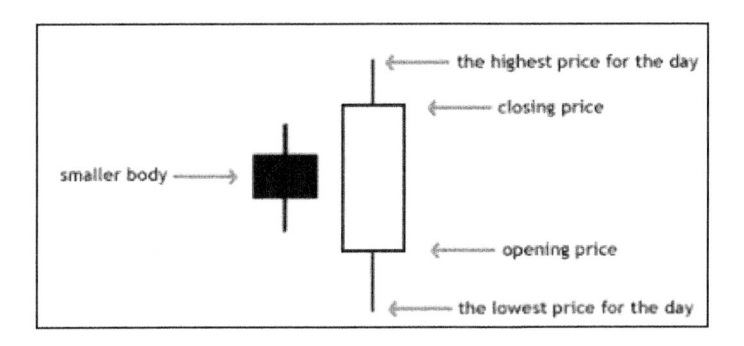

Three White Soldiers Bullish Reversal Candlestick Pattern

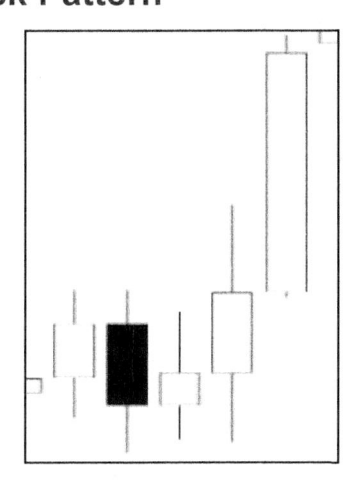

This formation is a revered bullish reversal sign that is generated towards the end of a bearish channel. The 'Three White Soldiers' consists of three bullish consecutive candles. Each of them posts a closing value that is higher than that of the previous one. The next diagram illustrates the 'three white soldiers.'

Shooting Star Bearish Reversal Candlestick Pattern

This famous formation is represented by just one candlestick that is often created towards the end of a well-defined bullish trend. After the candlestick opens, price surges higher during the early part of its creation only to retract sharply later to generate an extremely large wick (the difference between highest and closing prices), which ideally should be double the size of the body.

The central candle in the next diagram illustrates a 'shooting star.'

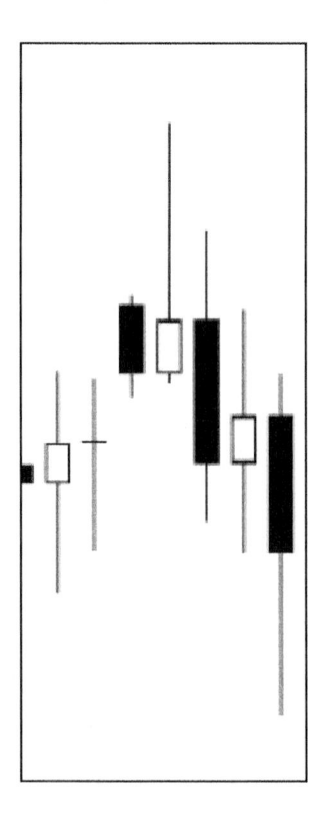

Dark Cloud Cover Bearish Reversal Candlestick Pattern

This pattern comprises two candlesticks that are produced towards the end of a bullish trend, which consists of a large bearish candlestick that follows a long bullish one. The last candlestick must open above the highest value of its predecessor but then close at or beneath the middle value of the body of the first bullish candlestick. An example of a Dark Cloud Cover is displayed in the following diagram.

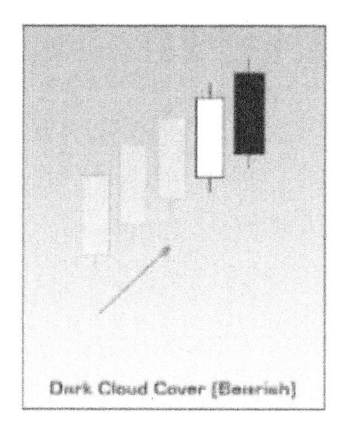

Bearish Engulfing Reversal Candlestick Pattern

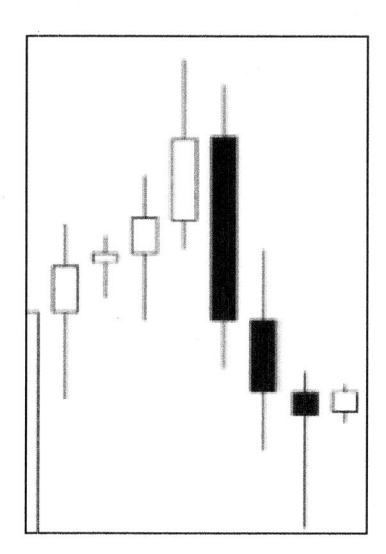

This revered pattern is an effective bearish reversal indicator that is generated via the usage of two candlesticks. The first one displays a bullish white body that is utterly engulfed by a second much larger black bearish candlestick. The next diagram demonstrates a Bearish Engulfing pattern depicted by the two central candlesticks.

Continuation Patterns

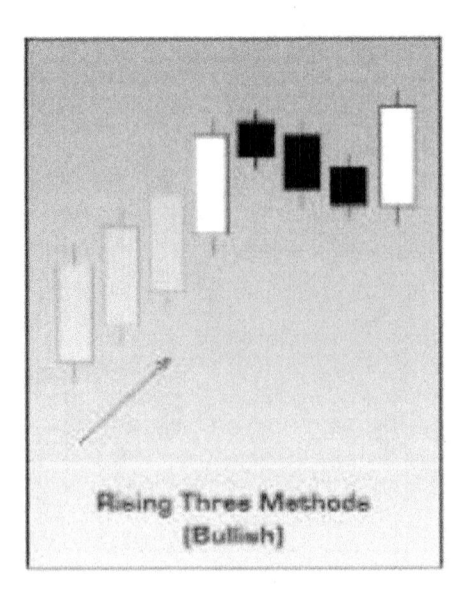

Rising Three Methods Bullish Continuation Candlestick Pattern

This pattern is normally generated during the middle of a current bullish trend and is a strong indication that price will resume its path higher after the structure has been completely formed. The Rising Three Methods comprises five candlesticks.

The first candlestick exhibits a sizeable bullish body. The following three candlesticks possess smaller bearish bodies with each one closing beneath its predecessor. The last candlestick has a very large bullish body that must close above the highest value of the preceding four candlesticks of the pattern. The following figure displays the Rising Three Methods formation towards the far right.

The Upside Three Gap Bullish Continuation Candlestick Pattern

This pattern is produced during a bullish trend and comprises three candlesticks. The first two possess long bullish bodies that are separated by a distinctive gap. The last candlestick sports a long bearish body and closes by filling the fore-mentioned gap. The right side of the next diagram illustrates the Upside Three Gap pattern.

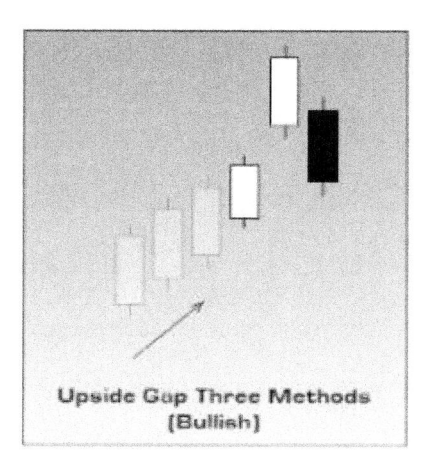

Upside Gap Three Methods (Bullish)

Bullish Separating Lines Continuation Candlestick Pattern

This pattern is often generated during bullish uptrends and signifies that the price of an asset is set to move even higher following a brief pause. As the reliability of the 'Bullish Separating Lines' is not particularly high, you are always advised to use additional verification tools whenever you detect it.

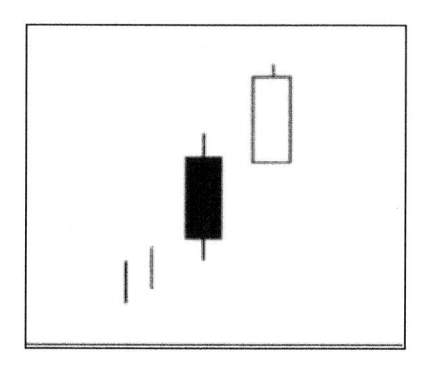

Bearish on Neckline Continuation Candlestick Pattern

This pattern is frequently encountered when the price of an asset has been descending within a well-constructed bearish channel for some extensive time. The 'Bearish on Neckline' is a bearish continuation sign that indicates that the present bearish trend will most likely continue following a short respite.

The pattern comprises two main candlesticks. The initial one opens by gapping lower and possesses a bearish body. The second component exhibits a bullish body but closes below the closing price of the first candlestick. The right-hand side of the next figure demonstrates the main attributes of the 'Bearish on Neckline'.

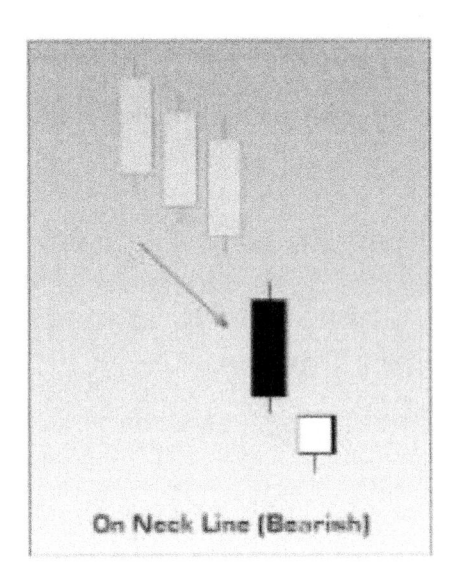

Downside Tasuki Gap Bearish Continuation Candlestick Pattern

This famous pattern possesses a three-candlestick structure which is normally created during a strong bearish trend. The 'Downside Tasuki Gap' is a reliable continuous sign indicating that price is very likely to recommence its downward path following a minor pause.

The initial two candles exhibit bearish bodies which are divided by a significant gap. The third candlestick in the sequence possesses a small bullish body that closes by only partially filling the fore-mentioned gap. The right-hand side of the next figure displays all the pertinent features of the 'Downside Tasuki Gap'

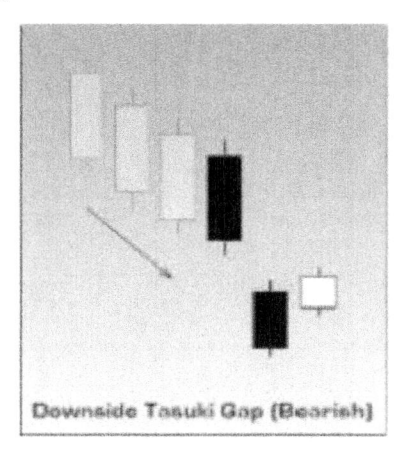

Downside Tasuki Gap (Bearish)

Bearish Thrusting Continuation Candlestick Pattern

This pattern comprises two main candlesticks and is produced whenever the price of an asset is declining in value within a well-constructed bearish channel. The 'Bearish Thrusting' indicates that the current downward is very likely to recommence its path downwards after a brief respite. However, as the reliability of this pattern is not especially high, you should always incorporate the usage of additional techniques or tools to verify that price is undeniably set to plummet lower. The following diagram displays all the main features of the 'Bearish Thrusting'.

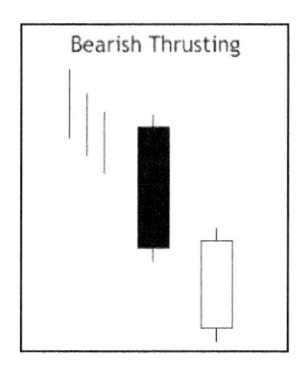

Bearish Thrusting

When it comes to analyzing traded assets such as futures, bonds, stocks, and so on, a commonly seen pattern on the candlestick is the Doji.

Doji

When you see it, you will notice that it has a length that is minute. What this means is that there is a minute trading range, with the closing and opening price being the same. The Doji is meant to show the level of indecision that is found in the market. If the market, at the moment, isn't trending properly, the Doji won't be significant at that movement. This is because these markets that are not trending show a high level of indecision. If you notice that the Doji has either a downtrend or uptrend, what this means is that buyers are currently losing conviction if it is seen in an uptrend format. If it is noticed in the downward format, which means that the sellers are currently losing conviction.

Types of Doji

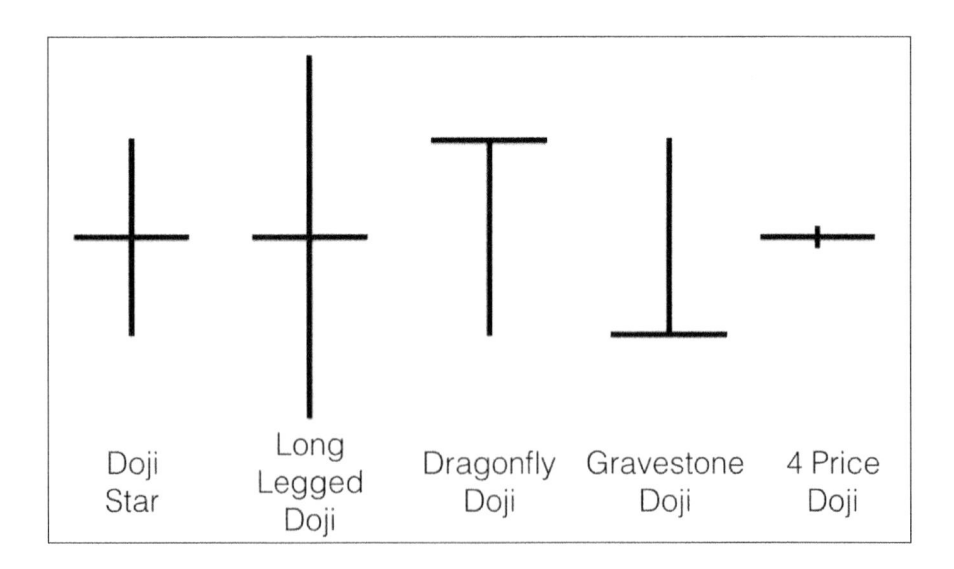

Doji Star | Long Legged Doji | Dragonfly Doji | Gravestone Doji | 4 Price Doji

Neutral Doji

This type of Doji forms when it is noticeable that both the closing and open prices are both equal. Typically, Dojis without interference have a neutral pattern.

1. Long-legged Doji

This is a reflection of a high amount of indecision that one faces concerning where the underlying asset is going in the future.

2. Gravestone Doji

If you see a long upper shadow, this means that the trend's direction may be getting close to the main turning point.

This occurs when you notice that the underlying asset's closing and opening price are equal while happening at the lowest part of the day.

3. Dragonfly Doji

When you notice the long lower shadow, it means that the trend's direction may be getting close to the main turning point. You will see it when the asset's closing and opening price are similar. This happens typically in the highest part of the day.

The Doji acts as a significant trend reversal indicator. This situation usually is actual when you noticed a large amount of trade, which is following a heightened movement in any direction.

When you notice the following, you should know that there is an excellent chance that a downtrend will occur within the next few days. If the market has seen as an uptrend, thereby trading using a higher high than what was seen in the previous days, and if the high doesn't hold, thereby closing in the lower ten percent of the trading range of the day, then this will occur, and vice versa.

As a horizontal line, the 4-Price Doji line shows that the close, open, low, and high are equal.

Tweezers

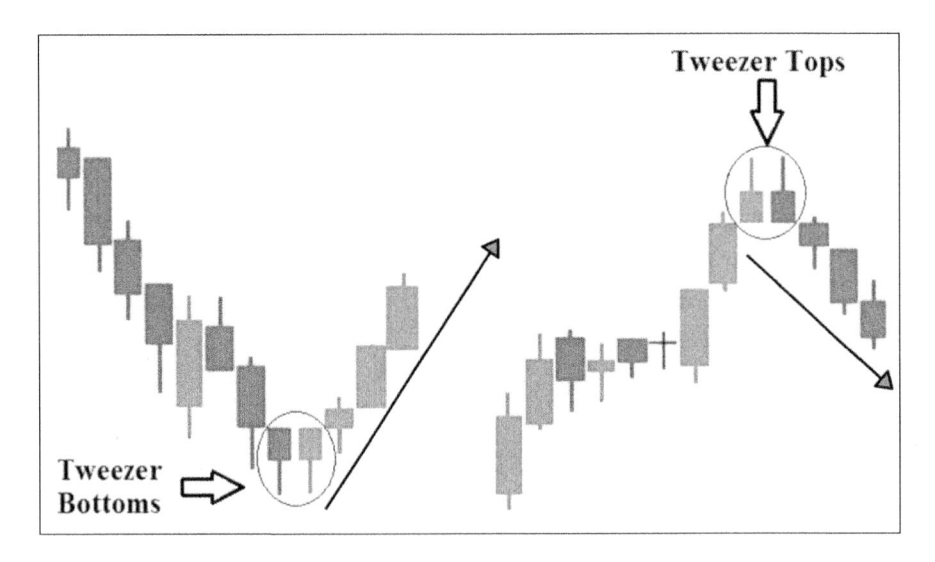

Tweezers came into existence when Steve Nison, the person that popularized candlestick charting in the West region, showed the pattern in "Japanese Candlestick Charting Techniques." You can see tweezers in different forms, but they have several similar characteristics.

They sometimes show at the market-turning points, and they can be utilized in running analysis. This is meant to show if there is a probability of reversal occurring. They are also utilized broadly when trend traders want to see trade signals.

Before the candlesticks came to the West, the Japanese had already been utilizing this for long centuries. They made use of them when they wanted to trade things. This started in the 17th century, thereby making the charts a lot popular. When it comes to monitoring the price data, these charts are the perfect ways of doing such.

A candle's body is usually formed by the disparity that exists between the close and open. Those thin shadows that you see on the different parts of the candle show the low and high during that period.

The red or dark candle translates to the open that was above the close. The green or white candle means that the price ended above how it opened. It indicates a shift in trend

The tweezers are meant to act as the bottoming and topping patterns. This pattern ends up showing the change in the direction of the trend. It is also used to confirm if the signal is correct because tweezers tend to happen a lot.

You will see a topping pattern if the two candlesticks' highs happen close to a similar level tailing the advancement.

The bottoming pattern happens when the two candlesticks' lows happen close to a similar level when a decline happens.

An extra set of criteria involves the first candle possessing a real big body, while the second one can have any size. This means that both candles may sometimes look differently.

Let's use an example. The top of the tweezers may have a first candlestick that is very strong, ending close to the high. On the other hand, the second candle may take the form of a Doji that won't end close to the high but may possess the same high seen in the first candle.

Importance of the Pattern

The tweezer is known to look like a different reversal candlestick pattern, and this is important. Examples of topping patterns are dark cloud cover and bearish engulfing pattern. The bottom pattern that you should consider watching is a piercing pattern and a bullish engulfing pattern.

These candlesticks do not look like tweezers every time, but whenever they take the form of tweezers; they input some significance to the pattern. Usually, special tweezers patterns tend to display a substantial alteration in the momentum from a day to the next one.

If you notice a sound up bar tailing a shooting start candle or a hanging man candle, then you should not assume that it is a significant reversal pattern. This is true especially when the price ends beneath the real body of the second candle inside the other couple of candles.

The bottoming pattern is usually the strong down candle that is tailed by the hammer. A short-term bottom is usually formed when a close appears on top of the hammer body candlestick patterns, in most cases, happen, and the same can be said for tweezers. Whether they are significant or not is dependent on their look.

If you notice a general trend while the tweezers happen in a pullback, it shows that this is a prospective entry point. It shows that the pullback gas ended, and there is an excellent chance that the price may swing to the trending direction once more.

When you make use of tweezers like this, the pattern's success rate tends to be heightened. In a bottom pattern, you will notice that stop-loss is put beneath the lows of the tweezers.

In a topping pattern, you will notice that the stop-loss is put on the highs of the tweezers. It is important to note that the tweezers do not give a profit target, meaning that you should base the target on several factors like overall momentum and trend.

Morning Star

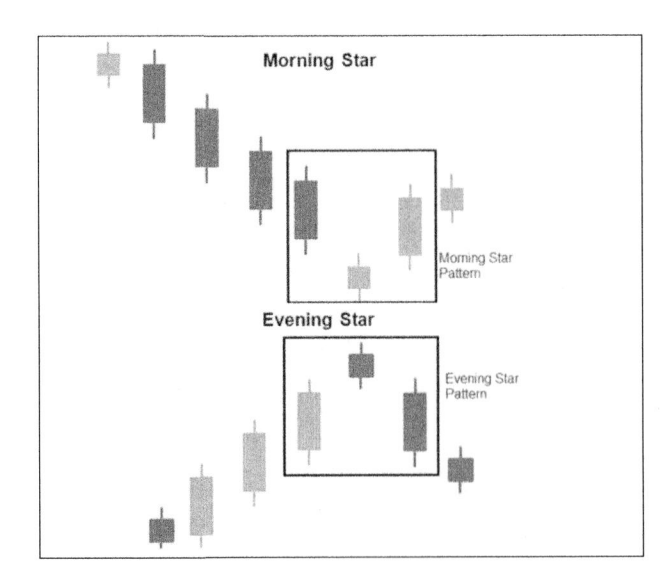

This is a visual pattern that shows three candlesticks that end up being a bullish sign to technical analysts. The morning start is formed by following the downward trend while showing the beginning of an upward climb. This is a symbol that there was a reversal in the prior price trend. When traders see the morning star pattern forming, they go ahead to see if there is any confirmation that a reversal in trend is occurring. They do this by making use of other indicators.

Since it is only a visual pattern, you don't have to do any calculations. The morning star usually begins after three sessions. If it doesn't come then, it is not coming. You can use technical indicators to see if a morning star will form anytime in the future.

OPTIONS

Chapter 12: Wave Analysis: Elliott Wave Decomposition

Ralph Nelson Elliott has developed an approach to interpret wave market movements. His work focuses on hourly Dow Jones quotations and is released from 1938, arousing interest due to the emergence of fractals and chaotic movements.

Elliott's research leads him to the following conclusion: the continual changes in the stock market reflected a fundamental harmony of nature. Thus, he notes that variations in the Dow Jones Industrial Average (DJIA) construct visible figures that return in the same forms, although they may vary in duration and amplitude.

These observations will allow him to develop a theory, known as Elliott's Wave Theory. It combines the psychological dimension borrowed from Charles Dow and the harmony of nature identified by the mathematician Fibonacci. It consists of a set of empirical rules to interpret the evolution of the leading stock indices. This tool is powerful because the rules and principles stated by Elliott are supposed to contain all the action of the market. The main advantage of the Elliott Wave Method is to set up scenarios, set targets and has points of invalidation, a universe of possibilities being known.

This approach is fascinating because it allows one to consider the cyclicality of the financial markets. Indeed, stock prices evolve cyclically: a rise or a fall will never appear in time and will be punctuated by movements of consolidation or correction. Elliott was one of the first writers to highlight the concept of action/reaction which posits that each impulsive movement must be followed by a corrective movement, the impulsive movement being more critical in amplitude than the corrective movement.

For example, in an uptrend, the amplitude of impulsive (bullish) waves is generally more robust than that of corrective waves (downs) and vice versa.

During a marked trend, it seems evident that the market can blow after an impulsive movement. This phenomenon can easily be explained by profit-taking. New entrants (buyers in an uptrend and sellers in a downtrend) are waiting for the presence of a low point to position themselves, which will allow the resumption of the dominant trend. The high strength of Elliott's waves is to be a complete method that emphasizes the two most essential elements in trading that are price and time.

Elliott Wave Decomposition

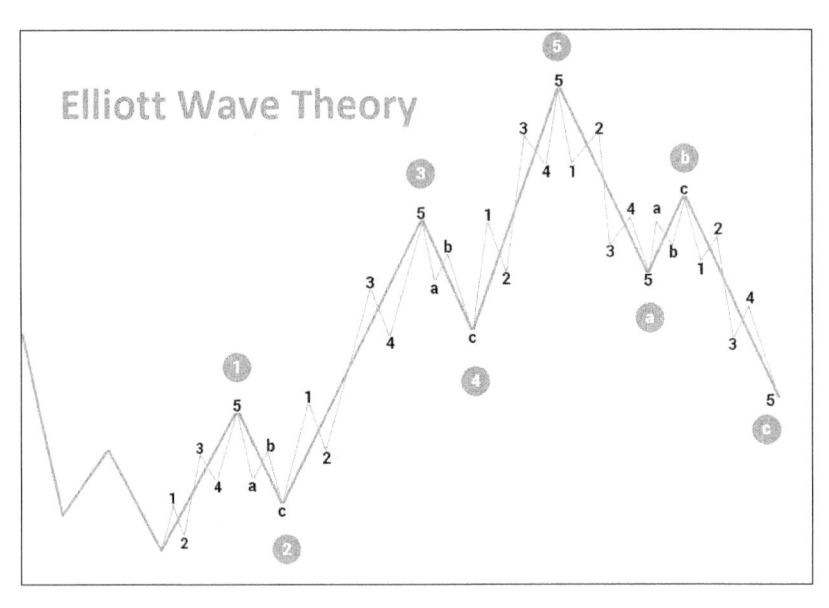

In various articles that were published in the Financial World in 1939, Elliott indicated that the market's bottom rate was a cycle of eight waves, containing five waves of the rise and three waves of decline.

The three waves of decline are a correction of the five previous waves of increase. For Elliott, every impulsive movement is followed by a corrective movement. An impulsive movement is composed of five waves of a lower degree of which three are impulsive and two are corrective. The corrective movement is composed of three waves, two of which are corrective, and one is impulsive.

We will first describe the decomposition of the five waves contained in the impulsive movement:

The first wave represents the arrival of precursors on the markets. The latter anticipates the market turnaround and the imminence of an impulsive movement. They seek to return at the very beginning of the movement and correspond to the initiated investors mentioned by Charles Dow.

The second wave very often corresponds to a reliable correction of the first impulsive movement. It represents the entry of contrarians who play the decline because they believe that the market remains in a bearish phase.

The third wave is usually that of followers and professional investors. The news is positive, and the operators are rushing on the title, causing a robust upward acceleration. It's the most potent impulsive wave, and it's never the shortest.

The fourth wave is profit-taking by operators who took advantage of the sharp rise in a wave. Nevertheless, the trend remains bullish and it is not questioned.

The fifth wave is the last impulsive wave of significant impulsive movement. It corresponds to the entry of late followers, who have observed the rise without positioning themselves and who are eager to enjoy the movement like others. Generally, they are the first victims of the market downturn. This wave is also characterized by a depletion of the technical indicators which often draw a bearish divergence and point the breathlessness of the trend in progress and the imminence of a correction.

On many impulsive waves, it is not uncommon to note the presence of an "extension": it is a wave of impulse which is prolonged, and which marks the power of the wave in question. This extension usually takes shape on a single impulsive wave, which allows analysts to take the measure of other waves. Thus, if the first and third waves are of the same length, the fifth will undoubtedly be an extension. The rules set out by Elliott are supposed to contain all the action of the market.

According to Elliott, this decomposition is found in whatever the period is chosen. Some analysts do not hesitate to make a comparison with the theory of chaos, developed primarily by Mandelbrot. According to this theory, there would be an order in apparent disorder, and images taken at different scales (short term, long term) may have striking similarities.

They forget, however, that the principal concerned, Mandelbrot, does not take Elliott's waves seriously. But let us leave aside these sterile quarrels and interest us in the most important: this method is popular, it is followed (the trader must, therefore, integrate it into his arsenal) and it is even sometimes effective!

Four Basic Principles and Five Rules

Several principles are governing Elliott's waves, which we will summarize into basic principles: Action is followed by a reaction: markets never go up in a single time; the impulse waves, movements in the direction of the primary tendency, break down into five waves of a lower degree, and the corrective waves, movements against the primary trend (bullish or bearish), are decomposed into three waves of a lower degree.

When a movement in eight waves (five up and three down) ends, a complete cycle comes to an end, and this cycle becomes two subdivisions in the immediately higher degree wave; whatever the time horizon, the way of counting is the same because the market is moving at the same pace. The rules stated must imperatively be applied during a count and will be controlled over time.

Corrective Waves

There are several types of corrective waves (zigzags, flats, etc.)

In a 5-step movement, corrective waves always correct the previous upward movement. The following properties are the most commonly observed: wave 2 corrects wave 1 and wave 4 corrects wave 3. Elliott, along with several top-flight analysts, noted that corrective waves regularly corrected the impulsive movements of a certain percentage.

Standard Wave Retracement Ratios 2

Wave 2 is often the strongest and corrects waves 1. It traces the previous move at a minimum of 38.2% to 50%, but the standard retracement is 61.8% and can go up to a maximum of 76.4%.

Standard Wave Retracement Ratios 4

Wave 4 represents profit-taking. The correction is never strong and stands at least 23.6%, the standard is 38.2% and they never retrace more than 50%. If the correction is greater than 50% then it is probably necessary to question its count because it is probably a wave 1. In summary, wave 2 corrects strongly (61.8% is the standard ratio); while wave 4 is profit-taking (the standard ratio is often 38.2%).

Can We Distinguish a Corrective Wave from a True Reversal of the Trend?

A correction was then drawn, and the prices have depressed the two previous low points without that preventing the title from continuing its ascent. Indeed, this corrective movement corrects the entirety of the previous movement.

The corrective movement corresponds to a true reversal of the trend if and only if the corrective wave sinks the low point of the previous impulsive movement. If not, the current trend remains healthy and nothing comes to question it.

The Rule of Alternation

This rule is a powerful principle of Elliott's waves. The principle is simple: if a wave 2 corrects strongly, then the correction in wave 4 will be weaker. Conversely, if wave 2 corrects weakly, expect an impulsive wave 3 but also a correction in wave 4 powerful.

The second property of alternation rules is based on the simplicity or complexity of the correction. At a wave 2 simple usually follows a complex wave 4. Conversely, if wave 2 is complex, then wave 4 will be simple.

Impulsive Waves

Impulsive waves are linked together by Fibonacci ratios. Thus, the objective of wave 3 is often obtained in the following way: we multiply the length of the wave 1 by 1.618 and we postpone the result obtained on the bottom of the wave 2. Often, wave 3 will go to hit this objective before correcting in wave 4. But during powerful movements in extension, the ratio will be higher than 1,618. The following ratios are usually taken: 2-2,618-3 and so on. If wave 2 is weakly traced (less than 50%), expect a powerful wave 3 and project it with ratios above the standard of 1.618.

Advantages

The main advantage of Elliott's method of waves is that it forces the analyst and the trader to imagine different counts, which is an excellent preparation to face the different eventualities.

A good "elliottist" is never closed. He will always highlight in his analysis a favorite scenario (the one that has the best chance of unfolding) and an alternative (a scenario that would invalidate his ideal scenario).

Disadvantages

The first disadvantage of Elliott waves is the learning time they require. Does the time devoted to training Elliott's waves necessarily find a justification? I will answer that it may be interesting for a trader to know the basics of Elliott's waves and their fundamentals, but that the signals provided by this method do not seem sufficiently convincing to devote too much time.

The waves of Elliott fascinate many stakeholders, so much so that they become slaves. This method makes it possible to identify turning points with a confusing precision. Nevertheless, the trap of this method of analysis is to force the countdown in a situation where none seems apparent. The analyst then stubbornly searches for movements in five times where there are none.

This danger is well illustrated by the well-known Elliott Wave Advisor Prechter, who became famous in 1987 for predicting the stock market crash with this method. In the 1990s, his market diagnosis was extremely negative, and he hammered in all the media that the US market was about to enter a prolonged bearish phase. This analyst was trapped by his method. He fell in love with it instead of considering it for what it is: a simple analytical tool. The moral of this story is two-fold: the markets are always right, and the trader who fights against this reality may pay very dearly.

Chapter 13: Tools and Indicators for Options Trading

There are plenty of indicators that traders and investors use to enhance their trades. We shall review just a few of these and discover the best way of applying them to our trades to maximize profitability. It is crucial to understand that none of these indicators will make you profitable from the onset. Therefore, do not break your back trying to find the best or most profitable trade indicators. Instead, focus more on learning about a couple of extremely effective indicators as well as the strategies and methods used alongside them. Experts believe that trading strategies are more profitable when you apply the few indicators that you have mastered.

1. Moving Averages

Moving averages are among the most important trade indicators used by swing traders. They are defined as lines drawn across a chart and are determined based on previous prices. Moving averages are really simple to understand yet they are useful when it comes to trading the markets. They are extremely useful to all kinds of traders, including swing traders, day, intraday, and long-term investors.

You need to ensure that you have some moving averages plotted across your trading charts, all with different periods.

For instance, you can have the 100-day moving average, the 50-day, and the 9-day MA. This way, you will obtain a much broader overview of the market and be able to identify much stronger reversals and trends.

How to Use Moving Averages

Once you have plotted and drawn the moving averages on your charts, you can then use them for many purposes. The first is to identify the strength of a trend. What you need to do is to observe the lines and gauge their distance from the current stock price.

A trend is considered weak if the trend and the current price are far from the relative MA. The farther they are then the weaker the trend is. This makes it easier for traders to note any possible reversals and also identify exit and entry points. You should use moving averages together with additional indicators, for instance, the volume.

Moving averages can also be used to identify trend reversals. When you plot multiple moving averages, they are bound to cross. If they do, then this implies a couple of things. For instance, crossing MA lines indicate a trend reversal. If these cross after an uptrend, then it means that the trend is about to change direction and a bearish one is about to appear.

However, some trend reversals are never real, so you have to be careful before calling out one. Many traders are often caught off guard by these false reversals.

Therefore, confirm them before trading using other tools and methods. Even then, the moving average is a very vital indicator. They enable traders to get a true feel and understanding of the markets.

2. RSI – Relative Strength Index

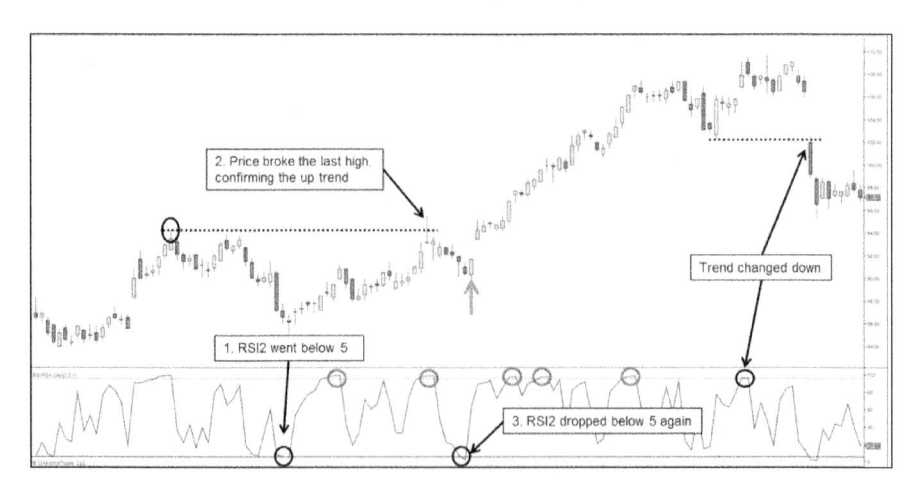

Another crucial indicator that is commonly used by swing traders and other traders is the RSI or relative strength index. This index is also an indicator that evaluates the strength of the price of a security that you may be interested in.

The figure indicated is relative and provides traders with a picture of how the stock is performing relative to the markets. You will need information regarding volatility and past performance. All traders, regardless of their trading styles, need this useful indicator. Using this relative evaluation tool gives you a figure that lies between 1 and 100.

Tips on RSI Use

The relative strength index is ideally used for identifying divergence. Divergence is used by traders to note trend reversals. We can say that divergence is a disagreement or difference between two points. There are bearish and bullish divergent signals. Very large and fast movements in the markets sometimes produce false signals. This is why it is advisable to always use indicators together with other tools.

You can also use the RSI to identify oversold and overbought conditions. You must be able to identify these conditions as you trade because you will easily identify corrections and reversals.

Sometimes securities are overbought at the markets when this situation occurs, it means that there is a possible trend reversal and usually the emerging trend is bearish. This is often a market correction. When security is oversold, it signals a correction or bullish trend reversal but when it's overbought, it introduces a bearish trend reversal.

The theory aspect of this condition requires a ratio of 70:30. This translates to 70% overvalued or over purchased and 30% undervalued or oversold. However, in some cases, you might be safer going with an 80 to 20 ratio just to prevent false breakouts.

4. Volume

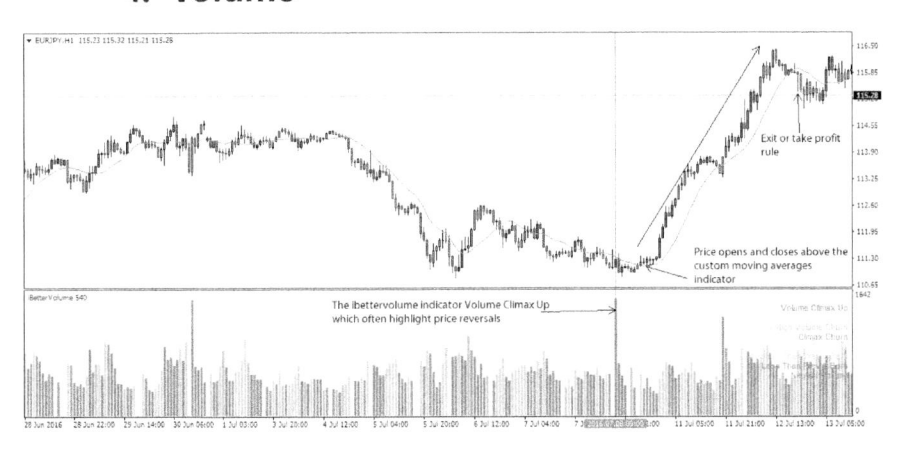

When trading, the volume is a crucial indicator and constitutes a major part of any trading strategy. As a trader, you want to always target stocks with high volumes as these are considered liquid. How many traders, especially new ones, often disregard volume and look at other indicators instead!

While volume is great for liquidity purposes, it is also desirable for trends. A good trend should be supported by volume. A large part of any stock's volume should constitute part of any trend for it to be a true and reliable trend.

Most of the time traders will observe a trend based on price action. You need to also be on the lookout for new money which means additional players and volume. If you note significant volumes contributing to a trend, then you can be confident about your analysis.

Even when it comes to a downtrend, there should be sufficient volumes visible for it to be considered trustworthy. A lack of volume simply means a stock has either been undervalued or overvalued.

5. Bollinger Bands Indicator

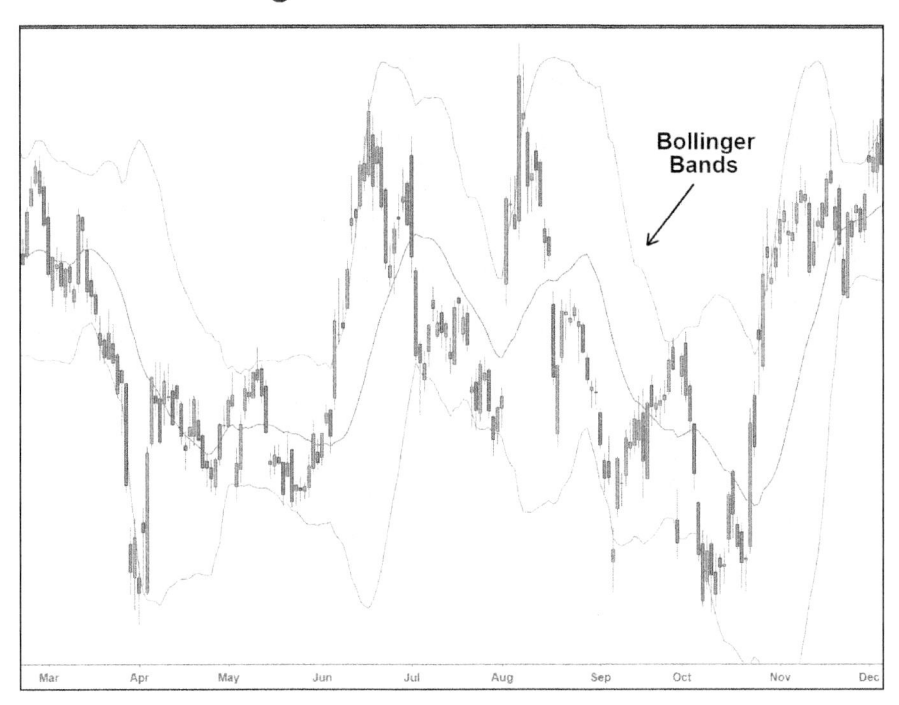

One of the most important indicators that you will need is the Bollinger band indicator. It is a technical indicator that performs two crucial purposes. The first is to identify sections of the market that are overbought and oversold. The other purpose is to check the market's volatility.

This indicator consists of 3 distinct moving averages. There is a central one which is an SMA or simple moving average and then there are two on each side of the SMA.

These are also moving averages, but are plotted on either side of the central SMA about 2 standard deviations away.

6. Accumulation and Distribution Line

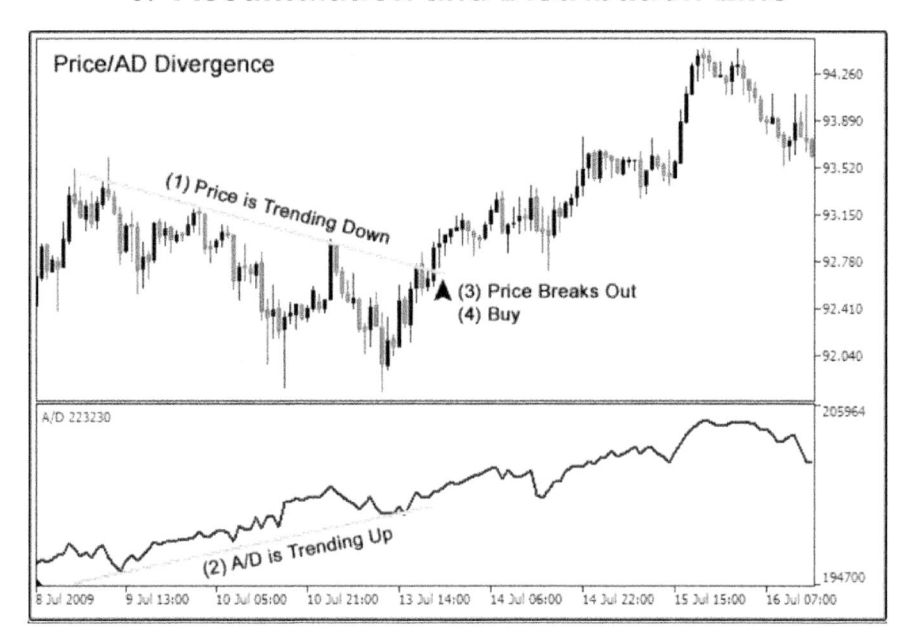

Another indicator that is widely used by swing traders is the accumulation/distribution line. This indicator is generally used to track the money flow within security. The money that flows into and out of a stock provides useful information for your analysis. The accumulation/distribution indicator compares very well with another indicator, the OBV, or the on-balance volume indicator.

The difference, in this case, is that it considers the trading range as well as the closing price of a stock.

The OBV only considers the trading range for a given period.

When security closes out close to its high, then the accumulation/distribution indicator will add weight to the stock value compared to closing out close to the mid-point. Depending on your needs and sometimes the calculations, you may want to also use the OBV indicator.

You can use this indicator to confirm an upward trend. For instance, when it is trending upwards, you will observe buying interest because the security will close at a point that is higher than the mid-range. However, when it closes at a point that is lower than the mid-range, then the volume is indicated as negative and this indicates a declining trend.

While using this indicator, you will also want to be on the lookout for divergence. When the accumulation/distribution begins to decline while the price is going up, then you should be careful because this signals a possible reversal. On the other hand, if the trend starts to ascend while the price is falling, then this probably indicates a possible price rise soon. It is advisable to ensure that your internet and other connections are extremely fast especially when using these indicators as time is essential.

7. The Average Directional Index, ADX

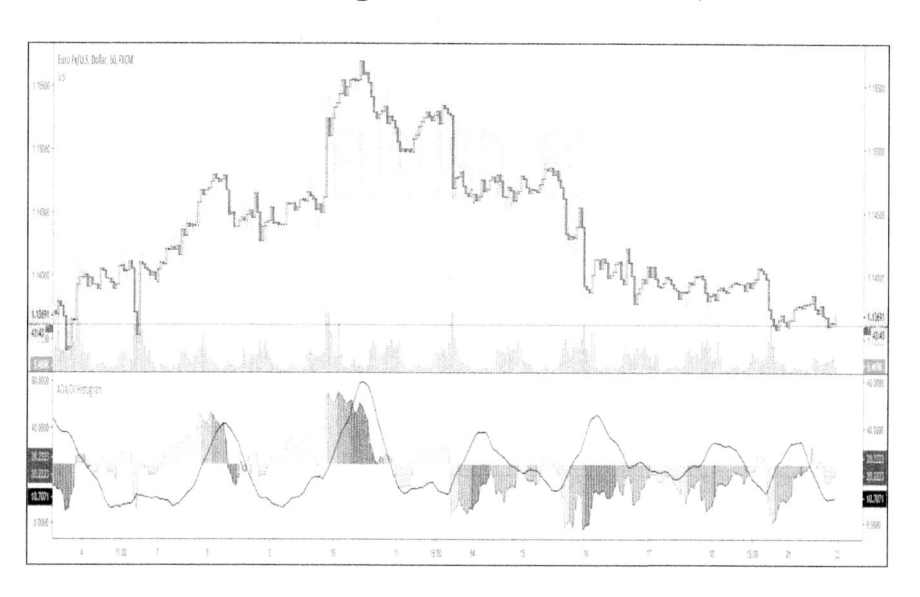

Another tool or indicator that is widely used by swing traders is the average directional index, the ADX.

This indicator is a trend indicator and its purpose is to check the momentum and strength of a trend. A trend is believed to have directional strength if the ADX value is equal to or higher than 40. The directional could be upward or downward based on the general price direction. However, when the ADX value is below 20, then we can say that there is no trend or there is one but it is weak and unreliable.

You will notice the ADX line on your charts as it is the mainline and is often black. Other lines can be shown additionally. These lines are DI- and DI+ and, in most cases, are green and red respectively. You can use all three lines to track both the momentum and the trend direction.

8. Aroon Technical Indicator

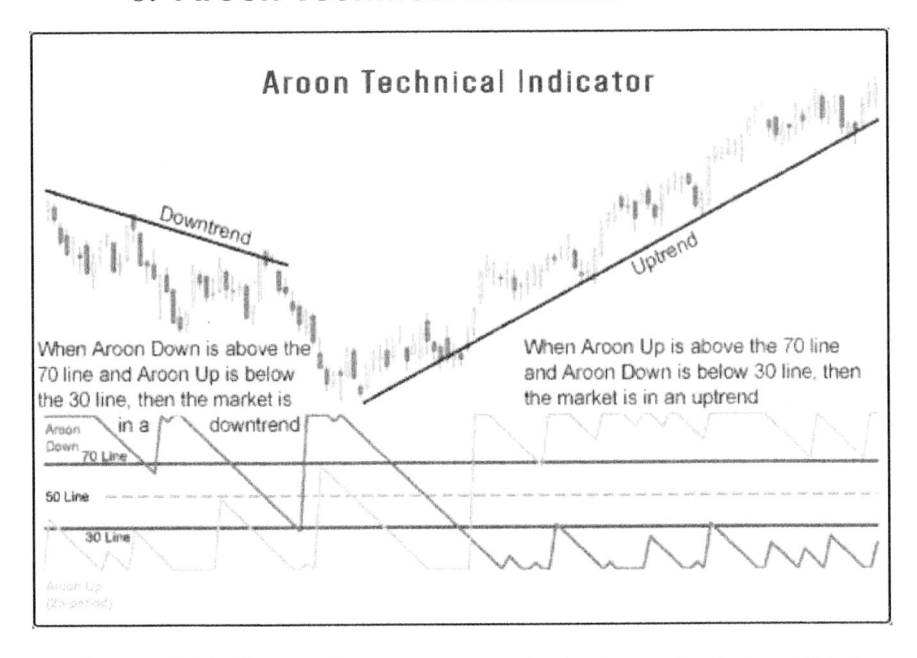

Aroon Technical Indicator

When Aroon Down is above the 70 line and Aroon Up is below the 30 line, then the market is in a downtrend

When Aroon Up is above the 70 line and Aroon Down is below 30 line, then the market is in an uptrend

Another useful indicator that you can use is the Aroon indicator. This is a technical indicator designed to check if certain financial security is trending. It also checks to find out whether the security's price is achieving new lows or new highs over a given period.

You can also use this technical indicator to discover the onset of a new trend. It features two distinct lines which are the Aroon down the line and the Aroon up line. A trend is noted when the Aaron up line traverses across the Aaron down line. To confirm the trend, then the Aaron up line will get to the 100-point mark and stay there.

The reverse holds water as well. When the Aroon down line cuts below the Aaron up line, then we can presume a downward trend.

To confirm this, we should note the line getting close to the 100-point mark and staying there.

This popular trading tool comes with a calculator that you can use to determine many things. If the trend is bullish or bearish, then the calculator will let you know. The formulas used to determine this refer to the most recent highs and lows. When the Aroon values are high, then recent values were used and when they are low, the values used were less recent. Typical Aroon values vary between 0 and 100. Figures that are close to 0 indicate a weak trend while those closer to 100 indicate a strong trend.

The bullish and bearish Aroon indicators can be converted into one oscillator. This is done by making the bearish one range from 0 to -100 while the bullish one ranges from 100 to 0. The combined indicator will then oscillate between 100 and -100. The number 100 will indicate a strong trend, 0 means there is no trend while -100 implies a negative or downward trend.

This trading tool is pretty easy to use. What you need to, is first obtain the necessary figures then plot these on the relevant chart. When you then plot these figures on the chart, watch out for the two key levels. These are 30 and 70. Anything above the 70-point mark means the trend is solid while anything below 30 implies a weak trend.

OPTIONS

Chapter 14: Strategies for Options Trading

Bull Call Spreads

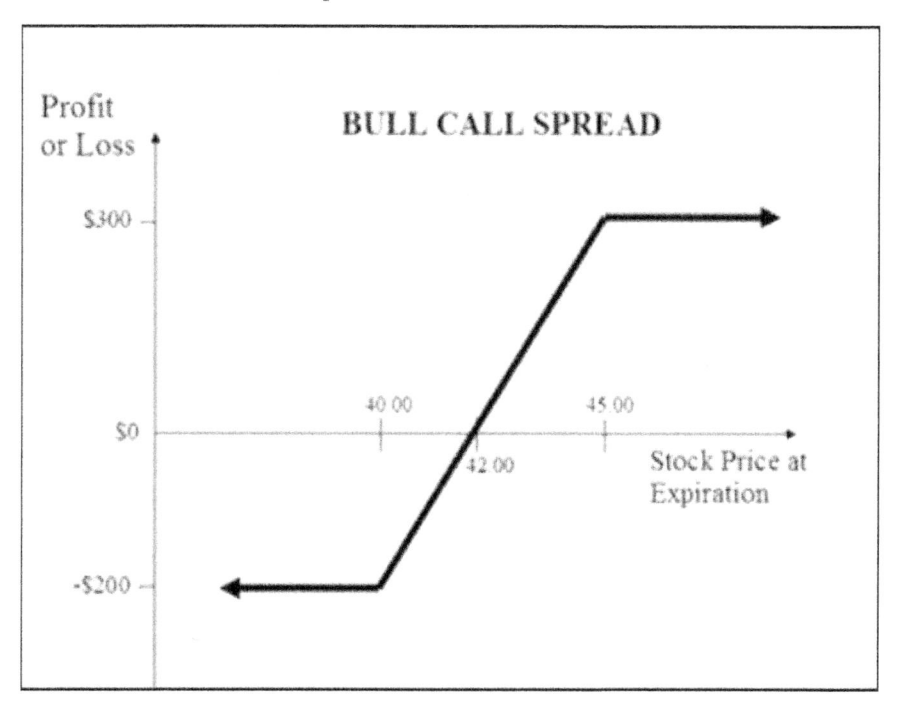

BULL CALL SPREAD chart showing profit/loss vs. stock price at expiration, with breakeven at $42.00, max loss -$200 below $40.00, and max profit $300 above $45.00.

The first type of vertical spread we'll be looking at is the bull call spread. This is a bullish trading strategy and works best in the middle portions of trending markets. I'll address why this is so. For now, keep in mind that while this is a bullish strategy, it works best when bullishness is beginning to slow down, and you observe the ranges getting larger.

You can utilize this in the earlier, more forceful, part of trends but this isn't the most efficient use of it. In those portions, you're better off simply buying a call and letting its premium rise. The covered call works well in those environments too.

Either way, the bull call spread has two legs to it. You will be buying one call and selling another. Thus, the long call leg of the trade covers the short call. Let's take a look at the legs in more details

Trade Legs

The first leg you should establish is the long call leg. This needs to be an at the money or slightly out of the money call that you're sure will move into the money soon.

The objective is to use this leg to make the majority of the profit in this trade. In essence, you're substituting the long stock position from the previous two strategies with a long call position.

Establishing a long stock position meant that you needed to protect it somehow which is why we had to incorporate the third leg in the case of the collar. With the covered call, given the investment nature of the trade, downside protection is moot since you'll be holding onto it for the long term anyway and the objective is to hold onto your investment no matter how much it dips (assuming the dip isn't catastrophic.)

The second leg of the bull call spread is the short call. This is written out of the money at a point where you think the price will advance too, even if it does so sluggishly. Much like with every other strategy we've looked at, you want both of these options to expire at least 30 days or more from the trade date. This helps you capture and avoid the risk of time decay.

Like the collar, the bull call spread can be adjusted, and its greatest power lies in a good adjustment. This allows you to remain in the market at a low cost. Adjustments depend on what the market scenario looks like. You should deploy this in times when bullishness is starting to be challenged by bearishness and thus, you will enter with the knowledge that the trend is still strong but there are some headwinds ahead.

You should place your short call at a level beyond the most relevant resistance ahead.

Once the price breaches this level, you should move it a few points higher to where the next resistance level could potentially be and so on. Alternatively, if you feel that the counter-trend presence is becoming far too much, you could let the market take you out of the position and close your long and cover your short position.

Bull Put Spread

BULL PUT SPREAD

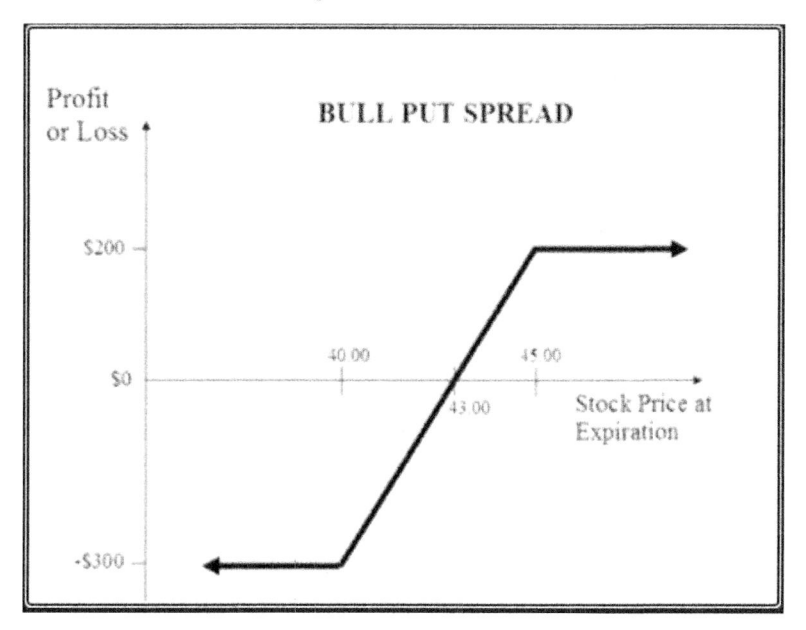

Profit or Loss: $200, $0, -$300
Stock prices: 40.00, 43.00, 45.00
Stock Price at Expiration

The bull put spread strategy seeks to take advantage of the same set of market conditions that the bull call spread seeks. So, what is the difference between the two? Aside from the obvious fact that one strategy uses calls and the other uses puts, there are many subtleties that you ought to be aware of.

The strategies do not contradict one another, in case you're wondering. Think of it as having two choices to pursue depending on what market conditions look like. If you're wondering how to determine the conditions which are ideal for each strategy, then the first step is to take a look at the bull put spread and understand how it works.

Trade Legs

Like the bull call, the bull put is a two-legged trade. The first leg involves establishing a long-put position that is out of the money and is below a strong support level. This long put is what caps your downside risk in case things go wrong. In addition to this, the long put also covers the next leg.

This is a short put which is written near or at the money. This leg is the primary profit-driving instrument for the trade. I'd like to point out here that the structure and positioning of the puts are very different from that of the calls. With the bull call spread, you were capping your maximum gain on the trade by writing an OTM call.

Here, you're not capping any gains and you are capping your loss via a trade leg. In the bull call spread, your maximum loss was automatically capped as a part of the trade structure. You could argue that this is what is happening here as well, but it's pretty clear that how the strategies do this is very different.

The next major point of difference is in the results trade entry gives you. The bull call is net debit trade, but the bull put is a net credit trade. Net debt trades have you realize your maximum loss upon trade entry. Net credit trades realize your maximum gain upon entry. This means that you earn your maximum profit on entry and if all goes well, your options will maintain themselves.

Like the bull call spread, you can adjust the trade depending on market conditions. Given that your upside is not capped, adjustments will need to be made primarily if the market turns downwards and if you see your puts move into the money. In this case, you will need to readjust the spread lower and exit your primary position. Thus, the adjustment scenarios in the bull put strategy aren't as varied as they are in the others we've seen so far.

If the trade works in your favor, you can establish a higher spread using the same principles you used to establish the initial one.

Bear Call Spread

Expiration P/L Graph: Bear Call Spread

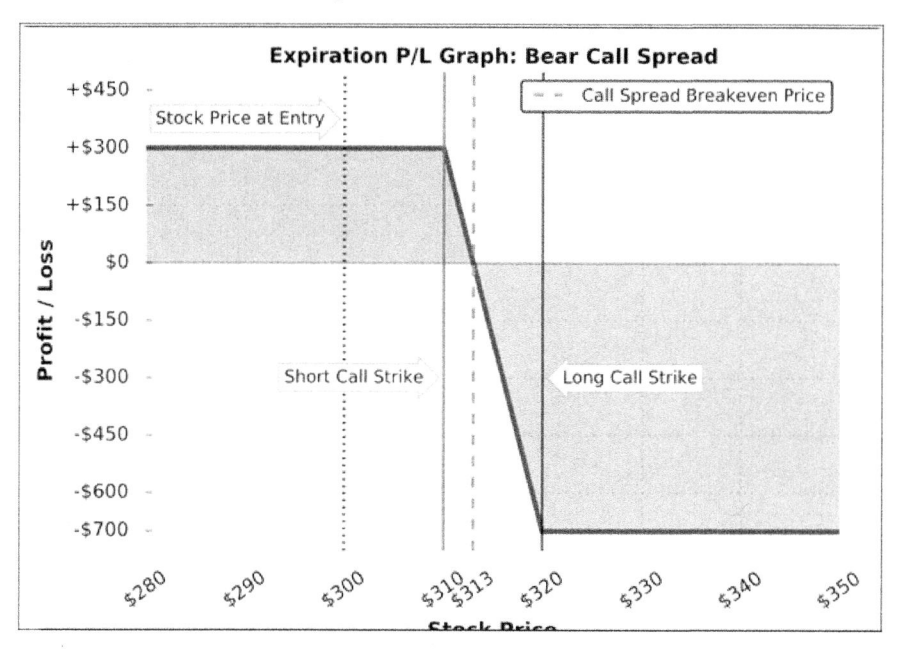

If you can use call spreads to take advantage of bullish conditions, you can use them to take advantage of bearish ones as well. In case you're wondering, it is possible to do this with puts as well, and much like what we saw with the bullish spreads, you have a choice of using either call or put spreads to do this. For now, let's take a look at bear call spreads.

The bear call spread has two legs to it, much like the bull spreads do. As the name suggests, you'll be setting up calls as part of this strategy. Let's take a deeper look at the two legs now.

Trade Legs

The first leg you want to establish is a long call position. The long call is placed at a level that is beyond a resistance zone and is the leg that limits your risk. The call itself is placed out of the money. The further away the call is, the greater your risk in the trade is.

The second leg to establish is the primary profit-driving leg of this trade. This is a short call you will write as close to the money as possible. The exact placement of this level is a tricky thing since you don't want it to move into the money. If it does, you'll have to wind up both legs of the trade and take your maximum loss amount.

Bear call spreads are net credit trades, which means you'll capture your entire gain upon trade entry. As such, like other options trading strategies we've seen thus far, you don't need to do anything special to maintain the trade.

You can adjust it as well but given that this is a net credit trade, there isn't much you can do in terms of adjustment beyond working out another spread level in case the original trade doesn't work out.

Bear Put Spread

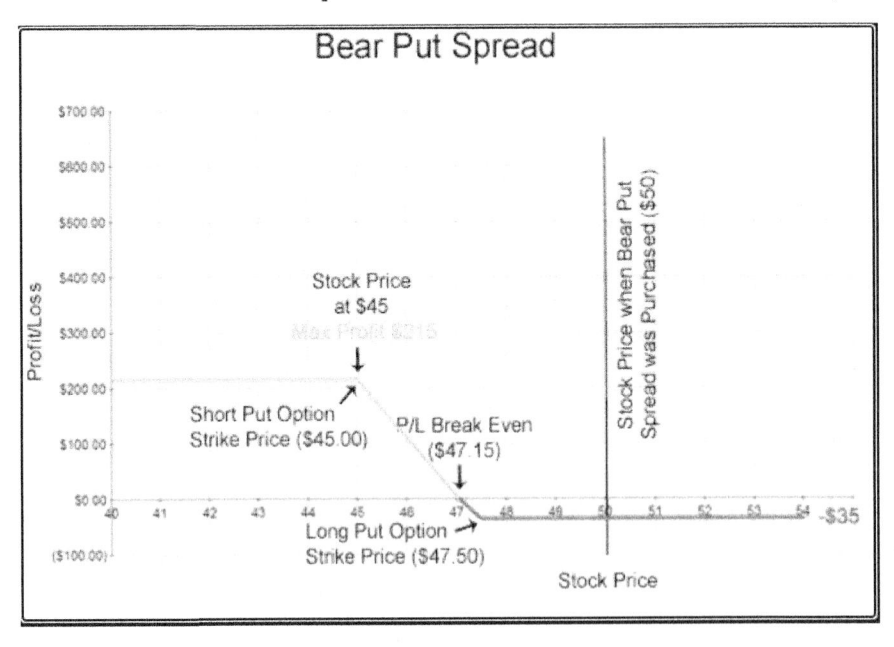

The bear put spread is the bearish cousin of the bull call spread because it is a net debit trade that seeks to capture more of the upside in a bearish movement. By now, hopefully, you've got a hang of how vertical spread trades are set up so let's quickly run through how this trade works. Like the other three, it has two legs to it: A long put and a short put. The long put is established at the money or as near to the money as possible and is the primary profit driver in this trade. The short put is written out of the money, a few levels below, and functions as a profit target of sorts.

The aim of this trade, like with the bull call spread is to capture as much of the market movement as possible. Hence, adjustments play an important role here. Once the market moves close to your short call, you can adjust your target downwards and move your long call leg up.

The timeline for this trade is the same as that of the others. You're looking at establishing options that are at least 30 days or so away from the trade entry date to avoid or capture as much of the time decay as possible. Using our TSLA example with a market price of $478.15, let's assume that we write the TSLA 450 option expiring a month from now.

This will net us $23.90 in premiums. We can go long on the 475 put option which will cost us $36.05. Thus, the net debit on the trade and our maximum loss is $12.15. Our maximum gain is limited to the strike price of the OTM put and this is $25.

Iron Condor

An iron condor is one of the most popular options strategies. This is an income-producing strategy, and an iron condor is sold for a net credit (keep this in mind, there is a lot of misinformation about iron condors).

An iron condor is sold using a call credit spread, and a put credit spread, all in the same trade. The two options with inner strike prices will be sold. So, for example, suppose that a stock is trading at $200 a share.

You could sell a call option with a strike price of $205 and buy a call option with a strike price of $210. Simultaneously, you would sell a put option with a $195 strike price and buy a put option with a $190 strike price. As long as the stock price stays in between the inner strike prices–ranging between $195 and $205 in our example–you will make a profit. So, we use an iron condor when you expect the stock price will not change very much over the lifetime of the options. All options used in an iron condor have the same expiration date. To pick your strike prices, determine where support and resistance are. You want to set the strike price of the put option you sell a bit above the support price and set the strike price of the call option you sell a little below the resistance price. Then set the outer strike prices slightly above the resistance price level for the purchased call option and below the support price level for the purchased put option. Many traders make a full-time living strictly selling iron condors. The chart has the following form.

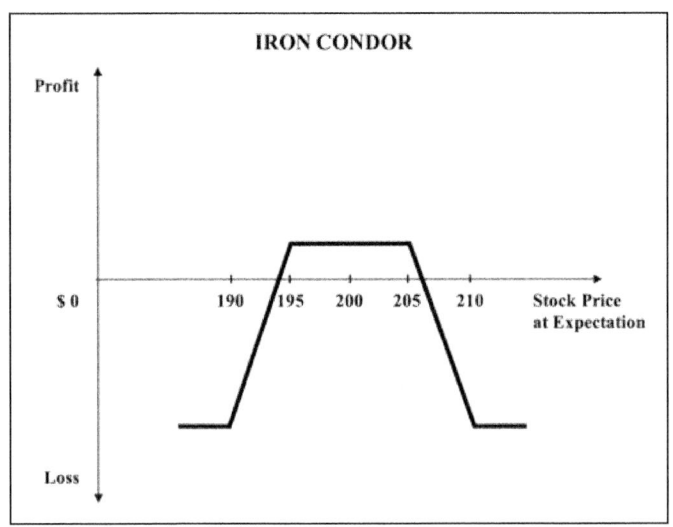

IRON CONDOR

You will receive a net credit for the call credit spread, and a net credit for the put credit spread. The total credit received is your maximum profit. If the stock remains in between the inner strike prices, this is when you will earn profits.

One advantage of the iron condor is that losses are also capped. The maximum loss, should the stock move to the upside, is the difference in strike prices of the two call options. Should the stock move downward, the maximum loss is the difference between the strike prices of the put options.

Using our example here would be a $5 loss (per share—total $500) if the stock moved below $190, or above $210.

There are plenty of options trading strategies to choose from. Some are suitable for beginners while others should only be practiced by advanced options traders who know the market well and have the experience to back them.

Even if a beginner is advised not to practice a particular strategy at that point in his or her career, being aware that the strategy exists is useful as this allows the trader to be aware of alternatives as well as gives this person strategies to work toward to make their daily trading more efficient and profitable.

The strategies listed below and expanded into an overview have been placed in alphabetical order for easy reference.

Covered Call Strategy

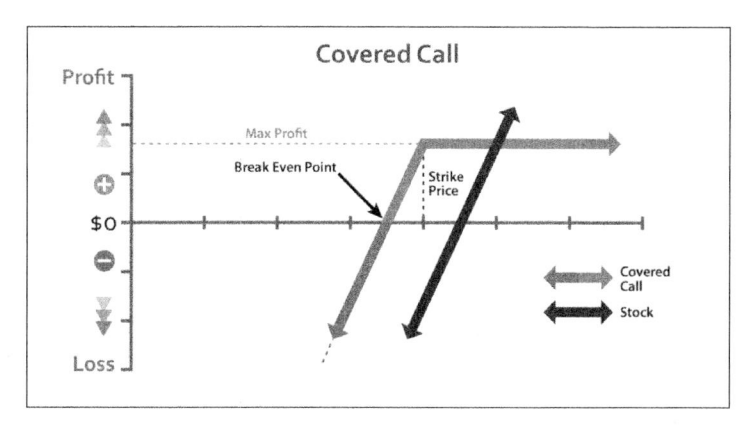

This strategy is also known as a buy-write because it relays the fact that this is a two-part process whereby the trader first buys the associated asset then sells the right to purchase that asset via an option. Stock is the most common associated asset with this strategy.

The trader lowers the risk because they own the asset and receive a premium payment from the contract holder. While the asset may still be in the owner's possession after the contract has expired, if the trader decides not to exercise the right, the owner needs to be willing to part with the asset if the trader does indeed decide to exercise that right.

The profit earned by the seller is achieved if the asset price meets or goes above the strike price on or by the expiration date. This is calculated with this formula:

Premium + (Strike Price - Asset Price) = Potential Profit

This profit is limited.

Breakeven is calculated like this:

Purchase Price of the Asset - Premium = Breakeven

This strategy appeals to many investors because there is guaranteed payment of the option premium whether or not the option holder decides to exercise the right to the option. The seller can set up a regular income stream in markets that are bullish or comparatively neutral. There is also the benefit of the seller being covered from risk due to ownership of the asset. The risks include the seller losing due to the asset price potentially decreasing below the breakeven point and potentially experiencing an opportunity cost if the price of the asset skyrockets.

Credit Spreads

This strategy describes the selling of a high-premium option while purchasing a low-premium option type, which is a call or put, to make a profit when the spread between the two options narrows. The options will have the same expiration date but different strike prices, hence the profit potential.

The appeal of credit spreads is that they have lowered risk if the price movement goes against the trader, making losses limited. The seller benefits from the premium payment.

The disadvantage is that profits are limited, just like losses.

There are different types of credit spreads. They include:

- Bear call spread, which is a beginner-friendly strategy. It employs a bearish outlook that relies on the price of the associated asset decreasing modestly. The trader buys 1 out of the money call option and sells 1 in the money put option. Profit is gained by finding the difference between the option premium and the commissions paid. Loss occurs when the asset price increases below the strike price.

- Bull put spread, a beginner-friendly strategy with a bearish outlook that relies on the price of the associated asset decreasing substantially. The trader buys 1 out of the money put option of a higher premium and sells 1 on the money put option of a lower premium. Profit is gained by finding the difference between the option premium and the commissions paid. Loss occurs when the asset price decreases below the strike price.

- Iron butterfly spread, which involves 4 transactions. The options trader is buying 1 out of the money call option, selling 1 at the money call option, buying 1 out of the money put option and selling 1 at the money put option, all with the same expiration date and associated asset. This is a complex strategy that is not recommended for beginners.

- Short butter spread, which entails 3 transactions. The transactions are buying 1 out of the money call/put option, selling 1 out of the money call/put option and buying 1 at the money call/put option. They all have the same expiration date and associated asset. This is also a complex strategy that is not recommended for beginners.

Debit Spreads

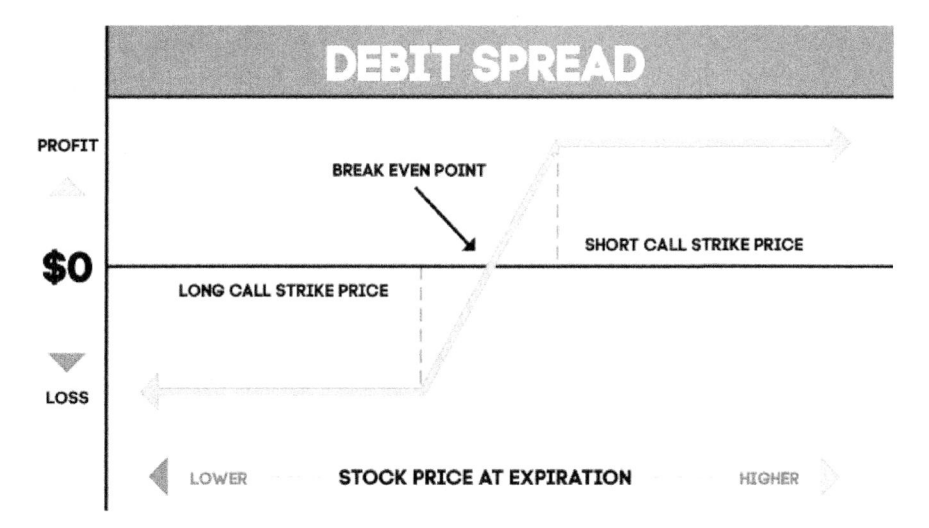

This strategy describes the buying of a high-premium option while purchasing a low-premium option type to make a profit when the spread between the two options widen. Just like with credit spreads, the options will have the same expiration date but different strike prices, which leaves the potential for profit.

The benefits of debit spreads include limited losses and being able to predict losses and profits better. The disadvantage is that profits are limited.

There are different types of debit spreads as well. They include:

- Bear put spread, which is a bearish strategy that requires 2 transactions, which are the buying of 1 at the money put option and the selling of 1 on the money put option. This is done because the trader is betting that the price movement of the associated asset will go down. Profit is earned when the price of the associated asset is the same as the strike price of the put option.

- Bull call spread, which is a bullish strategy that includes 2 transactions, which are the buying of 1 at the money call option and the selling of 1 out of money call option. A trader implements this strategy when he or she thinks that the price movement of the associated asset will go up modestly. Profit is gained when the price of the associated asset is the same at the strike price of the short call option.

- Butterfly spread, which is a neutral strategy that involves 3 transactions whereby the trader buys 1 in the money call option, sells 2 at the money call option and buys 1 on the money call option. Both profits and losses are limited by this type of spread strategy. Profit is gained when the price of the associated asset remained the same on the date of expiration.

- Reverse iron butterfly, which is a volatile strategy that involves 4 transactions. These transactions are the selling of 1 out of money put option, buying 1 at the money put option, buying 1 at the money call option and selling 1 out of money call option. Profit is gained when the price of the associated asset falls.

Rolling Out Options

This strategy involves closing one option, then, replacing it with an identical option to manage a winning or losing position. This management comes in the form of the newly opened position having the same associated asset but varied terms. These terms are typically the adjustment of the strike price and how long the trader would like to hold a long or short position.

Rolling can be done in 3 ways. They are:

- Rolling up, which is the process of closing an existing option position and simultaneously opening a similar position with a higher strike price.

- Rolling down, this is the process of closing an existing option position and simultaneously opening a similar position with a lower strike price.

- Rolling forward, this is the process of moving an open position to a different expiration date so that the length of the contract is extended.

This strategy is easy enough to be practiced by beginners.

Straddle Strategy

This strategy is employed so that the options trader protects himself or herself from loss whether the asset price moves up or down. There are short straddles and long straddles.

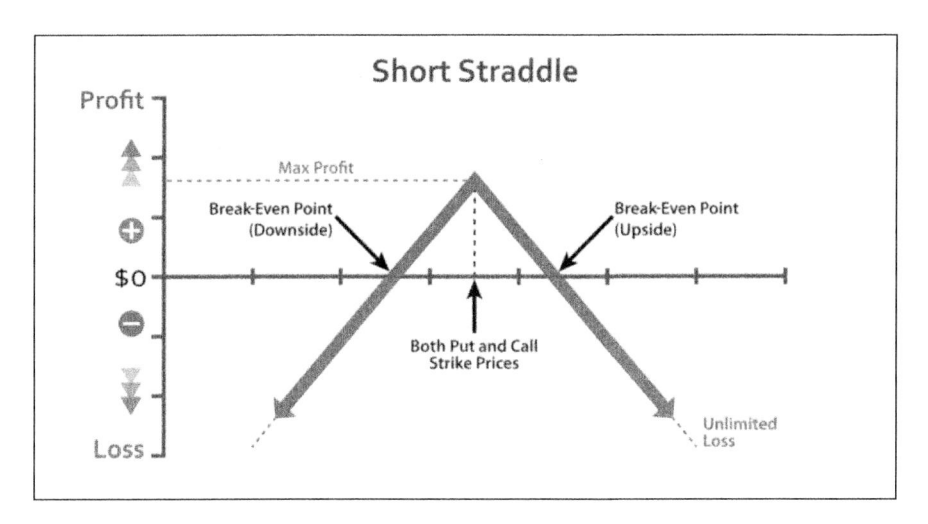

The short straddle is also called a sell straddle or a naked straddle. It is a neutral strategy that entails the trader selling 1 at the money call option and 1 at the money put option with the same expiration date, same strike price, and having the same associated asset. Profit from this strategy is limited and is calculated by finding the difference between the options premium and commissions paid.

Loss has the potential to be unlimited if the asset price moves sharply up or down.

The long straddle is also called a buy straddle. It is a neutral strategy and involves the trader buying 1 at the money call option and 1 at the money put option with the same expiration date, strike price, and associated asset.

The profit potential is unlimited and the risk of loss is limited.

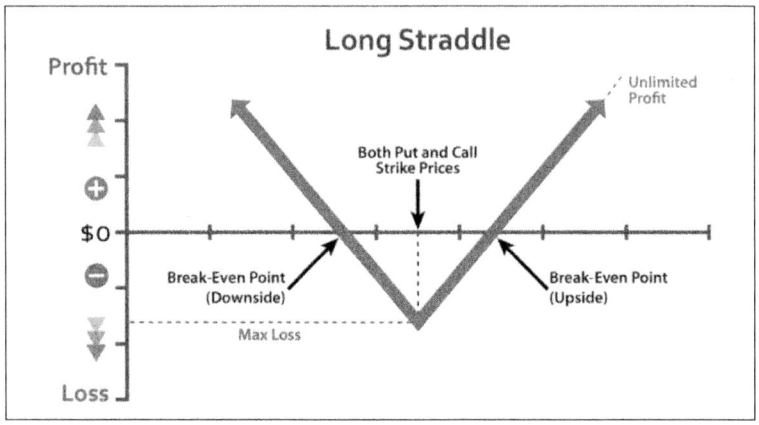

Strangle Strategy

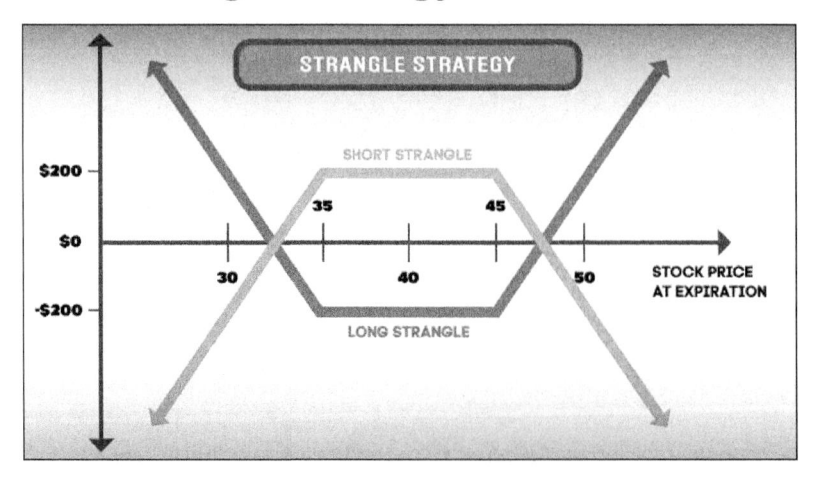

This is a strategy that is used when a trader bets that an asset price will move up or down but still gathers protection if he or she is wrong. Strangles come in both a long and short variety.

The long strangle is also called a buy strangle and it is a neutral options trading strategy. This strategy entails the trader buying 1 out of the money put option and 1 out of the money call option. This is done because the trader expects volatility on the market. Profit is potentially unlimited and happens if the asset price moves sharply up or down. Loss is limited and is the combination of the options premium and the commission paid.

The short strangle is also called a sell strangle. It is used as a neutral trading strategy and so the trader sells 1 out of the money put option and 1 out of the money call option. Both of these options have the same expiration date and the same asset associated. This is a short-term strategy used when the trader expects the asset price to remain relatively stable on the market. Profit is limited and is the difference between the option premium and commissions paid for that option. Risk is unlimited. Loss can be experienced if the price of the asset goes up or down sharply.

OPTIONS

Chapter 15: Money Management

How to Manage Money in Options

Seek not to get too emotional over wins or frustrated by losses to be effective in trading. Investing capital depending on gut instinct or word-of-mouth is a terrible way of investing. In all situations, a lack of rational reasoning contributes to one thinking the exchange would thrive. Greed has probably cost more to the market than fear. When an exchange is carried out on the grounds of expectation, it is fundamentally irrational and may result in quick actions made on bad judgment.

They also find it hard to reduce their losses whenever a market moves against such an entity. They can get deeply connected to trade and keep hoping for a change in trend. Given the economic, technological, and emotional factors that indicate it should be wise to take out significant returns, several people wanted to ride their market drop from the high in 2000. You should set targets and concentrate on what you've been doing to meet those goals. Set clear expectations on what you plan to do over the next three months, six months, or year. After that, you will create targets for the long run. By trying to write down your thoughts, you will get a clearer picture of what you'd like to achieve.

You'll focus on advancing the understanding, centralizing everything you've discovered, and reviewing the evidence before and during the exchange. That would offer you a big benefit over the average investor who's spending more based on sentiment than truth. The art of creating money will follow naturally.

When a person focuses on being the finest in their career, the money will flow seamlessly through them. Likewise, to be a good trader, instead of concentrating on the capital, you must focus on dealing properly. To get the max rewards and risks that incur, you must have defined endpoints. Your methodology should be well-organized and systematic. You would be able to witness by this technique why your transactions were financially beneficial. By knowing the performance approach, you'll find the keys to continuing achievements because you'll be likely to duplicate the cycle again and again and continue to increase your market size and net value.

Money Managing Rules

Managing money's first rule is never to sell assets that you can't afford to give up. Trading of money that is essential for everyday expenses would then adversely impact your judgment and clear thinking. Your trade becomes more sentimental than centered on proper analysis as well as factual information.The 2nd rule in managing money is to make sure you correctly distribute the threats to ensure longevity. You ought to have the resources ready to take benefit of if the stock takes big strategic movements.

Whether you have splintered your entire money in the market among two trades, you could find oneself quickly without any means of capitalizing on these market movements.

The 3rd rule of managing money is to receive a stable return on investment. The market strategy will be oriented to continuous benefit. If you continually profit in the market, you would then find one day that all the little profits also did turn into a profit's mountain.

Gaining a high return rate is the 4th rule of managing money. A vigorous approach may form part of your business strategy but must not be the primary business strategy. If you've mastered how to reliably raise money at a stable pace on the business, you should pursue more competitive tactics. One of the resources to reduce risk is good money management. This term indicates that discipline consists of planning not only the possible economic income, but also the possible losses to have at all times a plastic vision of the money you are risking.

Money management is a practice which the trader cannot renounce. Also, because the economic catastrophe is always around the corner. Just think of the most (sadly) famous Forex Trading statistic: about 90% of traders end the year at a loss! Regardless of the type of trading one is preparing to do, whether it is Forex trading, CFD trading, or others, money management can never be missing.

OPTIONS

Money Management Tips

The 2% Rule

Let me be clear, it is a fairly arbitrary indication, the result of a convention rather than a mathematical calculation. However, it is a common-sense rule based on the principle of prudence. It states that it is always good to invest, per single trade, no more than 2% of the entire capital. In this way, even in the worst-case scenario, dozens of trades would be needed before losing (almost) all the available capital. It is a widely used rule, therefore reliable.

For example, if we have € 10,000 and we decide to invest € 3,000 on a single operation, we expose 30% of our capital. It would be enough to open 3 operations in one day for having invested 90% of the capital.

If instead, we invest more like 10% per operation, we will end up with less than $ 15,000, or we would have burned well over 25% of our initial capital. The main problems always arise when it comes to recovering lost money: that's why money management strategies all aim to avoid, or at least limit, these situations.

The Question of Capitalization

Forex Trading has gained some success with ordinary people because of the barriers to entry, which are lower than other speculative investment activities.

This is mainly thanks to brokers who allow you to open accounts with small sums, often a few hundred euros. However, it is not recommended to operate if you have "few pennies" available. This is for two reasons: first, earnings are negligible; secondly, people are encouraged to use risky techniques to grind profits, for example.

Financial Leverage

Some brokers advertise themselves by placing the offer of "strong" financial levers as their main attraction, even if the authorities are trying to limit margin operations as much as possible. This is an attitude that, however legitimate, can mislead the less experienced trader, who can make leverage pass like any other instrument. Well, it is a real double-edged blade, also because the risk is not only to increase profits but also to increase losses exponentially! The advice, therefore, is to use levers that do not exceed the 1:50 ratio.

The Right Risk-Return Ratio

The risk-reward ratio is the ratio between the maximum possible loss and the maximum possible gain. The first term is determined by the stop-loss, the second term is determined by the take-profit (although some use the more complex trailing stops). However, by convention, it is good to plan your trade, therefore, the exit points, so that the maximum possible gain exceeds at least twice the maximum possible loss. The more prudent, then, refer to a ratio of 1:3.

The Whole Look

It often happens that the trader receives, or proceeds from, strong entry signals and, nevertheless, the subsequent trade proves to be bankrupt. This can occur for a variety of reasons, but the most frequent one has to do with volatility. If the market is volatile, and the signals are produced with too limited a temporal analysis, the signal is likely to prove false or misleading. So, before opening a position, take a look at the whole and verify that the market is not in a volatile situation.

Reinvest the Profits

A very prudent approach to money management is based on a simple rule: reinvesting profits. That is, given a precise period, always and only commit the earnings and not the initial capital, regardless of the 2% rule. This is a way to decrease the pressure since you have the feeling that you are not risking anything, but also to save money. Of course, the risk is to produce too low returns.

Call to the Frenzy

Scalping is the preserve of the more experienced. It is true, scalping is tempting to many. Firstly, because it promises huge profits, secondly because it is adrenaline. However, it is also very difficult to practice. The risk of not being able to bear the pressure and not being able to make decisions (and interpret the market) quickly is very high. So, before you open and close positions at a frenetic pace, think twice.

Martingale

Martingale is a very famous investment method, more outside of trading than inside trading, to be honest. It consists of investing, after a loss, exactly double what was invested in the previous trade. In this way, precisely for a mathematical question, even if one continues to lose large sums, once the victory has come this would reward the interests of all the previous defeats. Well, the martingale goes against all the principles of money management and even against the principles of prudence. It is truly capable of burning capital in a handful of trades. So, avoid it.

Always Set Stop-Loss and Take-Profit

Some hasty traders do not set the stop-loss or the take-profit but go arm in arm with a thorough market analysis. Well, it is always necessary to set these levels to limit the damage in case of losing trade to preserve the gains in case of winning trade. It is not even too difficult if you use the most basic approach, that is, the one that refers to supports and resistances (often corresponding to the minimum and maximum periodic).

How Much to Invest in Online Trading: Minimum Capital Required

Another fundamental point of money management where practically all new traders bang their heads is the following: the minimum capital for trading online.

The only rule that new traders seem to follow is the following: invest as much as the minimum deposit required by the broker.

And there is no bigger mistake a trader can make. Let's take an example. If a broker has a minimum deposit of only € 200, and we decide to invest this amount, what earnings could we expect? Well, following the 2-3% rule, we will invest from € 4 to € 6 per operation.

What are the problems that could arise in this situation?

- Too low to invest: broker trading platforms usually have a minimum amount to invest for each transaction, and it is said that they accept "small change" as in this case.

- Greed and boredom: emotions are one of the main problems of online trading. Investing such a small change will put a trader's patience to the test.

The result to which these two problems can lead is the same: not respecting the previous rule of 2-3% and increasing one's exposure to each operation.

In the first case, perhaps it will not even be possible to invest so little through the trading platform. What if the minimum investment to be made was € 10, or € 20 or even worse € 50? This is where a pillar rule of money management goes to be blessed.

Other traders, however, although perhaps they may invest so little, may soon stop doing so. The possible gains from these operations would be extremely small. A trader might say "hell, I'm wasting time making just a couple of euros a trade! Today I only made € 5 in earnings in a whole day! But who makes me do it?" and the next action will be to invest more.

The only golden rule, to always be respected, when it comes to choosing the capital to invest in online trading is: never invest more than you can afford to lose. If to open a trading account the broker asks for a figure too high for your pocket, you have two possible choices:

- Wait and put aside this figure, and a little more (because often starting with the bare minimum can be counterproductive as you have seen)

- Look for another broker

But never, and then never, will you have to decide to jeopardize money which, if lost, risks creating serious economic problems.

Importance of Proper Money Management Skills

As a trader, one of the most important skills you will need to develop is how to manage your money properly and how to keep as much of it as possible.

You need to learn how to save as much of your money as possible and avoid entering trades where you risk losing money. If you are unsure about a strategy, then do not implement it.

Your most crucial goal as a trader should be to preserve and protect your trading capital. This will enable you to last longer and grow your wealth and make big wins. For instance, there is a general rule that you should never spend more than 2% of your trading capital on a single trade. This means that if your trading capital is $100, 000 then no single trade should take more than $2,000. This way, should things not work in your favor, you stand to lose as little as possible.

Also, no matter how enticing or attractive a position seems, never place a larger amount than initially planned. Market positions on charts sometimes seem way too attractive, and we are inclined to invest more money for higher returns. However, the markets can be unpredictable, and chances of losing money or trades not working out as desired are always high. Therefore, avoid such temptations and stick to your trading plan. Also, check your account balance each month and then work out the amount that makes 2% of the total. For instance, if your account balance is $50,000, then 2% is equivalent to $1,000. As a swing trader, you cannot afford to lose more than this amount. This kind of approach will enable you to hold onto most of your money as well as stay safe even as you trade. Keep in mind that the premise of the swing trading strategy is to collect profits on half of each position's amount as soon as the stock moves and gains an amount that is equivalent to the original stop-loss.

OPTIONS

Chapter 16: Risk Management

Risk management has many different elements to both quantitative and qualitative. When it comes to options trading, the quantitative side is minimal thanks to the nature of options limiting risk by themselves. However, the qualitative side deserves a lot of attention.

Risk

So, what is risk anyway? Logically, it is the probability of you losing all of your money. In trading terms, you can think of it as being the probability of your actions putting you on a path to losing all of your capital. A good way to think about the need for good risk management is to ask yourself what a bad trader would do. Forget trading, what would a bad business person do with their capital?

Well, they would spend it on useless stuff that adds nothing to the bottom line. They would also increase expenses, market poorly, not take care of their employees, and be indisciplined with regards to their processes. While trading, you don't have employees or marketing needs, so you don't need to worry about that. Do you have suppliers and costs? Well, yes, you do. Your supplier is your broker, and you pay fees to execute your trades. That is the cost of access. In directional trading, you have high costs as well because taking losses is a necessary part of trading. With market neutral or non-directional trading, your losses are going to be minimal, but you should still seek to minimize them.

Risk per Trade

The quantitative side of risk management when it comes to options trading is lesser than what you need to take care of when trading directionally. However, this doesn't mean there's nothing to worry about. Perhaps the most important metric of them all is your risk per trade. The risk per trade is what ultimately governs your profitability.

How much should you risk per trade? Common wisdom says that you should restrict this to 2% of your capital. For options trading purposes, this is perfectly fine. Once you build your skill and can see opportunities better, I'd suggest increasing it to a higher level.

A point that you must understand here is that you must keep your risk per trade consistent for it to have any effect. You might see a wonderful setup and think that it has no chance of failure, but the truth is that you don't know how things will turn out. Even the prettiest setup has every chance of failing, and the ugliest setup you can think of may result in a profit. So never adjust your position size based on how something looks.

Calculating your position size for a trade is a pretty straightforward task. Every option's strategy will have a fixed maximum risk amount. Divide the capital risk by this amount, and that gives you your position size. Round that down to the nearest whole number since you can only buy whole number lots when it comes to contract sizes.

For example, let's say your maximum risk is $50 per lot on the trade. Your capital is $10,000. Your risk per trade is 2%. So, the amount you're risking on that trade is 2% of 10,000 which is $200. Divide this by 50, and you get 4. Hence, your position size is four contracts or 400 shares. (You'll buy the contracts, not the shares.)

Why is it important to keep your risk per trade consistent? Well, recall that your average win and loss size is important when it comes to determining your profitability. These, in conjunction with your strategy's success rate, determine how much money you'll make. If you keep shifting your risk amount per trade, you'll shift your win and loss sizes. You might argue that since it's an average, you can always adjust amounts to reflect an average.

My counter to that is, how would you know which trades to adjust in advance? You won't know which ones are going to be a win or a loss, so you won't know which trade sizes to adjust to meet the average. Hence, keep it consistent across all trades and let the math work for you. Aside from risk per trade, there are some simple metrics you should keep track of as part of your quantitative risk management plan.

Drawdown

A drawdown refers to the reduction in capital your account experiences. Drawdowns by themselves always occur. The metrics you should be measuring are the maximum drawdown and recovery period.

If you think of your account's balance as a curve, the maximum drawdown is the biggest peak to trough distance in dollars. The recovery period is the subsequent time it took for your account to make new equity high.

If your risk per trade is far too high, your max drawdown will be unacceptably high. For example, if you risk 10% per trade and lose two in a row, which is very likely, your drawdown is going to be 20%. This is an absurdly large hole to dig your way out. Consider that your capital has decreased by 20% and the subsequent climb back up needs to be done on lesser capital than previously.

This is why you need to keep your risk per trade low and in line with your strategy's success rate. The best way to manage drawdowns and limit the damage they cause is to put in place risk limits per day, week, and month. Even professional athletes who train to do one thing all the time have bad days, so it's unfair to expect yourself to be at 100% all the time.

These risk limits will take you out of the game when you're playing poorly. A daily risk limit is to prevent you from getting into a spiral of revenge trading. A good limit to stick to when starting is to stop trading if you experience three losses in a row. This is pretty unlikely with options trades unless you mess up badly, but it's good to have a limit in place from a perspective of the discipline.

Aim for a maximum weekly drawdown limit of 5% and a monthly drawdown limit of 6-8%. These are pretty high limits, to be honest, and if you are a directional trader, these limits do not apply to you. Directional traders need to be a lot more conservative than options traders when it comes to risk.

Understand that these are hard stop limits. So, if your account has hit its monthly drawdown level within the first week, you need to take the rest of the month off. Overtrading and a lack of reflection on progress can cause a lot of damage, and a drawdown is simply a reflection of that.

Qualitative Risk

Quantitative metrics aside, your ability to properly manage qualitative things in your life and trading will dictate a lot of your success. Prepare well, and you're likely to see progress. You need to see preparation as your responsibility. I mean, no one else can prepare for you, can they? There are different elements to tracking your level of preparation so let's look at them one by one.

Health

You can't trade if you're physically unfit. If you have a fever or if you're suffering from some condition that makes it impossible for you to concentrate, forget about trading. You can rest assured that the other traders in the market will be more than happy to take your money.

When viewed from an options trading perspective, the risk is even more acute. All options strategies will require you to write options at some point, even the most basic ones like in this book. Even if your position is covered, making a mistake, and having an option you wrote be exercised by the buyer is an unpleasant thing that happens. Maintain a regimen of exercise and eat healthy food. Depending on how long you sit in front of your screen, you might even want to consider avoiding certain foods when in session. Heavy meals and food that makes you drowsy will cause your performance to dip, so avoid eating them when you're in the market. Also, don't exercise to such an extent that you're completely exhausted. The idea is to be fresh and alert, not fatigued and aching for a good sleep.

You might have an image of traders as being highly wired and as people who spend their entire lives in front of a screen. Well, most traders do sit in front of a screen most of the time, but the successful ones make time for other stuff in their lives as well. So don't try to copy some false vision here. Instead, do what feels comfortable to you while taking care to not slip into habits that are detrimental to your success.

Lifestyle

Your fitness is just one part of your lifestyle, of course. Is your lifestyle conducive to profitable trading? Are you someone who loves staying up at all sorts of odd hours and considers it perfectly normal to stumble onto a work task while hungover or worse?

Make no mistake; the market will make you donate all of your capital to it.

Many beginners underestimate how difficult trading is. This should come as no surprise since beginners by definition underestimate anything. What shocks most of them is the degree to which they underestimate the difficulty of trading successfully. Let me put it in writing for you: Trading is one of the most challenging things you will ever do in your life. The reason it is so difficult is due to the ever-changing nature of the market and the mental demands it places upon you. Another key lifestyle question to consider is the hours when you'll trade. Most of you reading this probably have full-time jobs and cannot spend your whole day in front of the market.

So, plan out when you'll trade and how you'll prepare yourself for the session. What routines will you carry out? If you're going to trade in the morning before work begins, how will you manage to do this? Will you work in a quiet place or in some noisy truck stop on the way to work? Options positions don't need a lot of maintenance, so there's not much need for this, but when will you check in on the market throughout the day? Will you check in a few times? Five times? Define everything to do with your routine.

Mental States

Trading is a mental activity. You don't need to lift or push anything physically. Therefore, it is crucial to ensure that your mental state is as optimal as it needs to be for you to execute properly.

Having a checklist or a mental check-in list works wonders for the trading process.

Before any trading, write down what's going through your mind and ask yourself how you feel. If you find that you're tired or frustrated and unable to focus properly, step away, and do not trade. If you're planning on sitting in front of your terminal for more than an hour, make it a habit to check in with yourself every half hour or hourly. This need not be a detailed examination, just a simple check-in with yourself to see how things are going.

Take your risk management tasks seriously, and the market will reward you with profits. Do not be the trader who stumbles into the market completely unprepared and then wonders why trading is so unforgiving. Above all else, seek to eliminate all sources of stress when it comes to trading. Take regular breaks and schedule months off from the market to recap and assimilate the things you've learned and need to improve.

Trading every single day of the year does not make sense. This isn't a job where you'll be rewarded with a certain salary for just showing up. You need to produce results, and to do so, you need to manage your downside carefully.

Chapter 17: The Market Environment

The market is a chaotic place with some traders vying for dominance over one another. There are several strategies and time frames in play and at any point; it is close to impossible to determine who will emerge with the upper hand. In such an environment, how is it then possible to make any money? After all, if everything is unpredictable, how can you get your picks right?

Well, this is where thinking in terms of probabilities comes into play. While you cannot get every single bet right, as long as you get enough right and make enough money on those to offset your losses, you will make money in the long run.

It's not about getting one or two right. It's about executing the strategy with the best odds of winning over and over again and ensuring that your math works out with regard to the relationship between your win rate and average win.

So, it comes down to finding patterns that repeat themselves over time in the markets. What causes these patterns? Well, the other traders of course! To put it more accurately, the orders that the other traders place in the market are what create patterns that repeat themselves over time.

The first step to understanding these patterns is to understand what trends and ranges are. Identifying them and learning to spot them when they transition into one another will give you a massive leg up not only with your options trading but also with directional trading.

Trends

In theory, spotting a trend is simple enough. Look left to right and if the price is headed up or down, it's a trend. Well, sometimes it is that simple. However, for the majority of the time you have both with and counter-trend forces operating in the market, it is possible to have long counter-trend reactions within a larger trend and sometimes, depending on the time frame you're in, these counter-trend reactions take up the majority of your screen space.

Trend vs. Range

This is a chart of the UK100 CFD, which mimics the FTSE 100, on the four-hour time frame. Three-quarters of the chart is a downtrend and the last quarter is a wild uptrend. Using the looking left to right guideline; we'd conclude that this instrument is in a range. Is that true though?

Just looking at that chart, you can see that short-term momentum is bullish. So, if you were considering taking a trade on this, would you implement a range strategy or a trending one? This is exactly the sort of thing that catches traders up.

The key to deciphering trends is to watch for two things: counter-trend participation quality and turning points. Let's tackle counter-trend participation first.

Counter Trend Participation

When a new trend begins, the market experiences extremely imbalanced order flow, which is tilted towards one side. There isn't much counter-trend participation against this seeming tidal wave of trend orders. Price marches on without any opposition and experiences only a few hiccups.

As time goes on though, the with trend forces run out of steam and have to take breaks to gather themselves. This is where counter-trend traders start testing the trend and trying to see how far back into the trend they can go. While it is unrealistic to expect a full reversal at this point, the quality of the correction or pushback tells us a lot about the strength distribution between the with and counter-trend forces.

Eventually, the counter-trend players manage to push so far back against the trend that a stalemate results in the market. The with and counter-trend forces are equally balanced and thus the trend comes to an end. After all, you need an imbalance for the market to tip one way or another and balanced order flow is only going to result in a sideways market.

While all this is going on behind the scenes, the price chart is what records the push and pull between these two forces.

Using the price chart, we cannot only anticipate when a trend is coming to an end but also how long it could potentially take before it does. This second factor, which helps us estimate the time it could take, is invaluable from an options perspective, especially if you're using a horizontal spread strategy.

In all cases, the greater the number of them, the greater the counter-trend participation in the market. The closer a trend is to an ending, the greater the counter-trend participation. Thus, the minute you begin to see price move into a large, sideways move with an equal number of buyers and sellers in it, you can be sure that some form of redistribution is going on.

Mind you, the trend might continue or reverse. Either way, it doesn't matter. What matters is that you know the trend is weak and that now is probably not the time to be banking on-trend strategies.

Starting from the left, we can see that there are close to no counter-trend bars, bearish in this case, and the bulls make easy progress. Note the angle with which the bulls proceed upwards.

Then comes the first major correction and the counter-trend players push back against the last third of the bull move. Notice how strong the bearish bars are and note their character compared to the bullish bars.

The bulls recover and push the price higher at the original angle and without any bearish presence, which seems odd.

This is soon explained as the bears' slam price back down and for a while, it looks as if they've managed to form a V top reversal in the trend, which is an extremely rare occurrence.

The price action that follows is a more accurate reflection of the power in the market, with both bulls and bears sharing chunks of the order flow, with overall order flow in the bull's favor but only just. Price here is certainly in an uptrend but looking at the extent of the bearish pushbacks, perhaps we should be on our guard for a bearish reversal. After all, the order flow is looking pretty sideways at this point.

So, how would we approach an options strategy with the chart in the state it is in at the extreme right? Well, for one, any strategy that requires an option beyond the near month is out of the question, given the probability of it turning. Secondly, looking at the order flow, it does seem to be following a channel, doesn't it?

While the channel isn't very clean, if you were aggressive enough, you could consider deploying a collar with the strike prices above and below this channel to take advantage of the price movement. You could also employ some moderately bullish strategies as price approaches the bottom of this channel and figuring out the extent of the bull move is easier thanks to you being able to reference the top of the channel.

As price moves in this channel, it's all well and good. Eventually, though, we know that the trend has to flip. How do we know when this happens?

Turning Points

As bulls and bears struggle over who gets to control the order flow, price swings up and down. You will notice that every time price comes back into the 6427-6349 zone, the bulls seem to step in masse and repulse the bears.

This tells us that the bulls are willing to defend this level in large numbers and strongly at that. Given the number of times the bears have tested this level, we can safely assume that above this level, bullish strength is a bit weak. However, at this level, it is as if the bulls have retreated and are treating this as a sort of last resort, for the trend to be maintained. You can see where I'm going with this. If this level were to be breached by the bears, it is a good bet that a large number of bulls will be taken out. In martial terms, the largest army of bulls has been marshaled at this level. If this force is defeated, it is unlikely that there's going to be too much resistance to the bears below this level. This zone, in short, is a turning point. If price breaches this zone decisively, we can safely assume that the bears have moved in and control the majority of the order flows.

Turning Point Breached

The decisive turning point zone is marked by the two horizontal lines and the price touches this level twice more and is repulsed by the bulls. Notice how the last bounce before the level breaks produces an extremely weak bullish bounce and price simply caves through this. Notice the strength with which the bears breakthrough.

The FTSE was in a longer uptrend on the weekly chart, so the bulls aren't completely done yet. However, as far as the daily timeframe is concerned, notice how price retests that same level but this time around, it acts as resistance instead of support.

For now, we can conclude that as long as the price remains below the turning point, we are bearishly biased. You can see this by looking at the angle with which bulls push back as well as, the lack of strong bearish participation on the push upwards.

This doesn't mean we go ahead and pencil in a bull move and start implementing strategies that take advantage of the upcoming bullish move. Remember, nothing is for certain in the markets. Don't change your bias or strategy until the turning point decisively breaks.

Some key things to note here are that a turning point is always a major S/R level. It is usually a swing point where a large number of with trend forces gather to support the trend. This will not always be the case, so don't make the mistake of hanging on to older turning points.

The current order flow and price action are what matter the most, so pay attention to that above all else. Also, note how the candles that test this level all have wicks on top of them.

This indicates that the bears are quite strong here and that any subsequent attack will be handled the same way until the level breaks. Do we know when the level will break? Well, we can't say with any accuracy. However, we can estimate the probability of it breaking.

The latest upswing has seen very little bearish pushback, comparatively speaking, and the push into the level is strong. Instinct would say that there's one more rejection left here. However, who knows? Until the level breaks, we stay bearish. When the level breaks, we switch to the bullish side.

Putting It All Together

So now we're ready to put all of this together into one coherent package. Your analysis should always begin with determining the current state of the market. Ranges are pretty straightforward to spot, and they occur either within big pullbacks in trends or at the end of trends.

Trends vary in strength depending on the amount of counter-trend participation they have. The way to determine counter-trend participation levels is to simply look at the price bars and compare the counter-trend ones to the with trend ones. The angle with which the trend progresses is a great gauge as well, for its strength, with steeper angles being stronger.

Next, you need to determine the turning point of the trend. The turning point is a level that is extremely well defended by the with trend players and will be attacked repeatedly by the counter-trend traders in long trends.

Chapter 18: Options to Pursue If Your Options Aren't Working

At this point, you may think that if the underlying stock for your option doesn't go anywhere or it tanks that you have no choice but to wait out the expiration date and count the money you spend on your premiums as a loss. That isn't the case. The truth is you can sell a call option you've purchased to other traders in the event it's not working for you. Of course, you're not going to make a profit if you take this approach in the vast majority of cases. But it will give you a chance to recoup some of your losses. If you have invested in a large number of call options for a specific stock and it's causing you problems, you need to recoup at least some of your losses may be more acute. Of course, the right course of action in these cases is rarely certain, especially if the expiration date for the contract is relatively far off in the future, which could mean that the stock has many chances to turn around and beat your strike price. Remember, in all bad scenarios buying the shares of stock is an option – you're not required to do it. In all cases, the biggest loss you're facing is losing the entire premium. You'll also want to keep the following rule of thumb in mind at all times – the more time value an option has, the higher the price you can sell the option for. If there isn't much time value left, then you're probably going to have to sell the option at a discount. If there is a lot of time value, you may be able to recoup most of your losses on the premium.

Let's look at some specific scenarios:

- The stock is languishing. If the stock is losing time value (that is getting closer to the expiration date) and doesn't seem to be going anywhere, you can consider selling the call option to recoup some of your losses related to the premium. The more time value, the less likely it is that selling the option is a good idea. Of course, the less time value, the harder it's going to be actually to sell your option. Or put another way, to sell it you're going to have to take a lower price.

- Suppose the stock isn't stagnant, but it's tanking. If there is a lot of time value left and there is some reason to believe that the company is going to make moves before the expiration date of your contract that will improve the fortunes of the stock when you can still profit from it, then you may want to ride out the downturn. This is a risky judgment call, and it's going to be impossible to know for sure what the right answer is, but you can make an educated guess. On the other hand, if the stock is tanking and there is no good news about the company on the horizon, you are pretty much facing the certainty that you're not going to be able to exercise your options to buy the shares. In that case, you should probably look at selling the option contract to someone more willing to take the risk. At least you can get some of the money back that you paid for the premium.

Now let's briefly consider the positive scenario. Buying options and then trading the stocks can feel like a roller coaster ride, and that rush is what attracts a lot of people to options trading besides the possibilities of making short term profits. Let's consider an example where the stock keeps rising in price? How long do you wait before selling?

There are two risks here. The first risk is that you're too anxious to sell and you do it at the first opportunity. That isn't a huge downside; you're going to make some profits in that case. On the other hand, it's going to be disconcerting when you sit back and watch the stock continuing to rise. That said, this is better than some of the alternatives.

One of the alternatives is waiting too long to buy and sell the shares. You might wait and see the stock apparently reaching a peak, and then get a little greedy hoping that it's going to keep increasing so you can make even more profits. But then you keep waiting, and suddenly the stock starts dropping. Maybe you wait a little more hoping it's going to start rebounding and going up again, but it doesn't, and you're forced to buy and sell at a lower price than you could have gotten. Maybe it's even dropping enough so that you lose your opportunity altogether. A volatile stock might suddenly crash, leaving you with a lost opportunity. The reality is that like everything else involved in options trading since none of us can see the future it's going to be flat out impossible to know if you are making the right call every single time. Keep in mind that your goal is to make a profit on your trades.

Don't get greedy about it, hoping for more riches than you see on the screen. In other words, the goal isn't to sell at the maximum possible profits.

Nobody knows what those are because it's going to be virtually impossible to predict what price the stock will peak at before the contract expires. Instead, you're going to want to focus on making an acceptable profit.

Before you even buy your call options, you should sit down and figure out a reasonable range of values that define ahead of time what that acceptable profit level is. Then when the stock price hits your target range, you exercise your options and sell the shares. You take your profit and move on, going to the next trades.

That is not a guarantee that you're going to make money on every trade, but it's a more rules-based system that gets you into the mindset of trading based on objective facts rather than relying on unbridled emotions.

Also, remember that you can exercise the option to buy the shares, and then hold them until you think you've reached the right moment to sell. At other times, you may want to exercise the option to buy shares and hold in your portfolio as a long-term investment.

OPTIONS

Chapter 19: Creating an Options Trading Plan

Now that we have taken some time to learn more about options and the benefits of trading in them, it is time to get started on the actual process of trading with them. We will make this easier by breaking things down into steps so that it is easier to understand. Sometimes as a beginner it is confusing to know where you should begin or what steps to take, so we are going to try to make this as easy as possible so you can be successful right from the beginning.

Getting Ready

Before you start with the actual process of trading, there are a few steps that you can take first. You need to have a good understanding of some of the basics, which we have covered a bit, such as the types of options available. The more information you have about options and what they are, the more prepared you will be to begin this journey.

Once you are pretty certain that you have a good grasp of trading and what comes with options, it is a good idea to think about why you want to go into trading. How much money would you like to make and what other goals are important to you during this time? It is always a good idea to be precise in your goals because you can develop your strategy around this. It also helps to break frustration and overspending from the start.

But the most important thing that you can do in this first step is to make sure that you create what is known as a trading plan. This is a plan that lists out everything that you want to accomplish such as your expectations, goals, and the guidelines that you will follow with your strategy. Those who don't go into this with a plan are the ones who add a lot of risk to the whole process.

Getting a Broker

The second step is to find a good broker to work with. The broker is the person who, at your request, will make the actual trades. Remember that they will require some fees and a commission for the work that they do, so factor this in when figuring out the costs of getting started with options. Do some research on the broker that you would like to work with. Some will offer their services at a discount, but you have to determine if they are a good choice for you or not.

When you first get started with your new broker, they will probably sit down and discuss some of the things that they like to do with trading and they will go over a risk assessment with you since you are a new customer. This risk assessment is when the broker will figure out how much risk you will feel comfortable with based on your investment and financial history, and then they can assign you a trading level to keep you safe. This is a good place to start to develop your strategy and will help the broker to provide you with the best services possible.

Choosing Your Underlying Assets

Since a contract with options is going to be a derivative of other securities, there are quite a few that you will be able to pick from. You can purchase and sell options contracts of things such as stocks, bonds, foreign currencies, commodities and so much more. This is great news because it allows you to work with what you are comfortable with and will give you a lot of flexibility in the process. The key point here is to do your research before entering the market because it is never a good idea just to pick out a bunch of options that you have no idea about simply because you can.

Managing Your Money and Your Risk

The next thing that you need to consider when you get started with options trading is to know how you can manage your risk and your money. Like any type of trading, options are known to be risky and if you just jump in without a plan and you aren't careful, you can lose a lot of money. When you are creating your trading plan, it should include some guidelines on the amount of risk that you will take, depending on the money amount that you are using.

Get this kind of plan in place right from the beginning and keep it there. Having this plan in place is going to help keep your emotions out of the game; if emotions get into the game, you may as well give up now because you will make bad decisions that will lose you a lot of money. This is true whether the emotions are excitement, greed, nervousness, or something else.

Before you make any decisions with trading, take a breath, look over your plan, and then make the decision that will stay closest to that plan. If you follow that good feeling that you have about a trade, you will often take on more risk and it could be disastrous. One way to help you keep a better hold on your risk and money is to use what is known as an option spread. This is when you will combine more than one position on your contract on the same security. This way, no matter which way the market goes, you will end up making some money off the process rather than losing out.

Diversifying

Another thing that you need to work on when you enter the stock market is diversifying. This makes a lot of sense and is one of the best ways to limit how much risk you are taking on. There are some choices that you can make when it comes to diversifying in options trading. You can choose to work on a variety of strategies, pick out different securities, work on different orders, and even invest in different types of options.

Position Sizing

This step sounds kind of fancy, but it is pretty simple. All that it means is that you will decide how much money, or how much of the capital that you are using, you want to spend on taking a certain position while trading. It is similar to diversifying because you probably don't want to spend all of your money sitting in one position.

When you stay in control of your capital, you can control your losses better and it is easier to protect yourself from big losses.

Planning Out the Trades

Once you have finished out some of the other steps, it is time to get with your broker and start options trading. Some of the steps that you need to do for this part include:

Forecasting: In this step, you need to make predictions about what will happen with the security, such as whether it is going to rise or fall. Having this forecast is going to determine the strategy that you will use and the options that will fit into that strategy.

Setting goals: In this step, you will have to decide what your goals are. You can ask yourself some questions for this one, such as how much you would like to make off the trade. This can help you determine whether or not the trade was successful when it is all done.

Choose the right strategies: There are a lot of great options trading strategies that you can choose and we will discuss them a bit more lately. But having a good strategy in place is going to help you be successful. Before you contact the broker about making a trade, you need to choose what strategy you would like to use.

Choose your position sizing: This is going to be the basic decision of how much money you would like to put into each option so that you have a good idea of the risks ahead of time.

Making the Trades

Once the other steps are done, it is time for you to contact your broker and work with them to place the orders that you want to work with. You should have already set up the funds with the broker, so it won't be too hard to get the orders going quickly. This is the point where you are entering into a trade and you should also spend some time writing out what circumstances need to happen when you want to exit the trade. Will you keep going until the contracts expire? Will you close them early when you receive certain information? Or is there some other determining factor about when you will exit? This is important because it helps you to have a good strategy for all parts of your trading.

Monitoring the Trades

After you place your orders and the broker has been able to make the trades for you, there are a few other things that you will need to do. It is not enough to just put in the money and hope that things go well. Instead, you need to spend your time monitoring the trades as they are in progress. What this

OPTIONS

means is that you have to keep good records about what is going on throughout time with your security so you can make good decisions about holding onto this option or whether it is time to close it or not. The choices that you will make during this particular stage will depend on whether you lose money or make a profit on the options that you chose.

And that is all that it takes to get into the options trading and start making the money that you want in the process. If you pick out a good trading strategy and a good process to work with along the way, this process can yield you a good return on investment without having to put in as much work as you find with the stock market. It can still be hard to do sometimes, but as you get better at your strategy and work hard to learn how this market works, you can make some good money in the process.

OPTIONS

Conclusion

There is no such thing as a "Get Rich, Quick" scheme, no matter what people say. People that are trying to convince you of this are lying to you. This book has the basic information for you to make a start on a new journey in your life, and although it is still a daunting concept, it is one that is very attractive.

The stock exchange and trading platforms are not for the faint-of-heart, and is a very stressful environment, even for the most experienced of traders. The basics in this book are enough for you to get started, but this is only the beginning of your learning journey. Educationally, this is a mere stepping-stone to give you the fundamentals needed to start trading options contracts.

There are many risks involved with options trading, but they can be less risky than trading stocks if attempted properly. The reason for this is because the contracts themselves that will give you access to the underlying stock at the original strike price are not very expensive. The real expenses are those that occur when you purchase the underlying stock itself.

Remember the basics. Don't go into trading without a defined entrance and exit strategy. This will cause pain and unnecessary losses and will defeat the ultimate purpose of trading options contracts. Refer to the case studies included here and elsewhere and learn from the mistakes that other traders have made in the past. A new trader does not have to reinvent the wheel when coming into their own in this business.

You don't have to go on this journey alone. You know what type of individual you are and many brokers will suit your type of personality and will help you build your skills and techniques to become a successful trader. However, don't forget that if you do prefer the prospect of working alone, then you have to make sure that you have educated yourself enough to make educated strategy plans and have the knowledge and techniques to work by yourself.

This will be one of the most stressful jobs that you will have if you choose to do this as your full-time career. Balance is crucial in this line of work. You need to find healthy outlets to help you cope with your emotions. Exercise and hobbies are great to distract yourself, and spending time with family and friends is needed to maintain balance. One needs to maintain balance in one's portfolio and rebalance it when it's stressed, and it's just as important to use the same technique with one's livelihood.

Always seek advice from people that are more experienced than yourself. Learning does not necessarily have to come from books and a computer screen. Some traders and brokers can give you the advice needed to become a successful trader. Some brokers will charge you to teach you, but if you can afford it, this is a worthwhile choice. Gaining knowledge and advice from someone that you can discuss problems is a much-needed boost for the new trader. But if you can't afford the fees of private brokers there are always other options. Many online sources offer you the same advice for free.

Sites like Investopedia, and even YouTube, are filled with experienced and successful traders who are offering their advice for free.

For you to become the type of options trader who you are striving to be, then you need to be able to learn and practice continuously. Start small and move up from there. Learn one or two concepts at a time and then implement the technique on a trading platform simulator. Continuously try this until you become more knowledgeable and more experienced. Many real traders take part in simulated games on these trading platforms as a form of gaining experience, so you won't just be trading against automated robots. Learn to be patient while you are practicing your newly learned skills. Do your market research and look for trends. Watch what certain stock prices do during certain periods. You need to learn to predict the probability of how stock prices will fluctuate. This is not a skill that can be learned overnight, and even the most experienced traders make mistakes with this type of predictive skill.

There is a multitude of causes that can directly influence market trends and stock prices. Anything from CEO's being fired, to forest fires in certain countries, to global pandemics can directly influence the prices of underlying assets of certain companies. This patience comes with a certain amount of logical observations. Sometimes it is better to invest in stocks for a long-haul (especially in a bearish market) and sometimes it is better to trade in options contracts for the possibility of large profits (especially in a bullish market).

Instead of looking for unfounded advice from financial channels on TV, instead watch the news because large events around the world can, and will, directly affect certain stock prices. Do not get greedy when trading, no matter how experienced you become. It is crucial to remember that one must only invest what they are willing to lose. There will always be risks involved here, and losses are going to occur time and time again. Even the most calculated risks don't always turn out to be profitable. Stick to your financial plan, and you can limit your losses before they start to destroy your capital. If you do need to alter a few ideas, stay within the bounds of your strategy, and don't deviate from it. This is when large losses can become a very unfortunate reality. Learn how to analyze market trends and be open to experimentation. The "John Smith" case study showed that experimentation could be a good thing. He noticed that the market was moving in a certain direction and, because of that, he adjusted a few things in his portfolio to see what would work. The buying of shorter options contracts and selling of longer options contracts worked very well for him in the bullish market that he experienced. This is just the beginning of your journey as an up-and-coming options trader. You will see that the more you try, the easier it will be for you to fall into a rhythm as you start your trading. Remember, if you don't have the funds to open a trading account just yet, it doesn't mean that your learning must be put on hold. Open a free simulator trading account with Investopedia and start practicing everything that you have learned about options trading. This is a great start to your new career path, and you will not be disappointed in choosing to change your life.

BOOK 3

SWING & DAY Trading
for Beginners

The Best Strategies for Investing in Stock, Options and Forex With Day and Swing Trading. Make Money and Start Creating your Financial Freedom Today

Written by **Mark Davis**

Table of Contents

Introduction 245

Chapter 1: Overview of Day Trading 247

Chapter 2: Pros and Cons of Day Trading 253

Chapter 3: Day Trading Orders 257

Chapter 4: Best Markets for Day Trading 263

Chapter 5: Technical Analysis 271

Chapter 6: Introduction to Candlesticks 285

Chapter 7: Fundamental Analysis 293

Chapter 8: Basic Day Trading Tips 299

Chapter 9: Strategies of Day Trading 303

Chapter 10: More Day Trading Strategies 313

Chapter 11: Best Platforms for Day Trading 321

Chapter 12: Stock Management 327

Chapter 13: The Dos and Don'ts of Day Trading 333

Chapter 14: Swing Trading 339

Chapter 15: Swing Trading Rules 345

Chapter 16: How Does Swing Trading Work? 349

Chapter 17: Swing Trading Vs. Day Trading 355

Chapter 18: Advantages and Disadvantages of Swing Trading 361

Chapter 19: Strategies of Swing Trading 363

Chapter 20: Swing Trading Psychology 367

Chapter 21: How to Manage Your Funds When Swing Trading 371

Conclusion 377

Introduction

Day trading and swing trading are two of the most excellent strategies that have been in practice in the stock markets for quite some time now on a daily basis. These two are quite different from each other, but also enjoy some standard features that can be detected in both types.

Although most traders have similar goals, using several dissimilar trading types, they accomplish those goals. Trading types can be personalized to suit the occasion constraints of a trader, expectations for advantages, and personal strengths. There's not a single trading style that's superior to any other, but it's significant to recognize your style to synchronize and think about all of your future efforts.

There are two-day trading types that are insecurely dependent upon the keeping time of the asset. All models should be conducted with the guideline of risk and likelihood in mind. Intra-day is for the single-hour duration or a solitary open-to-close conference. A day trader may carry out scalps and swings throughout the intraday time. It is called standard swing trading when a pledge is held overnight or for more than a few days to weeks.

Day trading is a practice connecting opening and closing positions within a similar day. Day traders fancy having no positions held during the night, as an alternative opting to close their positions each sunset, and reopening the positions the day after. Day trading is a temporary strategy intended to take advantage of negligible, intraday price swings, rather than longer-term market engagements. The significance of day trading is in jagged contrast to predictable low buying, holding, and then high selling speculation strategies. Hence, day traders will think differently from investors, absorbed in the market progress of an asset rather than its long-term perspective. That's why day trading approaches are characteristically focused on large quantities of technological analysis, which insist that the trader stay behind up-to-date with breaking news that may activate market unpredictability.

On the other hand, Swing trading uses automated analysis to conclude if, in the very near term, the personal stocks may or may not go up and about or downward. Through analyzing technical indicators, day traders are penetrating for stocks with a spike in market transformations — indicating the most excellent opportunities to buy or sell. The long-standing worth of a given stock is not of curiosity to swing traders. The swing trade is risky but based on sound methodology. The victorious swing trader only focuses on locking up considerable gains in short periods, representing the approach particularly susceptible to changeable financial shocks.

In day trading, you can discover more prospects by being inside and outside the markets. When you look at every economic map, you can see that there is approximately always an apparent long-term inclination. Still, maybe the market may not forever be in a confrontation or support position. You will (typically) enjoy gains by getting on and off the market within a substance of a few days, and find other markets that are set up for additional trades. This helps you to increase the risk and ties up a smaller amount of money instead of continuously having to find a boundary for new positions when you find innovative companies.

Chapter 1: Overview of Day Trading

Before the invention of online trading platforms, people could only engage in stock market trading through brokerage firms, financial institutions, and other trading houses. As more inventions related to the internet were made, it became easy for individual traders to invest in the stock market. One way you can make money on the stock market is through day trading.

Day trading is one technique that can help you gain a lot of income if used properly. However, it becomes a challenge for those who have little information or those who lack the right trading strategies. Sometimes, even the most experienced traders end up losing a fortune because of inadequate knowledge and planning.

Definition

Day trading is the purchasing and selling of securities within a single trading day in any marketplace at commonly stock markets and foreign exchange (FOREX) to obtain a compound of short-term loans. Day traders involved in this are fully investing in this trading activity with multiple learning sources, learning time and a good kind of capital often end up being so successful. Being successful in day trading means acquiring large chunks of profit amounts.

Day trading is a business that you can set up fast. The very first step is to define if you are a full-time or a part-time day trader. I will explain the basic tips for day traders. I will shed light on what kind of weapons you are going to need along the way. I assume that you have allocated the budget that you want to invest in your trading business. The first rule of a trading business is that you should not trade with the money that, if lost, is likely to dent your lifestyle. This money, in the world of trading, is known as 'scarred money.' When you are trading with scarred money, fear comes to haunt your decisions and you lose more often a winning bet. Don't let fear color your business decisions. If you do that, you will be making the worst possible trading choices and lose money in the end. If you get the chance to interview traders and brokers, you will realize this fact.

When day trading, you must ensure that each position you open closes by the end of the same day. This means that you cannot hold a position overnight. Instead, you must close the position in the evening and reopen it the next day. It is the opposite of long-term trading where you purchase stock, hold it for some time, then sell it off at a profit. That is why day trading is not considered a form of investment.

Individuals who engage in this kind of trade are known as day traders. As a day trader, you must master how prices move in the marketplace. This is important if you want to make a profit from each short-term price movement.

A trader can make an unlimited number of trades within a single day. However, beginners can limit themselves to one or a few trades depending on the amount of capital and time available. If a trade does not seem quite profiting at the end of the day, you may decide to let it continue to the next day. However, you will be required to pay some fee to your broker for this to happen.

How long each transaction lasts depends on the trader. Some complete trades happen in a matter of seconds or minutes, while others take several hours. Traders who purchase and sell multiple times within the same day, usually end up with high-profit volumes. Some traders prefer selling their stock as soon as a good profit has been realized. Others prefer to wait until the close of the day to end their positions.

Day Trading Requirements

The most important thing for any trading style, as well as for Intraday trading, is that organizing a trading diary that includes detailed risk management is essential. That is to say, an adequate and controlled risk / return ratio.

Day traders who engage in the business as a career always seek to improve their skills each day. They possess in-depth knowledge of the market as well as the strategies required to make good cash from the market. So, what are the requirements of a person to engage in day trading?

Master the Markets

In-depth knowledge of the functioning of the market and the main factors driving market movements is essential. A day trader must monitor the technical and fundamental indicators. One of the methods to understand how markets work is to study a multitude of fundamental strategies that have always existed in the markets.

This will complete your vision of the market and allow you to identify the opportunities that the different types of traders are looking for, and this can complete your opinion on an investment opportunity.

Discipline in Intraday Trading

In all aspects of life, discipline is important, but neglecting this discipline in intraday trading can be harmful and cause big losses. Success in the stock market without well-established discipline is practically impossible.

You need to be able to control prices in certain periods without making reckless decisions. It sounds simple, but it turns out to be one of the first problems for traders and requires a lot of discipline.

Sometimes the market follows the movements you had expected, but just because you can anticipate it, it doesn't mean you have to place the order.

It is essential to be disciplined as a day trader. Without discipline, it becomes difficult to record any successful transactions. Day trading depends on the volatility of stock prices. Traders are often interested in stocks whose price changes a lot during the day. However, if you are not disciplined enough in the way you select your shares, you may end up losing a lot despite the substantial price changes.

You may decide to trade on several industries, products, and assets, but the truth is – not all these opportunities are good for making a profit. If you are disciplined enough, you will spend time analyzing opportunities before investing in them. You will also open and close trades at the right time, and this will ensure that you minimize losses.

Market Experience – if you happen to engage in day trading without the requisite knowledge of the market, you may lose all your capital. You must be good at reading charts and carrying out technical analysis of the prices and market trends. You must also be able to carry out all the due diligence required to ensure you maximize the profits you realize from the trade.

Adequate Capital – like any other trade, you need sufficient amounts of money to day trade. You must understand that this should be risk capital that you are ready to lose in case the market does not perform in your favor. Preparing yourself this way will save you the emotional torture associated with loss of cash in the trade. You must invest in large capital if you want to make more significant returns.

A Good Strategy – several strategies are involved in day trading. You need these strategies to stay ahead of other traders on the market. Before you start trading, you must understand how to apply these strategies in your transactions. When used correctly, these strategies ensure more consistent returns and fewer losses.

Patience – day trading involves a certain level of waiting. You need to time when to enter the market and when to exit. Getting into the market blindly always results in a lot of problems. You must be patient enough to get into trades in good time.

Besides being patient, you also need to adapt to the changes taking place in the market. For instance, how a market appears at the beginning of the day is not the same way it will be at midday. You must be able to adjust your strategies to accommodate market changes accordingly.

Most successful day traders always seek to acquire these characteristics as a way of improving their business. Doing this requires a high level of mental as well as financial flexibility. You must be thick-skinned enough to risk your capital and accept any losses that come along. Remember, the main difference between successful and unsuccessful day traders lies in the profits. More profits depict you as a successful trader while fewer profits display you as one that is on the losing end. However, losing trades should not make you focus less because even professional day traders started by losing.

How to Get Started With Day Trading

Day trading is not something that should be taken lightly or on a whim. It will require you to be analytical, sound, and have a rehearsed strategy that will give you an edge for each trade that you made.

Check out some charts and ask yourself:

- How would you begin to purchase a trade?

- How would you sell a trade?

- How much are you willing to risk for trade and what is the necessary size of the position you would need to take?

- What would the odds be for profitable trades? What tendencies would it show if you took the trade 100 times?

The only method for answering these questions would be to implement a method of repeating these strategies over and over again. You will then need to monitor the results to get an exact science. The strategy will create a tendency for a simplified way to find the action price daily of any of the assets, as well as a strategy which someone else can learn. Investing profitably allows you to use a brokerage company that aligns with your financial priorities, educational requirements and personal style, choosing the right online stock broker that suits your needs, particularly for new investors, may mean the difference between an exciting new income stream and crushing disappointment.

Although there are no surefire means of guaranteeing returns on investment, there is a way for your success setting by the selection of the online brokerage that fits better to your needs. In this book, we will break down all the things to consider to find a suitable brokerage for your needs from an obvious (a platform that allows or not for securities trading in which you are interested) to a not obvious one as to how much easier is to have the support of human in actual when it is required by you.

Important Points

- Exposure to the capital markets is simple and cheap due to several discount brokers operating online portals.
- Different online brokers are tailored for a particular category of customers — from long-term buy-and-hold novices to professional, successful day traders.
- Finding the right broker online needs some due diligence to get the best out of your funds. Follow the measures and guidance to pick the right one on this topic.

Step No. 1: Know Your Needs

Step No. 2: Field Narrowing

Step No. 3: Fees Figure Out

Chapter 2: Pros and Cons of Day Trading

When I told my friends I started day trading, I got two types of reactions: those who didn't know anything about this world and thought that I was one of those big shots at Wall Street, who could be earning millions of dollars every year. And those who understood investing and trading since they were doing similar things themselves.

Day trading is a particular subject. Some traders believe that it's a get-rich-quick scheme. But remember, the faster you climb, the quicker and harder you fall. In other words, while you gain something faster than you think, you also lose a lot in return.

They were concerned that I was about to lose my money—let me correct that. I think they believed that I would go bankrupt. Of course, I lost capital, but I did not have to file for bankruptcy.

Perhaps these people also do not understand the simple fact that day trading is not for everyone.

Advantages of Day Trading

You should probably consider day trading if:

- With this methodology, you can earn money daily: The idea that it is a "get rich quick" scheme may be part truth since you get to make a profit after the market closes. For example, let us pretend that you invested $100 for 100 shares. The market fluctuation is in your favor, so when you sell it, you double your money, which means you now have revenue of $2 per share—not too shabby, right?
- You want to think less about your investments: Cause once the market closes, your trading ends with your win or loss. The main point is that you will not have to think about whether your stock value will fall the next day or whether the US dollar will be strong in the following week. You think day by day, moment by moment.

- You can build cash inflow and liquidity very quickly: This can be related to the first point. Because you can earn revenues and profits by the end of the day, you can also boost your assets, which then means you can buy more securities and increase your chance of earning more money in a short period. I highly encourage that you diversify your portfolio even if they belong to the same class (e.g., class of stocks) to protect yourself in profound market fluctuations, which are not that common anyway.
- You are better protected against market fluctuations: I mentioned just a while ago that diversification could help shield you from profound fluctuations in the market. But here is something to be happy about: The likelihood that it is going to dip extremely low is minimal. As expected, market prices can change very fast in the blink of an eye, but the movements are often small.
- You can be your own boss: As a retail trader, you call the shots. You decide how much to invest, where to put your money, when to buy or sell, how much you like to earn, the securities you like to trade, etc.
- You have help: You may be a beginner, but the learning curve is not as steep as it is with other securities or types of investing or trading. A variety of materials are available to make sure you do not have to trade blindly.

Disadvantages of Day Trading

If day trading is not as bad as others say, now why should I say it is not meant for everyone?

· It requires a lot of time. All types of work or endeavor need it. I still have to find one that does not, and if it is legal and right, then I am definitely in. But when I say a lot, I genuinely mean it. You see, although there are specific hours of the day when you trade better, you still have to be alert as long as the market stays open because you will never really know what is going to happen.

Stock prices could plunge, which gives you the perfect moment to buy blue chips or those that you can't afford before. If the European forex session is terrible, there is a good chance the US session will suffer the same fate as well.

It is almost the same scenario when we talk about other securities like bonds, hedge contracts, futures, or commodities.

Let us not forget too that you would have to do your research after or in between trading!

• **It is risky**. To be honest, life is all about and related to risk. You are surrounded by it. When you cross the road or drive the car, you run the risk of meeting an accident. When you sleep, there is still a good chance you will never wake up! Have you heard of the term idiopathic? In science, it means a disease or a condition happens with no known or determined cause. It is merely saying it occurred just because it can.

The levels of risk we face daily, however, can vary. In the world of day trading, it can be on opposite ends, depending on how you trade and how much you put in. The bigger the money, the more significant the possible loss. The higher the returns, the higher the chance of falling hard. Losing is all part of the game. The problem comes in if you lose everything—that is a possibility, you know.

• **It can make you emotional**. What has emotion got to do with day trading or any kind of trading for that matter? A whole lot than you can imagine.

I remember the first time I earned a profit in day trading. It was not much, for someone who is just beginning, it meant something. I was so ecstatic I tried to trade more. Sadly, I lost the next day what I gained and traded.

On the other hand, I know of friends who turn into monsters—angry, bitter, resentful, and irritable—once they begin trading. You can blame it on the pressure, sense of competition, pride, or whatever. Whether you like it or not, day trading can get to you, and in many days, it is not a pleasant activity to do.

The relationship between emotions and commerce is strong. Many studies have already shown that customers are more likely to buy items on impulse and buy products that capture their emotions. The theory or concept of scarcity to sell something is also based on emotion. By instilling fear—the idea that if they do not act fast, they can no longer take advantage of the offer—is what has earned several businesspeople millions or even billions of dollars. You can, therefore, not avoid being emotional—whether it is positive or negative—when you are trading. However, you should learn how to control it and decrease its influence and impact on your decisions.

• **It can make you complacent**. These days it is so easy to get confident or even cocky with day trading. After all, you have more tools and resources compared to many years ago. You even have auto programs that can do the trading for you just in case you want to have some me-time in the middle of the day. But complacency can be one of your biggest mistakes.

As you relax, that is when you become least prepared for the uncertainties.

Your software can bog down, the analyses it provides, you can be wrong, markets go down quickly without you knowing it—these things you could have resolved to minimize the effect on you only if you have paid attention and be more proactive or do your part.

• **There are fees**. A lot of people think that they can just trade for free. Of course, it does not work that way. You have different expenses and fees to pay, including commissions for every execution (e.g., buying or selling). And there are tax implications! Yup, you still have to pay your taxes because you are getting some profit from the transaction. In fact, taxes are higher for short-term investments such as those of day trading than the ones held for a long time, which is at least a year. But the good news is there are caps set. Also, if you're having a loss, you can write it off up to the number of your capital gains. In cases where you have more losses than gains in a year, you can go beyond the number of your capital gains and carry it over the succeeding year.

For instance, last year, you had a $10,000 of capital gains and a $15,000 loss. You can zero your capital gains liability, leaving you with $5,000 more loss. You can then further reduce your tax liability by $3,000 and offset the next capital gains this year with $2,000. If you declare $18,000 capital gains this year, then your total liability is only $16,000.

Chapter 3: Day Trading Orders

Stock trading involves a lot more than selling and buying of assets and securities. There are several orders used in each technique of trading. Each order is created to fulfill a particular task on the market. Let us look at some of the orders you can employ in day trading and how you can use them.

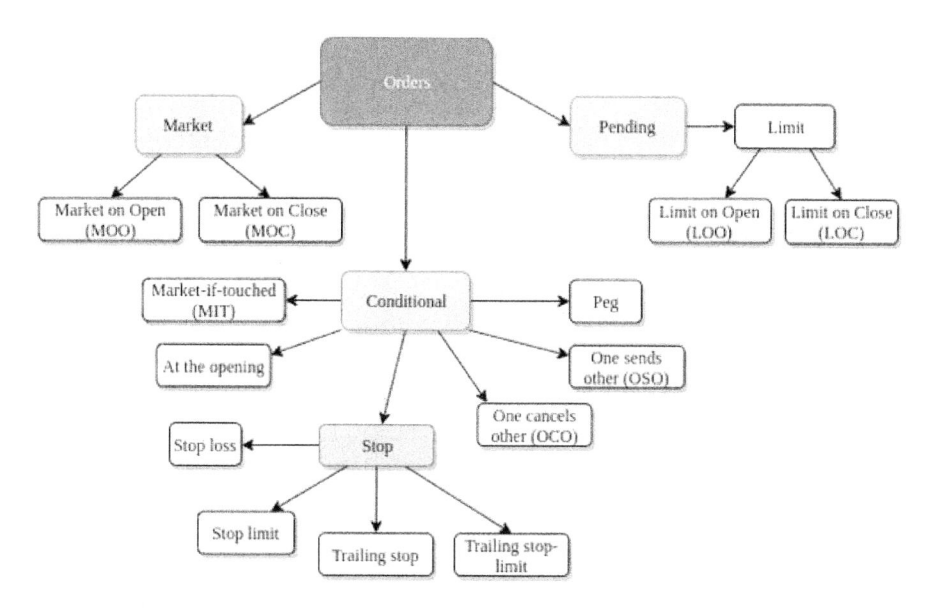

```
                           Orders
           ┌─────────────────┼─────────────────┐
         Market          Conditional        Pending ──→ Limit
        ┌──┴──┐                                   ┌──────┴──────┐
  Market on  Market on                        Limit on    Limit on
   Open       Close                             Open        Close
   (MOO)      (MOC)                             (LOO)       (LOC)
```

- Market-if-touched (MIT)
- At the opening
- Peg
- One sends other (OSO)
- One cancels other (OCO)
- Stop
  - Stop loss
  - Stop limit
  - Trailing stop
  - Trailing stop-limit

- Market Order is one of the easiest orders to raise: It can be divided into two – market orders for buying and market orders for selling. This order provides you information about the market price. For instance, if you create a market order to purchase a particular asset or derivative, you will be able to see a list of all the sellers on the market plus the price of their securities. If you raise an order to sell, you will gain access to a list of available buyers together with their bid prices. Day traders use market orders to enter or exit trades faster, especially when the prices are changing drastically.

The disadvantage of market orders, though, is that you can never tell the exact opening or closing price of a transaction. The prices always depend on the volume of the stock you decide to trade-in.

- A buy stop order is placed by day traders seeking to purchase stocks at a price that is higher than the current price: The order is filled when the price goes above the indicated stop price. The order is mostly used to restrict losses incurred on a short trade position when the market prices start moving in an unfavorable direction.

- Sell stop order is utilized when the price drops below the current stock price: When you raise this order, it can only be filled when the stop price is higher or the same as the current stock price. Day traders use this kind of order to exit long trades that have assumed a losing direction.

- Buy limit order is placed when the day trader wishes to purchase at a cost that is lower than the current stock price: This allows you to control the amount of cash you pay for a particular purchase position. When you create a buy limit order, you can only buy the stock at the current price or lower, not higher. One disadvantage of this kind of order is that you are never sure if it will be filled. If the amount of stock keeps going higher than the current price, then you will not succeed in purchasing any stock.

- Sell limit order is the opposite of the buy limit order: When you raise this order, you are indicating a willingness to sell a security or asset at a price that is higher than the current stock price. Like the buy limit order, you can only fill this order if the price rises above the current price. The aim of using this order is to make you generate profit from any long trades that you engage in.

- Buy stop limit order works the same way as the buy stop order, only that is working differently from the market order: This order gets completed when the price of the stock reaches the buy stop limit amount or less. It prevents you from paying more than the anticipated amount for each trade thus reducing the number of losses you may incur

- Sell stop limit order - sell stop limit order also plays the same role as the sell stop order, but does not mimic the market order: When you place this kind of order, it only gets filled when the stock price attains an amount that is equal or more than the stop limit price. Setting the wrong order for your day trading activities can cause you to end into problems. The more you practice how to use the orders, the more you will understand how and when to apply them.

What Day Traders Do Every Day

A typical day in the life of the day trader is often filled with lots of exciting activities. What the trader spends time doing during the day determines the amount of profit he makes at the end of the day. Some of the days are always smooth and less busy, while others involve a lot of activities.

Traders rise early enough to study the market as they prepare for the day. Depending on one's location, morning hours may present some excellent trading opportunities or some not so good ones.

Day traders always take advantage of this period because the prices are the most liquid and the most volatile. Here are some of the primary stages a day trader goes through each day:

1. Preparing for the Day

Day traders always take time to prepare for the day as a way of ensuring that things go as planned during the entire day. Some ensure that they get up at least an hour before the trading session begins. This is in order to:

- Go through the necessary strategies for the day and resolve any issues faced each day;
- Create a trading plan for the day or revise existing plans accordingly;
- Adjust account balances accordingly and determine how much they are ready to risk losing that day;
- Check any changes in price and financial news that can affect market direction,
- Analyze the trading platform to ensure it's still working well;

2. Trading Session

Day traders always make transactions the first few hours after the market opens.

Depending on how active the market is, some opt to trade for more extended periods, until most of the stocks become less volatile.

Although beginners in the trade always think that they have to spend a lot of time online to make a profit, this is not the case. Professional day traders only visit the trading platforms to enter or exit positions and set the necessary orders for the day. Once some orders are filled, trades associated with such orders always close automatically. This means that you do not need to spend all your time on day trading platforms to make a profit.

3. Review

It takes place at the end of the trading day. For some, the day can end as early as 11:00 am while for others; it may end as late as 6:00 pm. At this point, the trader goes through the day's business and notes down every activity and results of each trade.

This is where the trader also calculates the profits or losses incurred and notes down what needs to be done to improve future trading experiences. A basic review always consists of the number of hours spent on the trading platform and the number of positions completed successfully. It also consists of the number of successful or unsuccessful trades as well as the net profit or loss.

Without the right plan and strategy, day trading becomes a less exciting venture. However, traders who have mastered the necessary moves on the market always enjoy every bit of the business. The secret to becoming better at the trade lies in doing a lot of practice.

Trading Goals for Overcoming Constraints

Trading goals are different from ordinary goals. The main purpose of each trader is always to make a profit from each trade. However, day trading goals go beyond basic selling and buying of stocks at a profit. Several attributes define achievable day trading goals:

- They focus on the trading process and not the benefits. You probably know that the main focus of creating goals is making them specific and measurable. In day trading, you must ensure that the goals you make do not focus on the amount of money you wish to build over time. You should instead concentrate on the efforts you need to put into the process you use. When the process is perfect, the results will automatically be positive.

- They are defense-minded. If you set goals that are not defense-minded, you will end up pursuing trading opportunities only for the sake of financial gain. However, your goals should seek to protect your capital. Doing this will keep you in business even when you are not making any profit. You can do this by setting limit orders for each trading period. Also, you can outline a risk tolerance plan that indicates the amount you are willing to lose in every trade. With these figures in place, you can always customize your strategies and trading techniques to ensure that you do not exceed these limits.

- They are progressive. Sound goals allow you to get into the day trading business gradually. They ensure that you do not skip any step of the trading process and that you acquire the necessary training before jumping into the trade. You can do this by ensuring that you do not risk more than you are willing to lose. And that you do not depend on market indicators to make trading decisions all the time.

Setting clear, realistic goals is a must for every day trader. However, you must remember that your goals must never be profit-oriented. This is one grave mistake that most traders make. The right goals will always prevent you from over-risking your capital and overtrading.

Chapter 4: Best Markets for Day Trading

Trading in Stocks

The thought of trading in stocks scares away many investors. Individuals who have never traded are terrified by the fact that one can quickly lose money with wrong decisions. The reality is, stock trading is a risky activity. However, when approached with the right market knowledge, it is an efficient way of building your net worth.

So, what is a stock? A stock is a share. It is also termed as equity. It is a financial instrument which amounts to ownership in a particular company. When an individual purchases a stock or shares, it means that they own a portion or fraction of the company. For instance, say a trader owns 10,000 shares in a company with 100,000 shares. This would mean that the individual has 10% ownership of the stakes. The buyer of such shares is identified as a shareholder. Therefore, the more shares one owns, the more significant the proportion of the company which they own. Every time the value of the company shares rise, your share value will also rise. Similarly, if the value falls, your share value also declines. When a company makes a profit, the shareholders are also bestowed with the profits in the form of dividends.

Preferred stock and common stock are the two main types of stocks you should be aware of. The difference that lies between these stocks is that with common stocks, it carries voting rights. This means that a shareholder influences company meetings. Hence, they can have a say in company meetings where the board of directors is elected. On the other hand, preferred shares lack voting rights. However, they are identified as "preferred" shares or stocks because of their preference over common stocks. If a company goes through liquidation, shareholders with preferred shares will be preferred to receive assets or dividends.

Basing on the factors pointed out above, the stock market could be evaluated as follows.

Capital Requirements

According to the Pattern Day Trading Rule, the minimum brokerage balance you are required to maintain for you to trade in stocks is at least $25,000. Without a doubt, this is a lot of money to start with. Surprisingly, a lot of traders began with a lower amount than that. To understand how this rule applies, you need to know what it means to be a pattern day trader. This is the type of trader whereby they execute more than four traders within five business days in their margin accounts.

Leverage

There are two ways of trading in stocks. You could either choose to trade using a margin account or a cash account. With the margin account, it gives a trader the opportunity of buying their stocks on margin. Conversely, with cash accounts, you only buy the stocks for the amount of money present in your account. In other words, you will be trading with a leverage ratio of 1:1.

In a real-life example, say you make an initial deposit of $10,000 in your margin account. Since you deposited about 50% of the buying price, it means you are worth twice as much, i.e., $20,000. In other words, your buying power is worth twice what you deposited. Therefore, when you buy stocks worth $5,000, your buying power will reduce to $15,000. Your leverage ratio is, therefore 1:2. Traders with a good trading relationship with their brokers could have this ratio increased to even 1:8.

Liquidity

With regard to liquidity, you can be confident that trading in stocks is not a bad idea. There are over 10,000 stocks present in the U.S. stocks exchanges. Most of these stocks are traded daily. Dealing with these stocks guarantees that you evade the common issues of slippage or manipulation.

Volatility

A trader shouldn't worry about the volatility of the stocks market as they often go through cycles of high and low. This is not a bad thing as a trader simply needs to study when the markets are rising and be wary of the instances when markets seem to fall.

Basing it on these factors, would be correct to argue that stocks have got good volatility and liquidity. The only issue with stocks is that they have a high capital requirement.

Trading in Forex

Most traders would argue that trading in Forex is quite complicated. However, it's not. Just like any other form of trading, you have to stick to the basic rules. In this case, you need to buy when the market is rising and ensure you sell when the market is dropping. Trading in Forex involves the process of trading in currencies. In simpler terms, a trader exchanges currency for others based on individual agreed rates. If you have traveled to foreign countries and exchanged your currency against their local currencies, then you should understand how trading in Forex works.

At first, it could seem confusing to choose the best currencies, but a trader should simply go for major currencies. Some of the frequently traded currencies include the U.S. dollar, Japanese yen, European Union euro, Australian dollar, Canadian dollar, and Swiss franc.

An important thing you ought to understand about forex trading is that you need to trade in pairs. This means that when you are buying one currency, you should do this while simultaneously selling another. If you do some digging, you will notice that currencies are quoted in pairs, i.e., USD/JPY or EUR/USD. Below is an image showing how currencies are quoted in pairs.

Often, the most traded forex products include:

- USD/JPY

- EUR/USD

- GBP/USD

An important thing to keep in mind about forex trading is that the market is highly volatile. This means that a trader could quickly lose a lot of money within a single day. Before venturing into this market, a trader should take the time to understand this market in detail.

The forex market could be evaluated as follows.

Capital Requirements

With the number of brokers over the internet, it is relatively easy to begin forex trading. The best part is that different brokers will require varying amounts of capital from you. Hence, you could settle for the best, depending on how much you can afford. You can trade in forex with just $1,000 as your starting capital.

Leverage

Typically, leverage in the forex market stands at 1:100. This implies that if you have $2,000 in your trading account, you can trade $200,000. The ratio varies depending on the forex trader you deal with. Some traders offer leverage of 1:200.

Liquidity

Liquidity is not an issue in the world of forex trading. The only problem is that a trader doesn't have access to real-time volume data simply because the market is decentralized.

Volatility

Considering that there is high leverage in forex trading, it implies that little movement in the market could earn one colossal profit. The market's volatility is quite impressive, but not as volatile as the stock market. Basing on these factors, trading in forex is a smart move. A trader can begin trading with as little as $1,000.

Also, with the high leverage present in this market, it is easy to earn huge returns with the right moves.

Trading in Futures

Today, most traders prefer to trade in futures due to their flexibility and associated advantages.

The good news is that a trader can use almost any methodology to trade.

But in the trading in futures, the former is very risky compared to the stock one.

We have different futures contracts, including energies, currencies, metals, interest rates, food sector futures, and agricultural futures.

S&P 500 E-mini

Most traders will fancy the idea of trading in the S&P 500 E-mini because of its high liquidity aspect. It also appeals to most investors because of its low day trading margins. You can conveniently trade in S&P 500 E-mini around the clock not to mention that you will also benefit from its technical analysis aspect. Essentially, the S&P 500 E-mini is a friendly contract since you can easily predict its price patterns.

10 Year T-Notes

10 Year T-Notes is also ranked as one of the best contracts to trade-in. Considering its sweet maturity aspect, most traders would not hesitate to trade in this futures contract. There are low margin requirements that a trader will have to meet when trading in 10 Year T-Notes.

Crude Oil

Crude oil also stands as one of the most popular commodities in futures trading. It is a new market because of its high daily trading volume of about 800k. Its high volatility also makes the market highly lucrative.

Gold

This is yet another notable futures contract. It might be expensive to trade in gold; however, it is an excellent hedging choice more so in poor market conditions.

Capital Requirements

The amount of money required to begin trading in futures will vary. Some brokers will require a trader to have about $5,000. However, some would require only $2,000. A trader needs to choose the best broker who is flexible enough to allow them to trade with the little capital they have.

Leverage

Leverage will also vary depending on the type of futures you trade-in. The contract value will also have an impact on the amount of leverage that you will have.

Liquidity

Just like leverage, the liquidity aspects of futures will also depend on the futures you are trading. Accordingly, it is crucial for any trader to regularly check the respective volumes of contracts before trading on them.

Volatility

Futures are volatile. The advantage gained by using high leverage ensures that a trader makes a good profit with little price changes in the market.

Keeping the above factors into consideration, futures is an excellent market to trade. A trader can easily day trade with as little as $2,000. The high leverage ratio will also guarantee that huge profits can be earned.

Trading in Stock Options

Trading in stock options is almost similar to trading in futures. Here, a trader also buys stocks at a pre-established price and later sells when prices rise.

Capital Requirements

Stock options trading also affected by the Pattern Day Trading Rule. This means that your minimum capital requirements will be $25,000. If you engage in more than four trades in a particular week, then you should have about $30,000 in your trading account.

Leverage

Since there are many options to choose from, leverage will vary. The exciting aspect of stock options is that they have high leverage amounts.

Liquidity

Concerning liquidity, stock options are not that liquid. A keen eye on this market reveals that a few options are traded regularly. The low volume of trades is affected by the many options that traders can choose from. Fortunately, stock options are rarely manipulated by the market. Their values are not influenced by supply and demand.

Volatility

Stock options are highly volatile. From the look of things, stock options have similar pros and cons like trading in stocks. Most new traders will shy away from this form of day trading due to its high capital demands. Its high volatility could be scary to most investors as it makes the market to be unpredictable. This makes this form of trading to be very risky. Therefore, it is not recommended for new traders.

Chapter 5: Technical Analysis

Technical analysis is the method of using charts and other methods to analyze various data in options trading. Using these optical instruments, you have the chance to determine the direction of the market because they give you a trend.

This method focuses on studying the supply and demand of a market. The price will be seen to arise when the investor realizes the market is undervalued, and this leads to buying. If they think that the market is overvalued, the prices will start falling, and this is deemed the perfect time to sell.

Support and Resistance

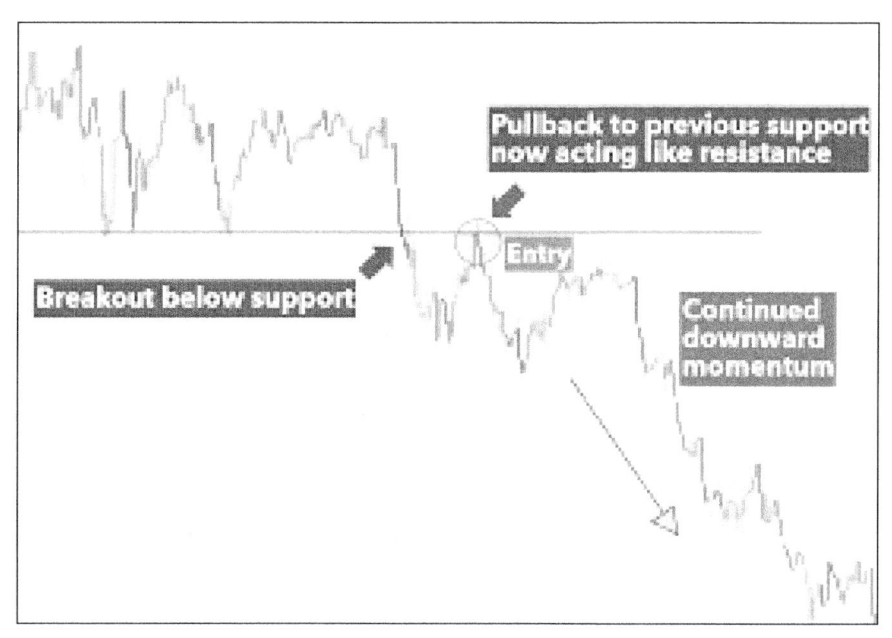

These levels occur at points where both the buyer and the seller aren't dormant. These levels are displayed on using a horizontal line extended in the past to the future.

The different prices will reach the support and resistance points in the future.

How to Apply Support and Resistance

• Using these points allows you to know when to call or put.

• Support and resistance give you a way to determine the entry point to use for a directional trade.

The Significance of Trends in Option Trading

Technical analysis works on the premise of the trend. These trends come by due to the interaction of the buyer and the seller. The aggressiveness of one of the parties in the market will determine how steep the trend becomes. To make a profit, you have to take advantage of the changes in the price movement.

To understand the direction of the trend, you ought to look at the troughs and peaks and how they relate to each other.

When looking for money in options trading, you ought to trade with a trend. The trend is what determines the decision you make when faced with a situation – whether to buy or to sell. You need to know the various signs that a prevailing trend is soon ending so that you can manage the risks and exit the trades the right way.

Characteristics of Technical Analysis

This analysis makes use of models and trading rules using different price and volume changes. These include the volume, price, and other different market info.

Technical analysis is applied among financial professionals and traders and is used by many option traders.

The Principles of Technical Analysis

Many traders on the market use the price to come up with information that affects the decision you make ultimately. The analysis looks at the trading pattern and what information it offers you rather than looking at drivers such as news events, economic and fundamental events.

Price action usually tends to change every time because the investor leans towards a particular pattern, which in turn predicts trends and conditions.

Prices Determine Trends

Technical analysts know that the price in the market determines the trend of the market. The trend can be up, down, or move sideways.

History Usually Repeats Itself

Analysts believe that an investor repeats the behavior of the people that traded before them. The investor sentiment usually repeats itself. Since the behavior repeats itself, traders know that using a price pattern can lead to predictions.

The investor uses the research to determine if the trend will continue or if the reversal will stop eventually and will anticipate a change when the charts show a lot of investor sentiment.

Combination With Other Analysis Methods

To make the most out of the technical analysis, you need to combine it with other charting methods on the market. You also need to use secondary data, such as sentiment analysis and indicators.

To achieve this, you need to go beyond pure technical analysis and combine other market forecast methods in line with technical work. You can use technical analysis along with fundamental analysis to improve the performance of your portfolio.

You can also combine technical analysis with economics and quantitative analysis. For instance, you can use neural networks along with technical analysis to identify the relationships in the market. Other traders make use of technical analysis with astrology.

Other traders go for newspaper polls, sentiment indicators to come with deductions.

The Different Types of Charts Used in Technical Analysis

Candlestick Chart

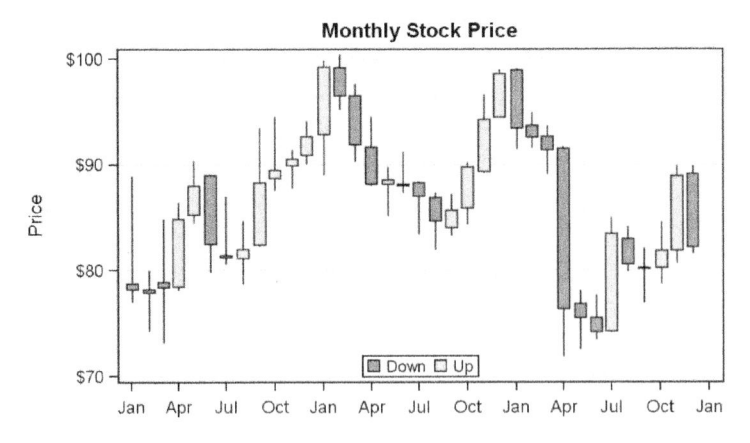

This is a charting method that came from the Japanese. The method fills the interval between the opening and closing prices to show a relationship. These candles use color-coding to show the closing points. You will come across black, red, white, blue, or green candles to represent the closing point at any time.

Open-high-low-close Chart (OHLC)

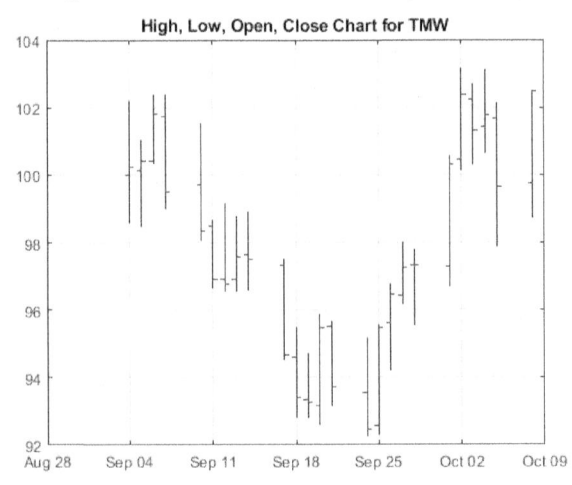

These are also referred to as bar charts, and they give you a connection between the maximum and minimum prices in a trading period. They usually feature a tick on the left side to show the open price and one on the right to show the closing price.

Line Chart

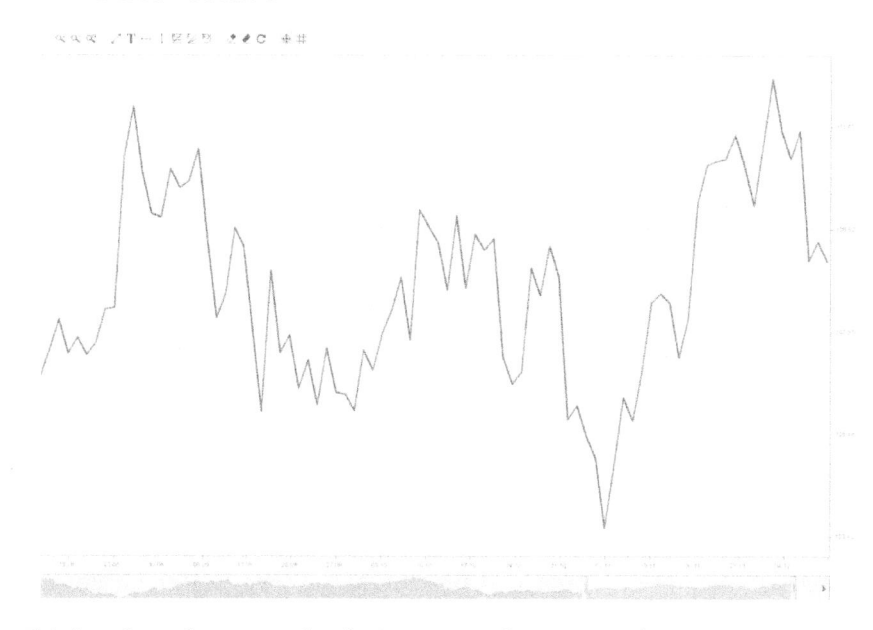

This is a chart that maps the closing price values using a line segment.

Point and Figure Chart

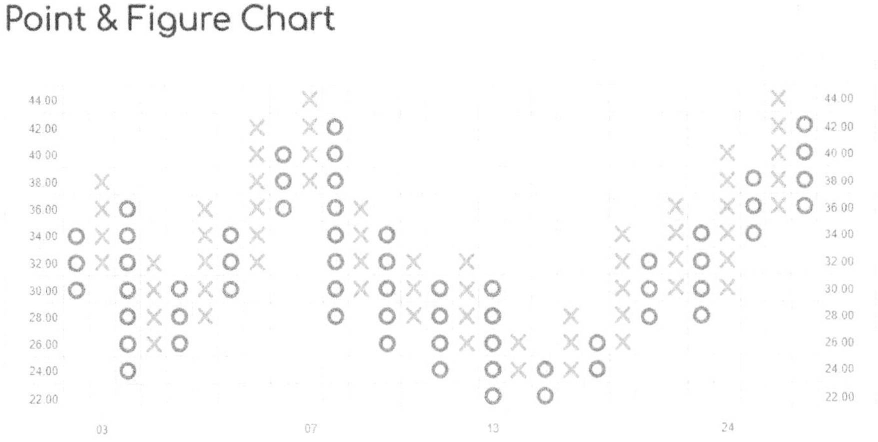

This employs numerical filters that reference times without entirely using the time to construct the chart.

Overlays

These are usually used on the main price charts and come in different ways:

- Resistance – refers to a price level that acts as the maximum level above the usual price.
- Support – the opposite of resistance, and it shows as the lowest value of the price.

[Support and resistance]

- Trend line – this is a line that connects two troughs or peaks.

- Channel – refers to the two trend lines that are parallel to each other.

- Moving average – a kind of dynamic trend line that looks at the average price in the market.

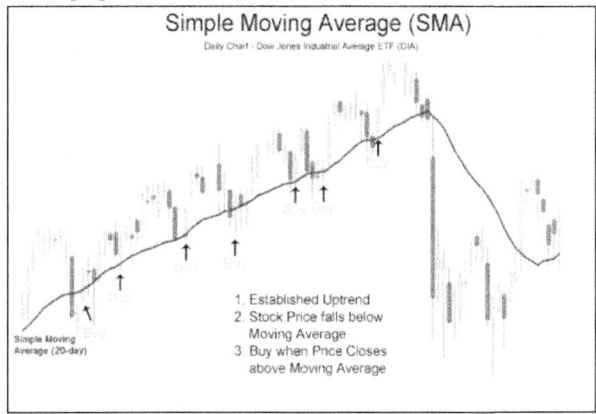

- Bollinger bands – these are charts that show the rate of volatility in a market.

277

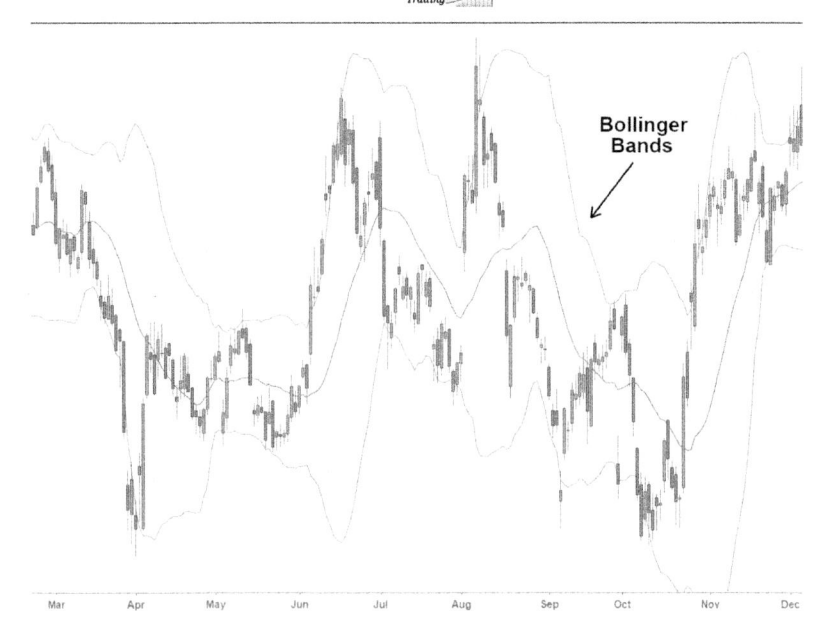

- Pivot point – this refers to the average of the high, low, and closing price averages for a specific stock or currency.

Price-based Indicators

These analyze the price values of the market. These include:

- Advance decline line – this is an indicator of the market breadth.

- Average directional index – shows the strength of a trend in the market.

- Commodity channel index – helps you to identify cyclical trends in the market.

- Relative strength index – this is a chart that shows you the strength of the price.

- Moving average convergence (MACD) – this shows the point where two trend lines converge or diverge.

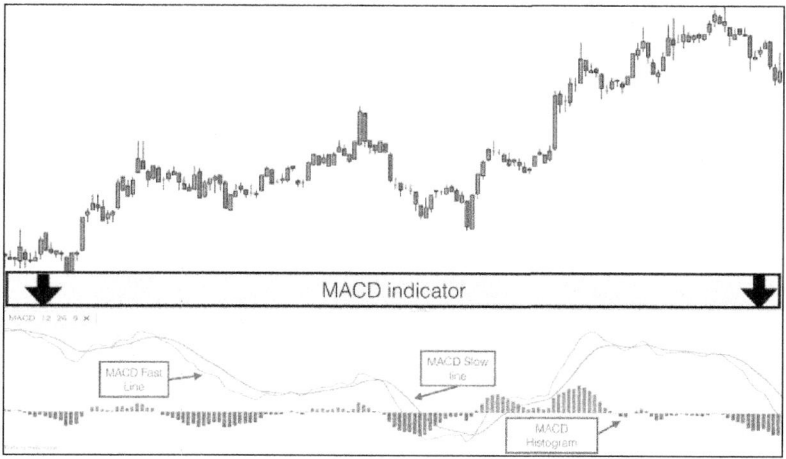

- Stochastic oscillator – this shows the close position that has happened within the recent trading range.

Stochastic Oscillator

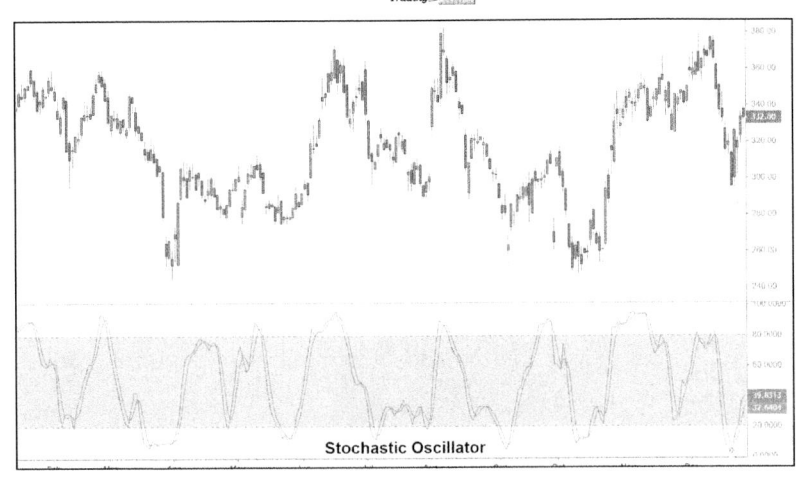

- Momentum – this is a chart that tells you how fast the price changes.

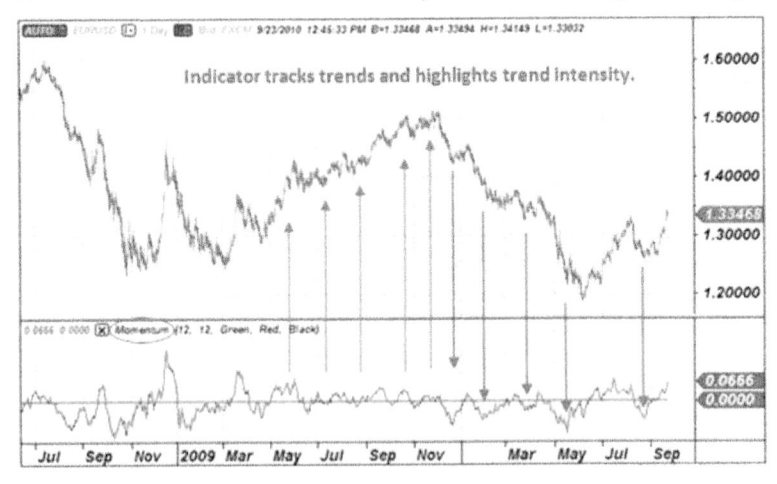

Indicator tracks trends and highlights trend intensity.

The Benefits of Technical Analysis in Options Trading

While the forecast for prices is a huge task, the use of technical analysis makes it easier to handle.

The significant advantages of technical analysis include:

Expert Trend Analysis

This is the most significant advantage of technical analysis in any market. With this method, you can predict the direction of the market at any time. You can determine whether the market will move up, down, or sideways quickly.

Entry and Exit Points

As a trader, you need to know when to place a trade and when to opt-out. The entry point is all about knowing the right time to enter the trade for good returns. Exiting a trade is also vital because it allows you to reduce losses.

Leverage Early Signals

Every trader looks for ways to get early signals to assist them in making decisions. Technical analysis gives you signals to trigger a decision on your part.

This is usually ideal when you suspect that a trend will reverse soon. Remember the time the trend reverses are when you need to make crucial decisions.

It Is Quick

In options trading, you need to go with techniques that give you fast results. Additionally, getting technical analysis data is cheaper than other techniques in fundamental analysis, with some companies offering free charting programs. If you are in the market to make use of short time intervals such as 1-minute, 5-minute, 30 minute, or 1-hour charts, you can get this using technical analysis.

It Gives You A Lot of Information

Technical analysis gives you a lot of information that you can use to make trading decisions. You can easily build a position depending on the information you get then take or exit trades. You have access to information such as chart patterns, trends, support, resistance, market momentum, and other information.

The current price of an asset usually reflects every known information of an asset. While the market might be rife with rumors that the prices might surge or plummet, the current price represents the final point for all information. As the traders and investors change their bearing from one part to another, the changes in assets reflect the current value perception.

If all this turns out to be true, then the only info you require is a price chart that gives all the price reflections and predictions. There isn't any need for you to worry yourself with the reasons why the price is rising or falling when you can use a chart to determine everything.

With the right technical analysis information, you can make trading easier and faster because you make decisions based not on hearsay but facts. You don't have to spend your time reading and trying to make headway in financial news. All you need us to check what the chart tells you.

You Understand Trends

If the prices on the market were to gyrate randomly without any direction, you would find it hard to make money. While these trends run in all directions, the prices always move in trends. The directional bias allows you to leverage the benefits of making money. Technical analysis allows you to determine when a trend occurs when it doesn't occur, or when it is in reversal.

Many of the profitable techniques that are used by the traders to make money follow trends. This means that you find the right trend and then look for opportunities that allow you to enter the market in the same direction as the trend. This helps you to capitalize on the price movement.

History Always Repeats Itself

Technical analysis uses common patterns to give you the information to trade. However, you need to understand that history will not be exact when it repeats itself. The current analysis will be either bigger or smaller, depending on the existing market conditions. The only thing is that it won't be a replica of the prior pattern.

This pans out easily because most human psychology doesn't change so much, and you will see that the emotions have a hand in making sure that prices rise and fall. The emotions that traders exhibit create a lot of patterns that lead to changes in prices all the time. As a trader, you need to identify these patterns and then use them for trading. Use prior history to guide you and then the current price as a trigger of the trade.

Enjoy Proper Timing

Do you know that without proper timing, you will not be able to make money at all? One of the major advantages of technical analysis is that you get the chance to time the trades. Using technical analysis, you get to wait, then place your money in other opportunities until it is the right time to place a trade.

Applicable Over a Wide Time Frame

When you learn technical analysis, you get to apply it to many areas in different markets, including options. All the trading in a market is based mostly on the patters that are a result of human behavior. These patterns can then be mapped out on a chart to be used across the markets.

Additionally, you can use the analysis in any timeframe, which is applicable whether you use hourly, daily, or weekly charts. These markets are usually taken to be fractal, which essentially means that patterns that appear on a small scale will also be present on a large scale as well.

Chapter 6: Introduction to Candlesticks

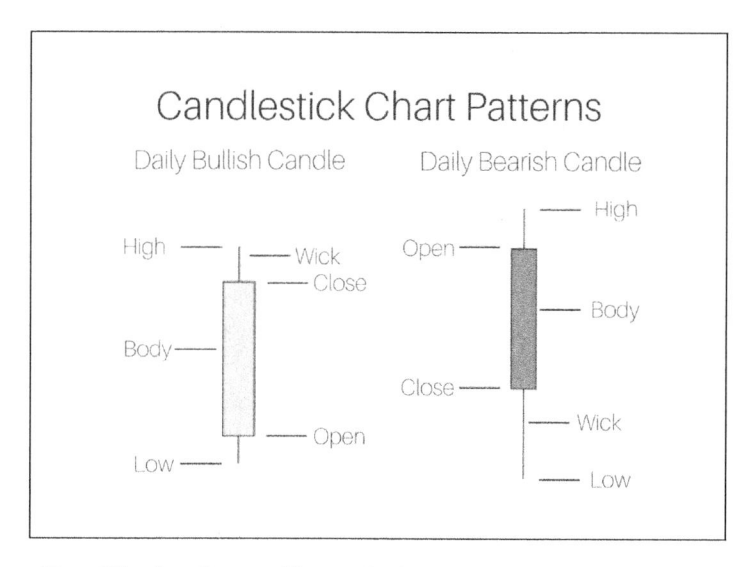

Candlestick Chart Patterns

Daily Bullish Candle — High, Wick, Close, Body, Open, Low

Daily Bearish Candle — High, Open, Body, Close, Wick, Low

Bullish Candlesticks

These charts are highly popular and are essential for any day trader. They display the prices for specific securities daily. By analyzing a candlestick chart, it is possible to know the day's highest and lowest prices, as well as the opening and closing price. In addition to this, the shape of the candle in the candlestick chart reveals more information. Specific colors denote this. The candle will be black or red when the stock closes at a lower price. However, the candle will be white or green when it closes at a higher price. The shadow of the candle in this chart also tells a story. It explains the highs and lows for the day, which can then be compared to the opening and closing prices.

So, in the final analysis, just the shape of the candle will vary based on all the movements taking place in a day's trade. This type of chart provides a straightforward analysis of pricing for the day.

Bearish Candlesticks

When a gambler goes to the races, they receive a thrill by watching everything unfolding live, right before their eyes. There is an equivalent for this in day trading, and this is referred to as Level II. A trader using this strategy is watching the trades being executed live, right before their eyes.

This is based on quotes from specific market makers. As everything unfolds, rapid decisions can be made to ensure that any small gain is capitalized on – in real-time.

ECN stands for Electronic Communication Network. This is an automated system that allows traders from different locations to trade with each other easily. It works by matching buy and sell orders. This system is great for a day trader who operates as an individual because by using an ECN, the trader can connect directly with a major brokerage. This cuts down on a middleman's fees and saves time, allowing for faster and more profitable trades. The added advantage of an ECN is that trading extends beyond the typical market hours, and includes after-hours trading.

In addition to these two tools, a chart can prove handy when reading information for data trading. Simply understanding the available information can go a long way in creating a foundation for success.

Discerning the information from day trading transactions would be a challenge if there was no mechanism to make it possible. All the information from day trading is arranged in different trading charts. By using these trading charts, a day trader can keep an eye on the markets they are trading on, making it easier to make informed decisions about when they should be making their trades. It also allows them to monitor the movements on the market consistently.

Candlestick charts were said to have come into existence a hundred years ago in Japan before the developed world created the bar charts and point-and-figure charts.

Homma, a Japanese man from the seventeenth century, was said to find out there was a relationship between the demand and supply of rice and its price.

It was said the markets were controlled a lot by how the traders felt.

Candlesticks end up displaying the emotion by physically representing the number of price movements using varying hues.

Traders tend to utilize candlesticks when they want to reach trading decisions.

This is usually dependent on those constantly occurring patterns, allowing one to forecast where the price direction would be in the short term.

Components of Candle Sticks

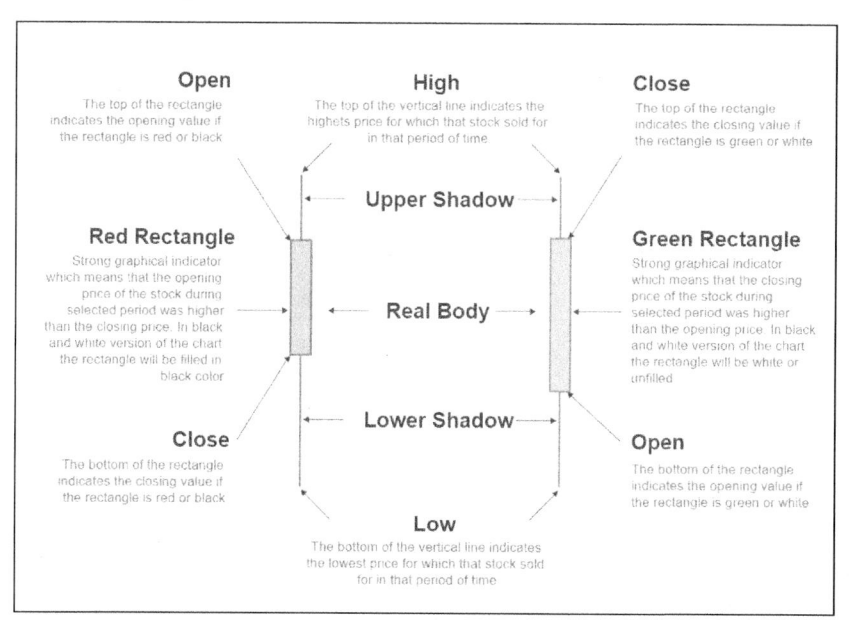

Open — The top of the rectangle indicates the opening value if the rectangle is red or black

High — The top of the vertical line indicates the highets price for which that stock sold for in that period of time

Close — The top of the rectangle indicates the closing value if the rectangle is green or white

Upper Shadow

Red Rectangle — Strong graphical indicator which means that the opening price of the stock during selected period was higher than the closing price. In black and white version of the chart the rectangle will be filled in black color

Real Body

Green Rectangle — Strong graphical indicator which means that the closing price of the stock during selected period was higher than the opening price. In black and white version of the chart the rectangle will be white or unfilled

Lower Shadow

Close — The bottom of the rectangle indicates the closing value if the rectangle is red or black

Open — The bottom of the rectangle indicates the opening value if the rectangle is green or white

Low — The bottom of the vertical line indicates the lowest price for which that stock sold for in that period of time

A daily candlestick bears similarity to a bar chart because it displays the daily low, high, and close price on the market.

The candlestick usually possesses a great aspect that makes up christened as the "real body."

The real body is that part that acts as the range of price between the closing and opening of a day's trading session.

If you see that the real body has either the black hue or is filled up, then it means that the closing position ended up being lower when compared to the opening position.

If you see that the real body came out empty, then the opening position was lower than the closing one.

Traders can change the hues in their trading platform. If you see a down candle, there is a great chance that it would be painted red and not black. For the up candles, they could be painted green and not white.

Traders use candlestick charts to find probable price movement depending on previous patterns.

When you are trading in any market, for that matter, candlesticks are awesome because they display the four price points, which are low, high, closed and open, in that time that the trader wishes for.

A lot of algorithms function with similar price details seen in candlestick charts. Usually, trading is affected by emotions, and this can be seen in a candlestick chart.

How to Read a Candlestick Chart

Many traders can't get past the use of candlestick charts as they offer a large number of details, as well as a design that ensures that you can easily read and understand it without any stress.

This chart got its name from the indicators or markers, from the fact that it has a body that resembles that of a candle, as well as a line showing at the top, which looks like a wick. This line is called the tail or shadow. Candlesticks also tend to possess a tail or shadow at the end.

When you look at the chart, you will notice that each candle has a low, high, open and closed price for that period that the trader desires.

If a trader decides to set the period to five minutes, it means that a brand new candle is formed every five minutes. It works well in an intraday chart.

They are not all candles, as they can display the price shown. There you will see the following:

Open Price

If you look at the candle body's bottom or top, you will see the open price. This depends on whether the asset is swinging lower or higher in five minutes.

If you notice that the price is moving up, then the candlestick is either white or green, while the open price is situated very low.

If you notice that the price is moving in a downward direction, then the candlestick is either black or red. You will also see that the open price is at its peak.

High Price

If a high price occurs in the candlestick period, then you will see it at the shadow's top or on the tail on top of the body. You won't see any upper shadow if the close or open price ends up being the largest.

Low Price

This low is shown by the shadow's bottom or the tail underneath the body. You won't see any lower shadow if the close or open-ended up is the lowest price.

Close Price

That price that ends up on the trade-in of a candle is seen as the close. The upper part shows whether the candle is white or green. If the candle is black or red, it shows in the lower part of the body.

When a candle occurs, it tends to be skewed once the price changes. Usually, the opening does not change, but the low and high prices will continue to change until the candle is completed.

The hue can also be altered as the candle develops. The candle can change from greenish to reddish hue if its recent price was once above the opening price but ended up falling below it.

If the period of the candle ends, the ending price is the closing price, which means that the candle is over. A new one will be developed.

Price Direction

When you look at the candlestick chart, it is easy to see where the price has moved while the candle was still in operation by looking at the position and hue of the candle.

If you notice that the candle has a greenish hue, the closing price has occurred above the opening price. This candle will be seen at the top and right corner of the previous one, except it has a different hue or is shorter than the last candle.

You can tell that the closing price was below the opening price if the candle has a reddish hue. This is also strengthened if the candle is below and to the right side of the previous candle. This is true except when it has a different shade or is shorter than the other candle.

Price Range

You can tell a candle's price range in a period by looking at the distance between the bottom of the lower shadow and the top of the upper shadow. It is easy to get the range by eliminating the low price from the high price. If you want to understand candlestick charts well, you need to create a demo trading account. You can also consider using candles on those web-based graphic structures that can be used for free. After signing up, choose candle as the chart type, then click on a one-minute time frame. This allows you to access a myriad of candles that can be fixed.

Try to find the meaning of each candle before you start looking for fantastic trading opportunities from candle patterns such as three black crows.

The candlestick has different elements:

The First Element: The Body Size

If you want to get a lot of information, you have to look at the candle body because it is the reservoir of knowledge.

When you see a long body, know that it has strength. If you notice that the body is getting bigger, there is an improvement in momentum.

If you notice that the candle body is shrinking, the momentum is slowing down. You can tell how prices have moved along the candle with the body.

Second Element: The Wicks' Length

When you look at the wicks, you can tell how volatile the price movements are. If the wicks are larger, then the price has moved about many times while the candle was living, but it ended up being rejected.

If the candle wicks end up being larger, it means that there was an improvement in volatility.

You will see this when a reversal occurs after the appearance of long trending phases. You can also see them at massive resistance and support levels.

The Third Element: The Ratio that Exists Between Bodies and Wicks

When you look at the candle, what do you see? Wicks or Longer bodies? When a high momentum trend occurs, long bodies with small wicks will become common.

If the level of uncertainty improves, you will see that volatility will increase while the bodies will be smaller. You will also see that the wicks have gotten bigger.

The Fourth Element: The Body's Position

This acts as the elongation of the prior point. Look at it, do you see a long wick that has a body on the other side? This normally shows rejection of some sort. You will notice indecision when the candle has a tiny body in its middle while having longer wicks.

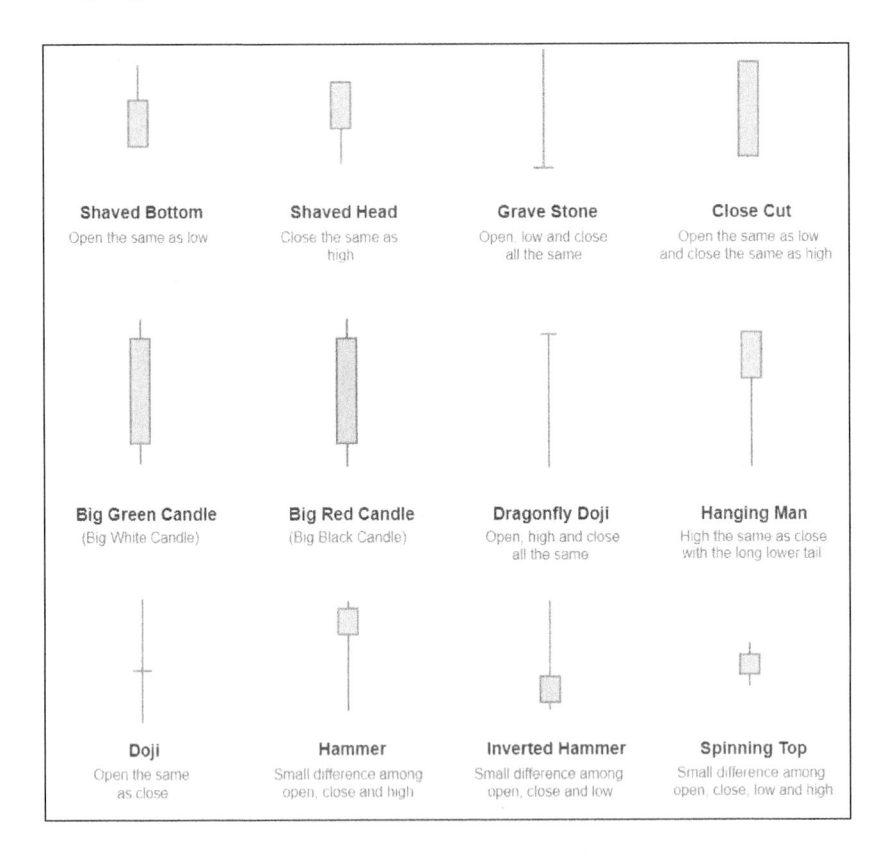

Shaved Bottom	Shaved Head	Grave Stone	Close Cut
Open the same as low	Close the same as high	Open, low and close all the same	Open the same as low and close the same as high

Big Green Candle	Big Red Candle	Dragonfly Doji	Hanging Man
(Big White Candle)	(Big Black Candle)	Open, high and close all the same	High the same as close with the long lower tail

Doji	Hammer	Inverted Hammer	Spinning Top
Open the same as close	Small difference among open, close and high	Small difference among open, close and low	Small difference among open, close, low and high

Chapter 7: Fundamental Analysis

The main purpose of fundamental analysis is to derive a quantitative value that can then be used by investors and traders to compare against a security's current prices. This way, an investor or any other finance expert will be able to compare the two values and determine whether a particular stock is overvalued or undervalued.

Fundamental Analysis

If you want to be a successful investor, then you have to learn about fundamental analysis. It is the most crucial aspect of any investment or trading strategy. Many would claim that a trader is not accomplished if they do not perform fundamental analysis.

The fact is that fundamental analysis is such a broad subject that what it entails sometimes differs depending on scope and strategy. It involves a lot of things such as regulatory filings, financial statements, valuation techniques, and so on.

Definition

Fundamental analysis can be defined as the examination, investigation, and research into the underlying factors that closely affect the financial health, success, and wellbeing of companies, industries, and the general economy.

It can also be defined as a technique used by both traders and investors to decide regarding the value of a stock or any other financial instrument by examining the factors that directly and indirectly affect a company's or industry's current and future business, financial, economic prospects.

At its most generic form, fundamental analysis endeavors to predict and learn the intrinsic value of securities such as stocks. An in-depth examination and analysis of certain financial, economic, quantitative, and qualitative factors will help in providing the solution.

Fundamental analysis is mostly performed on a company so a trader can determine whether or not to deal with its stocks. However, it can also be performed on the general economy and particular industries such as the motor industry, energy sector, and so on.

Foundations of Fundamental Analysis

The main purpose of fundamental analysis is to receive a forecast to profit from future price movements. There are certain questions that fundamental analysis seeks to answer. For instance, an investor examining a company may wish to know answers to the following questions;

- Is the firm's revenue growing?
- Is it profitable in both the short and long terms?
- Can if afford to settle its liabilities?
- Can it outsmart its competitors?
- Is the company's outlook genuine or fraudulent?

These are just a few examples of the numerous questions that fundamental analysis seeks to answer. Sometimes traders also want answers to questions not mentioned above. In short, therefore, the purpose is to obtain and profit from expected price movements in the short-to-near-term future.

Most of the fundamental analysis is conducted at the company level because traders and investors are mostly interested in information that will enable them to decide on the markets. They want information that will guide them in selecting the most suitable stocks to trade at the markets. As such, traders and investors searching for stocks to trade will resort to examining the competition, a company's business concept, its management, and financial data.

For a proper forecast regarding future stock prices, a trader is required to take into consideration a company's analysis, industry analysis, and even the overall economic outlook. This way, a trader will be able to determine the latest stock price as well as predicted future stock prices. When the outcome of fundamental analysis is not equal to the current market price, then it means that the stock is overpriced or perhaps even undervalued.

Steps to Fundamental Evaluation

There is no clear-cut pathway or method of conducting a fundamental analysis. However, we can break down the entire process so that you know exactly where to begin. The most preferred approach is the top-down approach. We begin by examining the general economy followed by industry group before finally ending with the company in question. In some instances, though, the bottom-up approach is also used.

Determine the Stock or Security

You need first to have a stock or security in mind. Many factors determine the stocks to trade. For instance, you may want to target blue-chip companies noted for exemplary stock market performance, profitability, and stability. You also want to focus on companies that constitute one of the major indices such as the Dow Jones Industrial Average or S&P 500. The stocks should have large trading volumes for purposes of liquidity.

Economic Forecast

The overall performance of the economy affects all companies. Therefore, when the economy fares well, then it follows that most companies will succeed. This is because the economy is like a tide, while the various companies are vessels directed by the tide.

There is a general correlation between the performance of companies and their stocks and the performance of the general economy. The economy can also be narrowed to focus on specific sectors. For instance, we have the energy sector, transport sector, manufacturing, hospitality, and so on. Narrowing down to specific sectors is crucial for proper analysis. There are certain factors that we need to consider when looking at the general economy. We have the market size, growth rate, and so on. When stocks move in the markets, they tend to move as a group. This is because when a sector does well then, most companies in that sector will also excel.

Company Analysis

One of the most crucial steps in fundamental analysis is company analysis. At this stage, you will come up with a compiled shortlist of companies. Different companies have varying capabilities and resources. The aim, in our case, is to find companies that can develop and keep a competitive advantage over its competitors and others in the same market. Some of the factors that are looked into at this stage include sound financial records, a solid management team, and a credible business plan.

When it comes to companies, the best approach is to check out a company's qualitative aspects followed by quantitative before checking out its financial outlook. We shall begin with the qualitative aspect of the company analysis. One of the most crucial is the company's business model.

Business Model

One of the most crucial questions that analysts and all others ask about a company is exactly what it does. This is a simple yet fundamental question. A company's business model is simply what the company does to make money. The best way to learn about a company's business model is to visit its website and learn more about what it does. You can also check out its 10-K filings to find out more.

You need to make sure that you thoroughly understand the business model of each company that you invest in. Most companies have very simple business models. Take McDonald's, for instance. They sell hamburgers and fries. At other times it is not easy to understand what a company does. For instance, the world's best-known investor, Warren Buffet, does not invest in tech companies because he simply doesn't understand what they do.

Competitive Advantage

We also need to take a closer look at a company's competitive advantage. Any company supposed to survive the long term needs to have a competitive edge over its competitors. A company with one such advantage has to be Coca-Cola because of the unique nature of its products. Others are Microsoft, Toyota, and Google. Their business models provide them with a competitive edge that is hard for others to compete with.

In general, a unique competitive edge is where a company has clear trade-offs and options for customers compared to competitors, a unique product or service, reliable operational effectiveness, and a great fit in all activities.

Management

Another crucial aspect of any serious company is its management. Any company worth its salt has to have top quality management in major positions. Investors and analysts usually look at the level and quality of management to determine their competences, experience, strengths, and capabilities. This is because they hold in their hands the fate of a company. Even a great company with excellent ideas and plans can fail if the management is not right.

It is advisable to find out how qualified, experienced, successful, and committed the leadership of a company is. For instance, do they have prior experience at senior levels? Is there a track record and can management deliver on its stated objectives? These are crucial questions that should be answered appropriately for a positive conclusion.

There are plenty of tools available to the ordinary investor to learn more about a publicly-traded company's management. One of these is the company's website. Such a site is a trove of information regarding top managers, such as the chief officers.

You can also check out the conference calls where company C-suite executives host press conferences and present quarterly earnings reports. Many analysts await such opportunities to ask any questions they may have.

We also have the management discussion and analysis sessions that take place at the start of annual reports. During these instances, top managers often speak candidly about a company's future outlook and things like that. Also, watch out for corporate governance. This has to do with a company's guidelines and policies in place. It refers to the relationship that a company has with the management, stakeholders, and directors. You can find these guidelines and policies in the company's charter.

Industry Factors

When conducting your company analysis, there are other factors that you will need to consider here. These factors include business cycles, competition, growth in the industry, government regulation, and others. It is advisable also to have an understanding of the workings of a specific industry that you are interested in.

You should endeavor to learn more about the customer served by the said industry. Some companies have millions of customers while others serve only a handful. A company that relies solely on a tiny number of customers for its revenue is considered a negative position and a red flag.

Government Policy

In countries such as the United States, government policy is extremely crucial. When conducting fundamental analysis, you really should take this into perspective because certain policies can completely kill an industry. Companies provide relevant information on their 10-K forms which you can always look into.

Market Share

Different companies within the same industry sometimes have to work hard to gain market share. There are sometimes a lot of companies fighting for a small share of customers, especially at a local level. If a company controls about 85% of the market, then it means it is a solid company with strong fundamentals.

A strong market share also means that a company possesses that competitive edge over its customers. It also means that the company is larger than its rivals and hence has a great future outlook.

Industry Growth

This is also another aspect that should be taken into account. Some companies may have everything else working for them, but future growth prospects may not be so bright. It is important to assess an industry and confirm whether there are any prospects for future growth.

Chapter 8: Basic Day Trading Tips

In day trading, the focus is buying and selling stock during the same day and consequentially, the techniques and tips are different against other types of trading. A successful day trader takes advantage of little movements in the prices. But this game may appear to be dangerous for the newbie traders. Costance and good strategy are a must here

Day trading demands that you gain sufficient knowledge about the stocks that you want to buy. As already mentioned and suggested, day traders need to keep themselves up-to-date with the latest knowledge of events of news happening around. This includes the general economic outlook and the Fed's interest rate plans. For example, when the COVID-19, a deadly virus, hit hard at the global economy at the start of 2020, the world markets started panicking. Dow Jones fell flat more than once. The oil market crashed because the global food supply chain, trade chain, and flight pattern got disturbed. Financial markets started reeling from the economic halt. Industries stopped working and cargo ships docked for an unlimited time.

All these factors accounted for the fall in the global financial markets, especially the oil market. Amidst this chaos, the Kingdom of Saudi Arabia (KSA) and Russia were caught up in a price war regarding the sale of oil. This further pushed oil to the downside. Suddenly, the oil market rose and made significant gains. The day traders who were aware of the news about US President Donald Trump's mediation between KSA and Russia bagged a significant amount of profits by buying early and selling when it touched its peak.

Another important thing is the rise in the prices of gold as oil fell to the ground. Over the years, it has become a tradition that whenever oil faces an uncertain future and the global markets react to panic across the world, gold strengthens its position. Day traders who carefully watch the markets and make an in-depth study of different commodities capitalize even on uncertain fluctuations in the markets. The takeaway is that you should do your homework. Better make a wish list of the stocks that you would like to trade-in and keep yourself aware of the latest news about those companies. Scan all the business news that comes your way by visiting reliable financial markets.

Day trading demands that you set aside plenty of time during the day and if you are prone to get carried away by distractions, you should reconsider your daily routines and habits. Don't take up this profession if you don't have sufficient time to spare. Day trading demands that the trader consumes sufficient time on tracking the markets and hunting down potential opportunities, which can pop up any time during the trading hours. The key is to move fast.

You are not supposed to gallop like a horse in the beginning. Instead, try to focus on one or two stocks at maximum during one season as tracking them will be easier. You can choose to buy fractional shares at the start just to get the taste as to how the markets will behave. If Apple shares are trading at $200, you can ask your broker to purchase $50 worth of it, which makes up the one-fourth of the total value of the share.

Don't trade in penny stocks. At the start, you might be looking for low prices and deals, but it is better to stay away from the penny stocks as much as you can. Their chances of hitting the jackpot are low. Many stocks trade under $5 per share and get de-listed from major stock exchanges. Unless you are sure that a real opportunity lies in your way, avoid buying them.

Stay realistic in your trading ventures. As you get into top gear in the world of trading, you should make sure that you don't miss out on some decent gains just because you behave greedily. Markets, at times, appear to be tricky; therefore, it is best to settle down for small profits rather than losing heavily by falling for greed. The key to a satisfying trading business is not to regret if you miss out on a potential profit-making opportunity. Markets, sometimes, behave in a tricky manner; therefore, it is in your best interest to be content on small profits. You can always have the chance to buy the same stock upon the next dip. Rest assured that the stock will rebound. Each small profitable deal will boost your confidence levels and offer you a chance to apply the strategy again.

If you are new to trading, you should know that trading on margins means that you are borrowing money from the brokerage firm to which you are registered. If you use margins appropriately, you can amplify the trading results. While you get excited about how much profits you can bag with the help of margins, you also should know the fact that the same is true for losses as well. If a particular trade goes against you, you will be posting some heavy losses. As a beginner, you need to stay in control of the amount you have invested. It is a better strategy to start without getting involved in margins.

Lots of orders that are placed by investors start executing when the market opens in the morning. This adds to volatility in the prices of commodities. A seasoned day trader will be able to recognize the patterns and pick the right profits at the right time, but as a beginner, it will be hard for you to analyze the patterns and understand them for profitmaking. It is better to let the market flow for 15 to 20 minutes before entering it. It settles down to a predictable pattern in a matter of time. The middle hours of the market usually are less volatile than the morning and the evening hours. Start by trading in this window. Day trading can turn out to be pretty risky and there is a higher chance of loss if you don't adhere to the advice of seasoned traders. You can end up posting significant losses in no time; therefore, it is recommended that in the wake of loss you set aside some funds that you can trade with. This money should be in addition to the money that you keep aside for your living expenses. This ensures that your risk quotient is lower and that you are not putting everything at stake. This also adds to your satisfaction as well.

One interesting tip is to limit your orders. When you place an order in the open market, it is executed at the fixed time at the best price available for that order. There is not a price guarantee for that. You should limit orders and it would help you trade with higher precision in uncertain times. Beginners often fall for unreliable sources of information such as SMS, emails, advertisements, and mails, which make claims about above-normal profits. I don't rubbish all the claims as bogus, but the fact is that you should do proper authentication for your transactions. Don't trust a random source of information.

Day trading will test you emotionally, psychologically, and financially. You need to stay calm and deal with each situation as calmly and smoothly as you can. Day trading demands from your discipline, time, and skills. It is not the skill that you can develop overnight. These tips can help you get started with day trading. Self-learning is always the best way to learn when it comes to day trading.

The basic thing is to be persistent in your approach. You should keep going even amid adversity. Just think of the last time you have learned something worthwhile or fun. Remember how you behaved when you started playing baseball or fishing. Did you become a master the very first time you did that? Did you behave awkwardly or were you smooth in handling the equipment? Did the bat drop from your hands? Can you recall a person who mastered it the first time? Even if there is anyone, he would be one out of thousands. No one masters anything from the first attempt.

You need time to build and polish your skills. You usually are pretty bad at first, but you learn to make it right over time because you have an urge buried down in your heart to make it better. If you are desperate to become a musician, you will become one someday. The same applies to day trading. It can be frustrating at the start. Don't try to give up on a couple of failed trades. You may lose some part of your capital while you desperately attempt to bag profits from a trade. If you have failed, you must push past this pain and keep your gaze fixed at the horizon. You must keep in mind the final destination. Only then you can get over the desperation and the frustration.

Chapter 9: Strategies of Day Trading

Here are some strategies in day trading:

1. Breakout

The breakout strategy is when the price clears a specified level with increased volume.

In a breakout strategy, the trader enters a long position after the asset breaks the above resistance. You can join in a short position, but once the stock breaks below support.

When you see a start of breakout you need to find the right instrument to trade. When doing this, the support and resistance levels are very important. The more frequently the price has hit these points, the more validated and important they become.

Entry Points

If prices are close or above resistance levels, you need to take a bearish position. If prices are close or below a support level, you need to take a bullish position.

Plan Your Exits

Using chart patterns will help you to make this process more accurate.

You can calculate recent average price swings to create a goal. For example, if the average price swing was 3 points in the last several price swings, this would be a reasonable target. Once you've reached that goal (your take profit level), you can exit the trade and enjoy the profit.

2. Scalping

Scalping is one of the most popular strategies. It's particularly popular in the forex market and is based on capitalizing on minute price changes.

You work with the quantity, and you will look to sell as soon as the trade becomes profitable. This is an exciting way to trade, but it can be very risky.

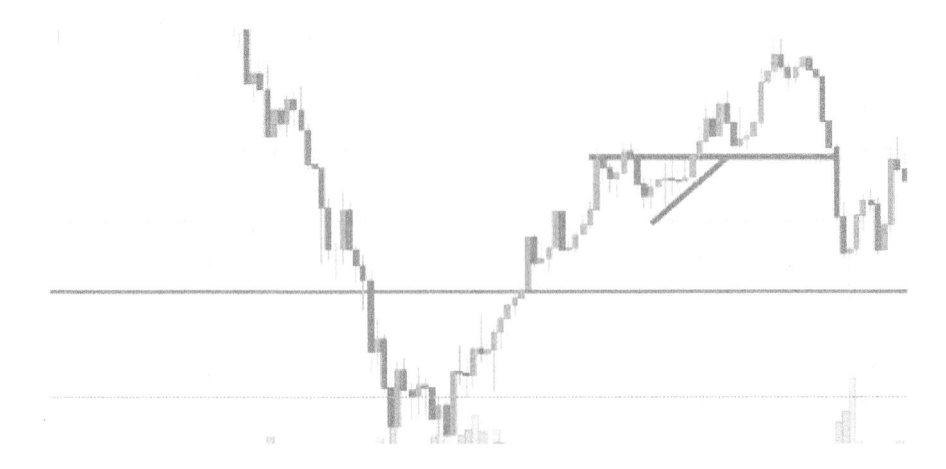

Be on the lookout for attractive liquidity, volatile instruments and keep an eye on the timing. You can't wait for the market; loss-making operations must be closed as soon as possible.

3. Momentum

This strategy is very popular and revolves around acting on news sources and identifying substantial trending moves supported by high volume.

There is always at least one stock that moves around 15-30% each day, so there's always an opportunity. You simply have to hold onto your position until you see signs of reversal for getting out.

Alternatively, you can fade the price drop.

This strategy is not complicated compared to others. Simple and effective if used correctly. When you operate with momentum, you must ensure you're aware of upcoming news and earnings announcements. A few seconds will make all the difference to your end-of-day profits.

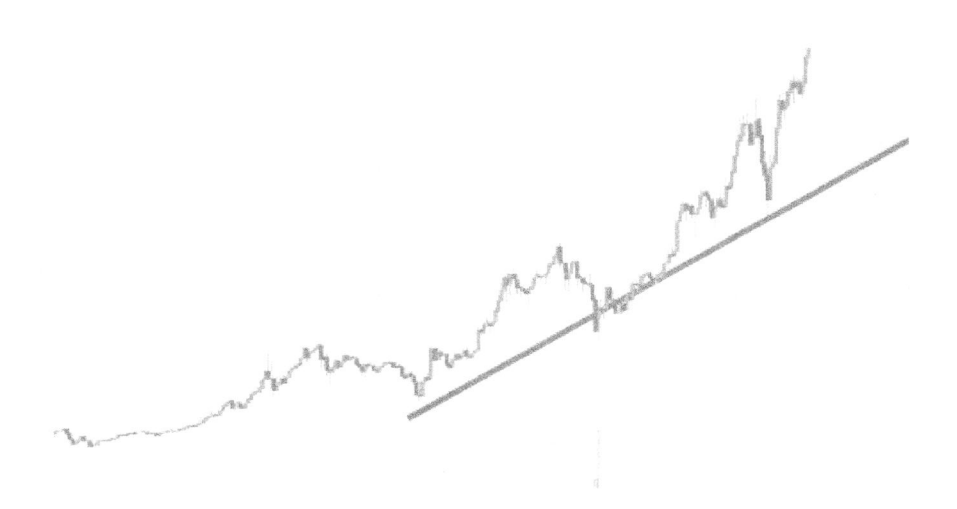

4. Reversal

Reverse trading is potentially dangerous, expecially when used by beginners. It's also known as pullback trending, trend trading and a mean reversion strategy.

This strategy defies basic logic as you aim to trade against the trend. You have to identify possible pullbacks plus predict their strength accurately. To be profitable using this strategy, you need in-depth market knowledge and experience.

The "daily pivot" strategy is considered a unique case of reverse trading, as it focuses on buying and selling the daily minimum and maximum pullback/reverse.

5. Using Pivot Points

It's fantastic for identifying and acting on critical support or resistance levels and It is particularly useful in the forex market. Range-bound traders can also use it to identify points of entry. In contrast, trend and breakout traders can use pivot points to locate key levels that need to break for a move to count as a breakout.

Indispensable for Intraday Traders:

1. The first thing that a beginner intraday trader should discover is his investor profile, that is, his aversion or tolerability towards risk.

2. Regardless of the intraday trader's risk profile, he must make sure to test his strategies in a risk-free environment, such as a demo trading account, a trading simulator, or backtesting.

3. The fundamental tool of the intraday trader is technical analysis.

4. The factors that should dominate and should not be missing in intraday trading strategies are volatility and liquidity.

Volatility is the entity of market movements. In short-term trading, high volatility is mandatory. This essentially reduces the selection of instruments to the major currency pairs and some cross pairs, depending on the trading sessions.

Liquidity is also important. A long-term trader can afford to give up 10 pips, but a short-term trader cannot because those 10 pips can be the total profit of the trade. Of course, this precision comes from the trader's ability to trade in the short term, but also from the liquidity of the market.

If there is little liquidity on the market, orders are not always executed at the desired price. This once again encourages day traders to trade certain instruments rather than others, and only for specific periods.

One or more strategies must be adopted to minimize losses and maximize benefits. Since market conditions vary from day to day, you should be able to follow them.

A profitable trader should be able to vary or adjust his intraday trading strategies daily and based on market conditions. For this, in addition to a lot of experience, a creative mind is needed.

Build a Trade Plan

Set the Rules for Exit

One of the main mistakes that most traders fail to understand is that they usually concentrate over 80% of their efforts in trying to look for signals showing buy. They, however, fail to look at where and when they should exit a trade. Most investors will not risk selling if they are down because they are usually not ready for losses. You should get over it or else you will never make it in the trading world. Don't take things personally, especially when you are making losses. It only indicates that your predictions were incorrect. Keep it in mind that professional/experienced traders often have more losing trades that the winning trades. You will still make profits if you can manage your investments and limit your losses.

Therefore, before entering a trade, clearly know yours exists. For every trade you do, ensure that you have at least two exit points. The first exit point is the stop-loss which will tell you to exit if you are trading negatively. You should ensure that you have a written exit spot and not memorizing them. Second, ensure that you have a profit target for each trade you perform. However, don't risk more than the percentage that you have set in your portfolio. Here are exit strategies you can choose:

- **Exit Strategy: Traditional Stop/Limit**

The most effective way to keep your emotions in check is by setting targets or limits and stops the moment a trade is entered into. You can use the DailyFX to research into the over 40 million traders. You will realize that most of the successful traders set their risk to reward ratio to at least 1:1. Before entering into a market, you have to analyze the amount of risk you are willing to assume and then set a stop at this level. At the same time, place your target at least many pips away. This means that if your predictions were wrong, your trade would be closed automatically, and this will be at an acceptable risk level. If your prediction is correct, the trade will be closed automatically after having your target. In either way, you will still have an exit.

- # Exit Strategy: Moving Average Trailing Stops

This exit strategy is also referred to as a moving average. This strategy is effective in filtering the direction a currency pair has trended.

The main idea behind this strategy is that traders are usually busy looking for buying opportunities, particularly when the prices are above a moving average. Traders will also be busy looking for selling opportunities, especially when the prices are moving below the average. Therefore, this strategy also considers the fact that a moving average can also be a trailing stop. This means that if a moving average cross over price, the trend is considered to be shifting.

When you are a trend trader, you would consider closing out the position the moment a shift has occurred. It is preferred that you set your stop-loss based on a moving average, as this is very effective.

- **Exit Strategy: Volatility Bases Approach Using ATR**

This technique involves the use of the Average True Range (ATR), which is designed to determine market volatility. It calculates the average range of the last 14 candles found between the high and low and thereby tells a trader the erratic behavior of the market. Traders can, therefore, use this to set stops and limits for every trade they do. A greater ATR on a given pair means a wider stop. This means if a volatile pair can generally be stopped out early, and thus will have a tight stop. You can adopt ATR for any time frame; a factor that makes to be considered as a universal indicator.

Set Entry Rules

We have set the exit rules to come before the entry rules for a reason. The reason is that exits are very important compared to entries. The entry rule is simple. For instance, we can have an entry rule like: "given that signal, B fires up and we have the minimum set target is suggested to be three times the stop-loss, from the fact that we give service, buying Y shares or contracts here is appropriated and allowed." Even though the effectiveness of most of these systems is determined by how complicated they are, it should also be simple enough to enable you to make effective decisions quickly. In many cases, computers usually make better trade decisions than humans and this is the reason why nearly 50% of all trades occurring today are generated on computer programs.

Computers have powerful information processing capabilities and will not want to think or rely on emotions to make decisions. If a given condition is met, then they will automatically enter. They will exit when the trade hits its profit target or when the trade goes the wrong way. Each of the decisions made by a computer is based on probabilities. Otherwise, if you rely alone on your thoughts, it will difficult for you or almost impossible to make trades.

Building an effective watchlist requires three basic steps. The first step is collecting a handful of liquidity components of leadership in each of the major sectors in the market. Secondly, you will scan through stocks that meet the general technical criteria fitting your approach to the stock market. Third, do a rescan on the list nightly to be able to identify and locate setups or patterns that can generate opportunities in the session to follow while at the same time culling out the issues you don't have interest on may be due to their technical violations or secondary offerings, etc.

Chapter 10: More Day Trading Strategies

Anyone who wishes to make money with the stock trading should have a better strategy on how to predict the trend in prices of the stock to maximize profits. The charts show the trends that have different patterns that a new person in the trade cannot easily interpret. The patterns in the trend have meanings that give signals to the trader on when to make a move by either buying or selling stock.

The ABCD Pattern

This is a harmonic pattern that is used to derive the other patterns of trade. This pattern is made up of three swings that are made up of the AB and CD lines, also known as the legs. The line BC is known as the correction line. The lines AB and CD are almost of the same size. The AB-CD pattern uses a downtrend that indicates that the reversal will be upward. On the other hand, the bearish pattern uses the uptrend than indicates there will be a reversal downward at some point. When using this pattern for trade, you have to know the direction of the trend and the movement of the market. There are three types of ABCD pattern: the classic ABCD pattern, the AB=CD pattern, and the ABCD extension.

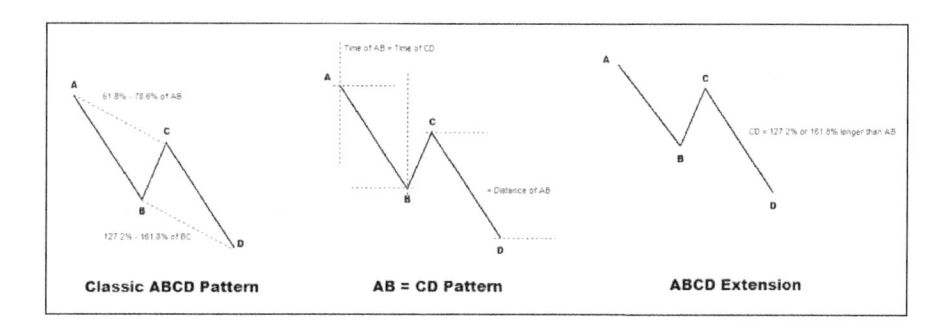

Classic ABCD Pattern   **AB = CD Pattern**   **ABCD Extension**

When using this pattern, remember that one can only enter the trade when the price has reached point D. Therefore, it is important to study the chart o at the lows and highs; you can use the zigzag indicator, which marks the swings on the chart. As you study the chart, watch the price that forms AB and BC. In a bullish trade ABCD, C should be at the lower side of A. The point A, on the other hand, should be intermediate-high after B that is at a low point. D should be a new point that is lower than B. as mentioned earlier, the entry is at point D, but when the market reaches point D, you should not be too quick to enter the trade, consider other techniques that would make sure that the reverse is up when it is a bullish trade, and down when it is a bearish trade.

Flag Momentum

In a trading market, there are times when things are good and the traders enjoy an upward trend, which gives a chart pattern that represents a bull flag pattern.

It is named as such because when you look at the chart, it forms a pattern that resembles a flag on a pole. The trend in the market is an uptrend, and therefore the pattern is referred to as a bullish flag.

The bull flag pattern is characterized by the following; when the stock makes a positive move with a relatively high volume, the pole is formed, when the stock consolidates on a lighter volume at the top, the flag is formed. The stock continues to move at a relatively high volume breaking through the consolidation pattern. The bull flag momentum is a trading strategy that can be used at any given time frame. When it is used to scalp the movements of price, the bull is used only on two instances of time frame: the second and the fifth minute time frames. The trading bull flags also work well when using daily charts to trade and can also be used effectively when swing trading.

It is simple to trade, but it is challenging to look for the exact bull pattern. This problem can be solved using scanners that help to look for stocks on the upward trend and wait for them to be in a consolidation position at the top. The best and free scanners that can be used to locate bull flags are Finviz and chart mill. Some tips can be used to indicate a bull flag. For example, when there is an increase in stock volume that is influenced by news, and when the stock prices remain high, showing a clear pattern for a pullback.

At this point, you can now check out when the prices break out above the consolidation pattern or on high volumes of stock. To make a move, place a stop order at the bottom of the consolidation. At this point, the ratio of risk to reward is 2:1, and it is the best time to target. The strongest part of the pattern is the volume of the stock, and it is a good sign that there will be a major move and a successful breakout. On the trend, it is also good to look at the descending trend as it gives a sign on the next breakout. This can be seen in the trend line that is found on at the topmost of the flag.

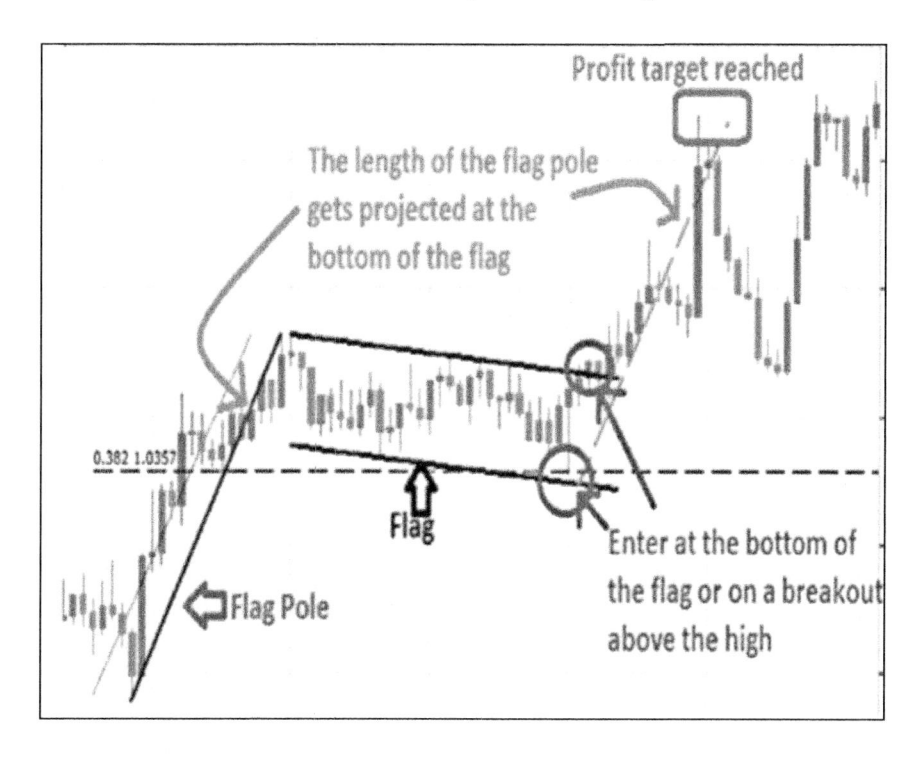

When used well for trading, the bull flags are effective tools of the trade; however, things can go wrong, and therefore one must be ready with an exit strategy. There are two strategies, one is placing a stop order at a point below the consolidation area, and the second method is using a moving average that is monitored within 20 days. Within 20 days, if the price of the stock is below the moving average, then it is time to close out the position and try out other trading routes.

Reversal Trading

Reversal trading, also known as a trend reversal pattern, is a trading strategy that indicates the end of a trend and the start of a new one. This pattern is formed when the price level of stock in the current trend has reached a maximum. This pattern provides information on the possible change of trend and possible value of price movement. A pattern that is formed in the upwards trend signals that there would be a reversal in the trend and the prices will go down soon. Conversely, a downward trend will indicate that there will be a movement of the prices and it will be upwards. For you to recognize this pattern, you have to know where specific patterns form in the current trend. There are distribution patterns that occur at the top of the market; at this point, traders sell more than they buy. The patterns that occur at the bottom of the markets are referred to as accumulation patterns, and at this point, traders buy more than they sell.

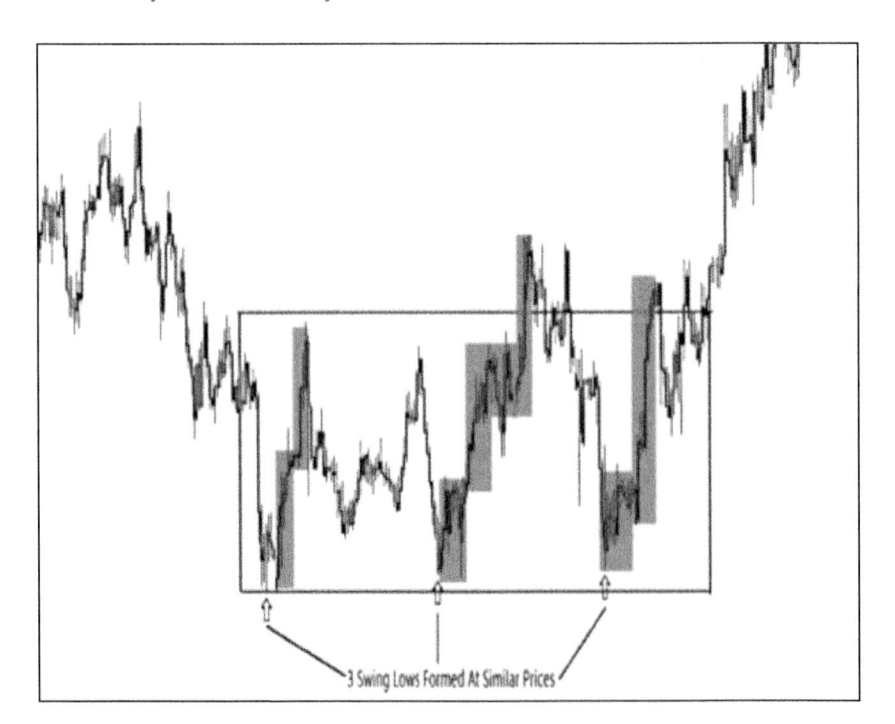

3 Swing Lows Formed At Similar Prices

Reversal trends are formed at all time frames, and it is because the bank traders have either place trades or are taking profits off the trades. The trend can be detected when multiple up and down formations are fully formed; they should be at least two upswings and two downswings indicating a bearish pattern. The swing highs of lows on the trend line depend on which reversal pattern is formed.

The highs or lows form at a similar price because the bank traders want to appear as if they are causing a reversal in the market, by getting all their trades placed at the same time. In the real sense that is not the case because they appear at different points of the trend.

Therefore, as a trader, you should wait for a clear and steady trend upward for you to sell in the case of a bullish trade and a steady trend downward for the case of a bearish trade for you to buy.

There are different types of reversal patterns. The double top reversal pattern is a pattern that has two tops on the chart. It looks like "M." The double top has its reverse type known as the double bottom pattern that resembles "W." The double bottom has two bottoms located either on the same support or at different supports.

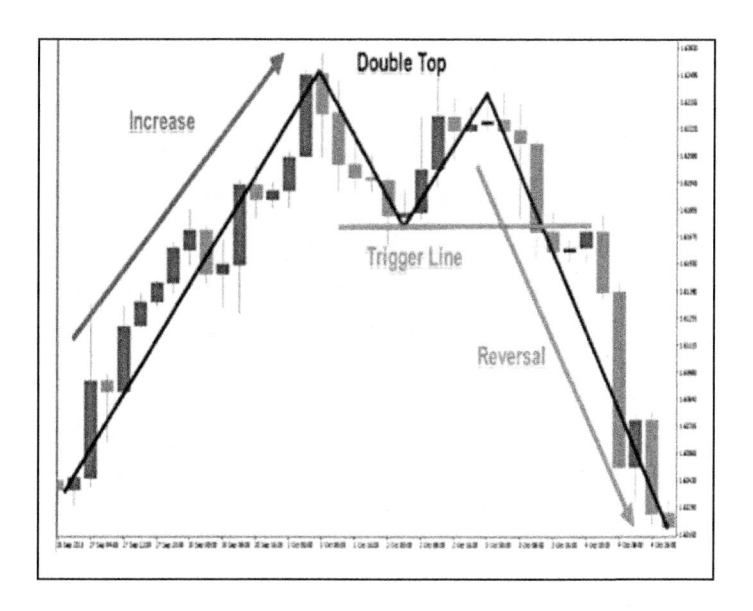

Another reversal pattern is the head and shoulders; this pattern resembled two shoulders and ahead. The two shoulders are tops that are slightly below the other top that is known as the head. The head and shoulders can also be represented in a descending pattern whereby the tops become bottoms.

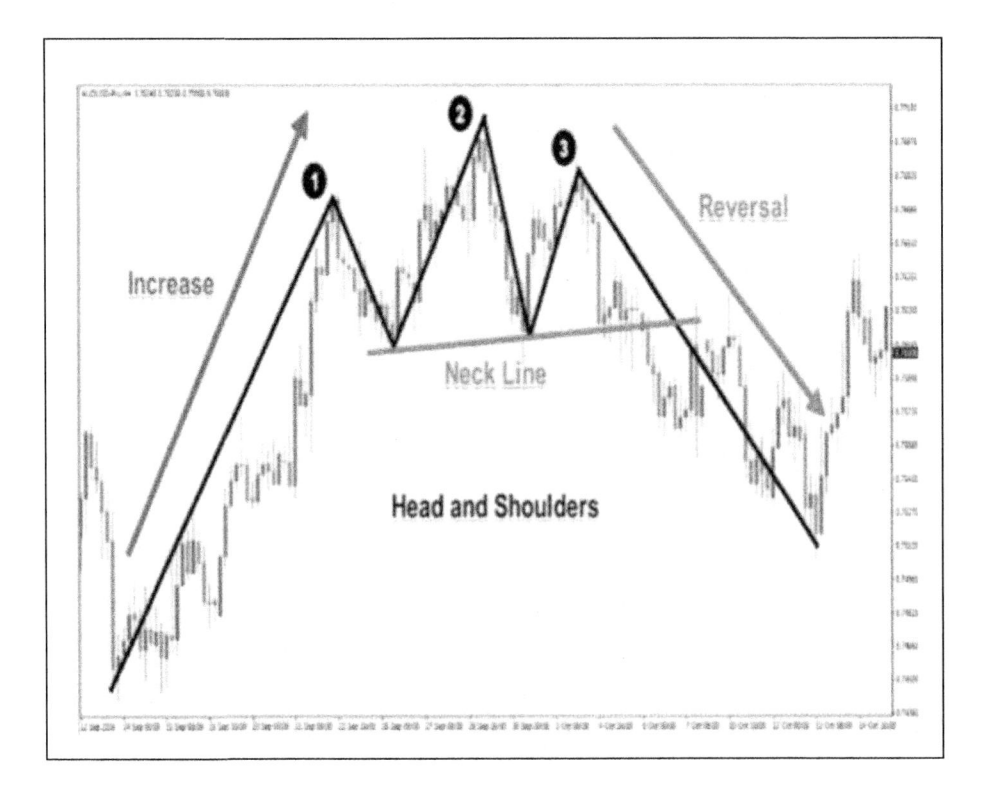

[Chart showing Head and Shoulders pattern with Increase, Neck Line, and Reversal labels]

Moving Average Trend Trading

This strategy of trading is common among traders and it uses technical indicators. A moving average helps to know which way the price is moving, if the moving average is inclined upwards, then the price is moving up, and if it is inclined downwards, then the price is going downwards.

Moving average can also help to show resistance or support of the trend, but this depends on the amount of time of the moving average. Support is shown when the trend of the price is downward, and at this point, the selling pressure reduces, and buyers start to step into the market. Resistance is shown when the trend in the price of the stock is upward. At this point, buying of stock reduces and sellers step in. It should be noted that the prices of trade stock do not always follow the moving average, but it is good to know that when the stock price is above the moving average of the trend, then the price trend is upward. Conversely, if the price is below the moving average, then the trend of the price of the stock is downwards.

Moving average is a powerful tool of the trade as it is easy to calculate, which makes it popular among traders. This tool of trade enables the trader to understand the current trend and identify any signs of a reversal. It also helps the trader to determine entry into the trade or an exit, depending on whether it offers support or resistance.

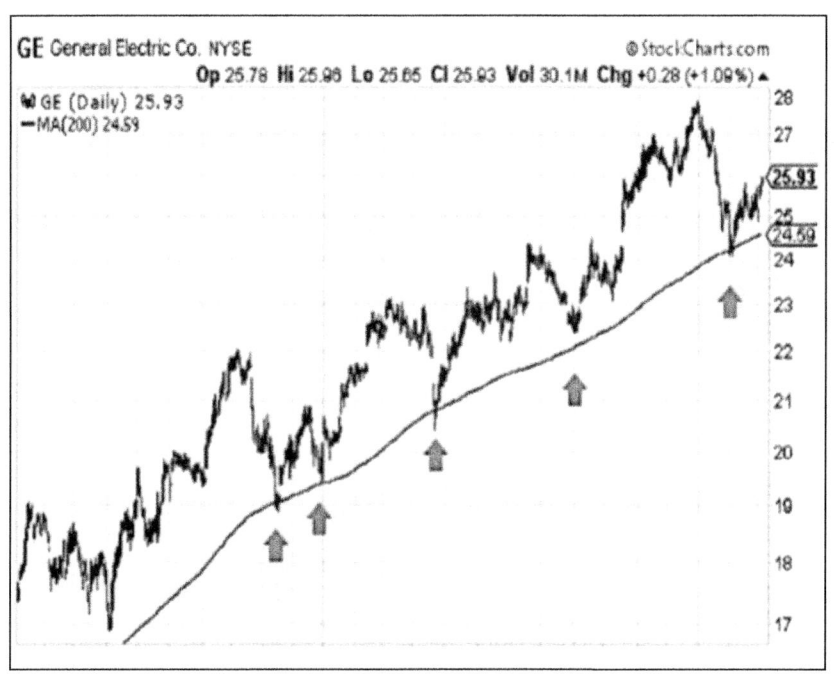

There are different types of moving averages. The simple moving average, which sums up five recent closing prices and calculates the average price, another one is the exponential moving average, whose calculation is a bit complex because it applies more weighting to the most recent data. When the simple moving average and the exponential moving averages are compared, the exponential moving average is affected more by the changes in prices that the simple moving average.

VWAP Trading

VWAP is the volume-weighted average price. It is a trading strategy that is simple and highly effective when you are trading in a short time frame.

For it to work for you, you must use different strategies, and the most common strategy is the waiting for a VWAP to cross above and enter long.

A VWAP that is across above gives signals to the traders that buyers would be entering the market, and there would be an upward movement of price. The bearish traders might short stock giving it a VWAP cross below, thus signaling the buyers to leave the market and take profits. VWAP can also be used as a resistance or support level for determining the risk of trade; when the stock trades above the VWAP, the VWAP is used as the support level, and when the trading is below the VWAP, the VWAP is used as a resistance level. In both cases, the trader is guided by it to know when to buy and when to sell.

When doing trading transactions, trading costs are determined by comparing the price of a transaction, against a reference or a benchmark, and the most common benchmark is the VWAP. The daily VWAP benchmark encourages traders to avoid risks of trading on extreme prices of the day by spreading their trades over time. This trading strategy favors those people who use market orders to trade rather than limit orders. This is because an opportunity cost arises from delays and passive trading.

Chapter 11: Best Platforms for Day Trading

You will need to accept the help of some outside 'forces' to succeed in the day trading business. Apart from your efforts, three things will decide if you can succeed or not at earning profits from day trading. These are trading platforms, charting software, and brokerage services.

Day trading was made popular by the electronic trading systems, also known as online trading platforms. These are computer software programs for placing buy and sell orders for different financial products. On online trading platforms, the speed of data feeds and fast execution of orders have made them very popular with day traders. This is one of the reasons why many people now prefer to become individual day traders and conduct their business from any place, especially from their homes.

This is in stark contrast to traditional trading, which usually happens on stock exchange floors where brokers yell on telephones and clients find it hard to get their desired trades executed immediately.

Electronic trading platforms also have another advantage. These relay live market prices to the clients' computer screen, which traders can use to decide whether they want to buy, or sell, or hold their positions.

Apart from an online trading platform, day traders also need to have sophisticated trading tools; such as charting software, account management tools, and newsfeed. In today's technology-driven age, one cannot imagine indulging in day trading with no charting software.

This software helps in the technical analysis of stock prices, based on which traders take to buy and sell decisions. Automatic or algorithmic trading is rapidly expanding. Big traders use automatic charting software to generate trading signals that are automatically executed on their behalf.

According to their trading styles, traders have different requirements. Trading software is also based on various trading styles. For day traders, the speed of execution and tools for chart analysis is very important. Brokerage houses provide trading platforms that fulfill these requirements and attract many day traders as their customers. Some other companies have nothing to do with brokerage services, but provide standalone charting software of excellent quality.

The third essential requirement for day trading is selecting a good broker who provides competitive brokerage rates. With every trade, day traders have to pay some fees to the broker, which is called brokerage or commission. Since day traders usually trade in every session and mostly execute more than one trade every day, they need a brokerage plan where the trading commission is at a minimum.

Take it this way; as the trading commission, traders incur a financial loss as soon as they place a trade, with every trade. Every trade has two legs; one buys and one sells. The brokerage is charged on both legs. To keep this money-outflow to a minimum, traders need a broker who provides them with necessary day trading facilities but does not charge hefty fees for this.

All these things, online trading platform, charting software, and broker's commission; will also constitute parts of your investment in a day trading business. You will need to research and compare various services and tools before making a final decision. Once you invest money in these "parts" of the business, it will not be easy to change.

Introduction to Trading Platforms

Trading platforms are technical tools created with computer software. These platforms are used for trade execution and managing open positions in the stock markets. Online platforms range from a basic screen to sophisticated and complex systems. The simple and basic trading platforms usually provide only order entry facilities, not much beyond that. Advanced trading terminals have many other facilities, such as streaming quotes, newsfeed, and charting facilities.

Day traders should consider their needs while selecting a trading platform. For example, are they at a beginner's level or professional?

No need to spend money on highly sophisticated platforms, when you are just beginning your day trading career. Different trading platforms are tailored to suit different markets: such as stocks, forex, commodities, options, and futures.

Based on their features, trading platforms can be divided into categories of commercial platforms and crop platforms. For day traders and retail investors, commercial platforms are more useful. These are easy to use and have many valuable features. On these platforms, day traders will find the news feed and technical charts good for day trading. Investors can use research and education-related tools. Prop trading platforms are more sophisticated and are customized for large brokerage houses that wish to provide a unique trading experience to their clients.

For beginners, it is advisable to go for some basic online trading platform that provides a simple and easy-to-understand interface. At the beginning of the day trading career, it will be difficult to adjust to the market volatility and learn new things with every trade. On top of that, any complicated trading program may confuse a novice day trader and cause losses instead of providing ease of business.

Day traders should consider two factors before choosing a trading platform; its price and available features. A live data feed is a must for any good platform. At the same time, it should not cost the moon and some more.

Therefore, the day trader will have to balance between the price and trading features. Going for a cheap platform may help cut costs, but it could provide delayed data, which will destroy your day trading business. On the other hand, a fancy trading platform will put a hole in your pocket and confuse you during trading by its overwhelming range of features.

Those, who day-trade in options, will need different charting features than those who trade in stocks. Similarly; day traders in forex markets will need different types of trading platforms. Carefully consider what tools are available on any online platform. If that suits your requirements and budget, make a final decision to purchase it.

Day Trading Software

Many day traders use computer software for automated trading. This takes away their headache of spotting the trend and deciding the trade entry and exit points. Also, they do not need to spend hours on chart analysis and reading economic news to understand what will happen in stock markets. Day trading software takes care of all their time-consuming and decision-making problems.

These days, trading software automatically analyzes chart signals, decide trade entry and exit points, profit booking and stop-loss levels, and execute the trade on behalf of the trader. The biggest advantage of automated trading is, it takes away the hazards of emotional trading.

Not everyone can control their emotions, especially in stock markets, where fear and greed overcome day traders. Under the influence of emotions, they do not spot the right trend and make trading mistakes. This is one of the very common mistakes in day trading, and most of the day traders who suffer losses, do so because they cannot control their emotions.

In such situations, automated trading software solves the problem by taking the emotions out of day trading. As machines, trading software can only focus on the facts and make trading decisions based on technical signals. These signals are generated by automatic chart analysis. Thus, the human error component is eliminated from machine trading. Automatic trading is also known as algorithmic (or algo) trading because trade signals are generated based on specific algorithms. Some traders prefer their customize algo-trading programs, where trade signals are generated based on specific signals.

Different types of automated trading programs are available nowadays. The simplest type of such program is standalone websites that provide trade signals for time-based subscriptions. These websites display trading charts, where real-time prices run through the session and generate intraday buy and sell signals. Day traders have to watch these signals and manually trade on their own trading platform. Such programs cost little, and day traders can continue their subscription, or discontinuous it, based on how much profit they make from it.

Choosing a Suitable Broker

In the day trading business, a brokerage service will be like your business partner, which will link you with the stock exchanges and give you a platform to execute your trade. Also, this service will demand a fee from you for every executed trade. Therefore, you will have to consider many points before you choose a broker for day trading.

A high brokerage can create setbacks in your profit-making efforts, and a low brokerage may hide some low-quality features of the trading platform. Since this brokerage service will be the medium through which you will execute your day trading business, compare different services before making your choice.

The first thing to consider will be; does the broker fit your needs? If you are going to focus only on day trading, then you must choose a service where the brokerage will be affordable for you.

Check its features, whether they are suitable for intraday trading or not. Choosing the right broker will be the first step in investing in your trading business. Investing in the right tools and services will provide a solid foundation for trading.

Different brokers cater to different trading and investing needs. Their tools and features are also tailored according to their customers' needs.

A brokerage service, which is focused on long-term investors, may not be a good fit for day traders.

In day trading also, various services are tailormade for day traders of forex markets, some other target day traders in commodities markets. For day trading in stocks, you will have to focus on brokers that have the most comprehensive features for stock traders.

The second most important step in finalizing a broker will be its trading fees and facilities. As a day trader, you will be placing more trades every day. Therefore, a low brokerage will suit your needs. Also, look for margin facilities for intraday traders, which will help you at a fraction of the original cost of trading. Check out the broker's trading platform. Does it provide a live data feed of markets; or, is there any delay in its price feed? For a day trader, going for a trading platform with a delayed price feed will be like committing hara-kiri. Getting the right price at the right time is a must for making correct trade decisions. Also, the broker's trading platform should have good speed and should not face connectivity problems. Check out social media forums to know what other customers of the broker say about its services.

As a beginner, it will be better to go with a simple brokerage plan that fulfills your basic day trading needs. In the initial stages, you will have to focus on learning how stock markets function and how to trade correctly. Once you have successfully established your day trading business, and feel confident about various trading tricks, you can think of upgrading your system and go for more advanced trading platforms and charting software.

Practice by Paper Day Trading

Everything can be learned with practice. Even the most difficult skills in the world can be mastered with regular practice. Sportspersons and actors are the best examples of what can be achieved by rehearsals. Since day trading can cause a loss of a significant amount of money, it is advisable that day traders start with paper trading first and upgrade to trading with real money once they become comfortable with the pace of stock markets.

In paper trading, everything else is real except money. Here, day traders see the real price charts, the real market data, and decide how they will trade without risking any real money. This is a sort of simulated trading, where day traders get to do real trades with fake money. This gives them a chance to learn from their mistakes, strengthened day trading techniques, and become familiar with stock market movements. This is just like actors rehearsing scenes before the real shoot begins.

Chapter 12: Stock Management

Building Up Your Watch List

The first step when you are ready to get started in day trading is to do some research. When you first wake up in the morning, look over your notes and your research and then use that information to create a good watch list. This watch list can be important because it can limit you down to just a few options that you plan to use for trading on that day. There are thousands of stocks on the market and making this watch list will make it so much easier for you to pick the right stocks to invest in. There are different methods you can use to create this watch list. But one of the best options is to use a scanner. These scanners can look for specific criteria that you want out of stock and can make things faster than trying to look through them all on your own. To make the scanner work, you just need to list out the requirements that you want the stock to meet and then the scanner will alert you as soon as it finds one that meets these.

Decide Which of These Stocks Work Best for You

After the scanner has given you a few options for stocks that meet your requirements, you can decide which of these stocks are the best. You may have a specific strategy that you would like to go with and then choose the stock that seems to be following that strategy the best.

You can always change strategies from one day to the next, or you can choose to stick with one strategy if it is serving your purpose. Make sure that you do not trade in the market for at least the first five minutes after the market opens. Some professionals wait even longer than these five minutes for the market to settle down.

There can be a ton of commotion and crazy ups and downs in the market during those first few minutes and investing at this time can hurt your profits. If you spend time looking at your scanner and then investigating the stocks that you receive, it will probably be at least five or more minutes before you are ready to enter the market anyway, but it is still important to be aware of this volatility and learn how to avoid it.

Put That Entry and Exit Strategy in Place

Now that you have a few stocks that are ready to go, you're probably excited to get into the market and start trading. Before you make that purchase, you need to finish up your strategies. This isn't just the overall strategy, but also the center and the exit strategy, so you know how to get into and out of the market at the right times.

The first strategy you should work with here is your entry strategy. This is the place where you are comfortable and will purchase your stock. You aim to get this entry point as low as you can so that you don't spend too much money and to increase your profits later on. When you look through the charts for that stock, you should be able to figure out a safe entry point that will provide you with a reasonable price on that stock.

Purchase the Stocks You Want

After you created your watch list and came up with your enter and exit strategies to keep you safe, it is time actually to go into the market and make your purchase. You will want to have all the criteria in place for that stock before doing this. But if you are working with a strategy, that is going to outline the criteria for you, so just follow that.

If you plan to work with your broker when doing day trading, you would just give them your order to get the trade started. The order is going to include a ton of information that can help the broker do everything that you want. This would include information on which stocks, in particular, you want to purchase, how many shares of each you want to purchase, how much you will spend on these stocks, when you want to enter the market, and when you want to exit the market. The broker is then able to take that information and place the order for you in the system.

Pay Attention to the Market Until the Trade Is Closed

You will quickly find that day trading has some differences compared to other stock trading options. Many other options are longer-term; you purchase the stock and then ride out the market, hoping that your choice will go up over some time.

But with day trading, you are only letting the trade occur in one day. The purchase of the stock, as well as the sale of it, all need to happen sometime between open and close of the same day.

This does make day trading a riskier option to work with compared to some of the other stock trading options. This means that you need to want the market and make some quick decisions on when to buy and sell your stocks. If you don't watch the market, then how are you going to be able to make these quick changes when needed?

Once you enter into a trade, you need to pay attention to the market and there may be times when the market changes quickly and you will need to make some quick changes to your position or close it out so you can earn more profits or keep the losses down as much as possible. Day trading is not one of those methods where you can place the order and then walk away. If you don't have the time to sit and closely watch the market, make sure not to place an order until you have more time.

Take Some Time to Reflect on That Trade and Write Down Some of the Information as Research Later

As a beginner in the day trading world, there are a lot of things to learn about the market. This is even truer if you have never invested in the past. As a trader, it is your job to learn as you go and make some changes if it is needed. But when you are learning a lot of strategies and keeping track of a large number of trades that are done in day trading, it can be hard to remember everything over time.

Getting a journal and writing down some of your mistakes, your tips, and more after each trade can make a difference. You don't have to write down a lot of information unless you want to. Just have a few lines or a paragraph. This may seem like it wastes your time. But if you ever get stuck on a trade later on, or if you are trying to figure out why you are in a slump and not getting the profits that you want, looking back through this information can make a big difference in how things go in the future.

Choosing and Purchasing Stocks

When buying a company's stock, a trader becomes a stakeholder or a part-owner of that company. The value of the trader's investment, therefore, depends on the general well-being of the business.

Therefore, when buying a stock, a trader should start with a company that he or she knows. In so doing, a trader gets a place to start and avoids buying stocks without understanding how the company intends to make money. Additionally, a trader should take into account the stock price and valuation. More experienced investors tend to look for securities that are cheap or undervalued to reap benefits when the stock price goes up.

Knowing How to Stop Loss

A broker places a stop-loss order once the stock reaches a particular level. A stop-loss helps to limit a trader's loss on a stock position.

For example, when a trader buys a share at $10 per share, he or she can place a stop-loss order for $8. Therefore, is the security's price falls beyond $8, the broker will sell the trader's shares at the prevailing market price.

A trader can know where to place his or her stop-losses by using the percentage method, the support method, or the moving average method. Many traders use the percentage method.

The percentage method involves calculating the percentage of stock a trader is willing to risk before he or she closes his or her position on the trade.

For instance, if a trader is willing to lose 10 percent of the value of security before he or she exits and the trader owns securities that are trading at $40 per share, the trader would place his or her stop-loss order at $36. That will be 10 percent below the market price of the security.

The support method also allows the trader to tailor his or her stop-loss level to the commodity that he or she is trading. As such, the trader needs to find the most recent level of support and place his or her stop-loss slightly below that level. For example, if the trader owns a share that is currently trading at $30 per share, and he or she finds $25 as the most recent support level. Therefore, the trader should place his or her stop-loss slightly below $25. Placing the stop-loss slightly below the support level gives the commodity's price space to come down and bounce back up before the trader closes his or her position.

The moving average method requires the trader to apply a moving average to his or her security chart. A moving average is a technical indicator that analyzes the price changes of stocks while reducing the impact of random price fluctuations.

A trader may want to use a long-term moving average as compared to a short-term moving average to avoid placing his or her stop-loss too close to the stock price and getting closed out of his or her trade too soon.

As soon as the trader puts the moving average, he or she should set his or her stop-loss immediately below the level of the moving average. For instance, if the trader's share is currently trading at $30 and the moving average is at $26, he or she should place the stop-loss below $26, to allow the stock price space for movement.

Knowing When to Sell

A trader should start selling his or her stock when he or she miscalculated the decision to buy the stock, when the stock price shoots up dramatically, and when the stock has reached an unsustainable amount.

A trader will know whether he or she made a profit or loss the minute he or she sells the stock. While the buying price may help the trader to know how much advantage he or she has gained, the selling price guarantees the profit, if any.

While selling a stock should not be a common occurrence because trading in and out of positions could be detrimental to a trader's investment, postponing the decision to sell the stock when it is the right time to do so may also yield unfavorable outcomes.

For example, a trader may buy a stock at $20 to sell it at $25. The stock price reaches $25, and the trader decides to hold out for a couple of more points. The stock hits $27, and the trader still holds out to maximize on profit should the stock price move further up. Suddenly, the price drops back to $24. The trader waits until the price hits $25 again, but this does not happen. The trader then gives in to frustration and sells the stock at a loss when the stock price hits $18.

Chapter 13: The Dos and Don'ts of Day Trading

The Do's of Day Trading Business

Here is a rundown of the things that you must do when you enter the day trading business. The basic thing is to be persistent in your approach. You should keep going even amid adversity. Just think of the last time you have learned something worthwhile or fun. Remember how you behaved when you started playing baseball or fishing. Did you become a master the very first time you did that? Did you behave awkwardly or were you smooth in handling the equipment? Did the bat drop from your hands? Can you recall a person who mastered it the first time? Even if there is anyone, he would be one out of thousands. No one masters anything from the first attempt. You need time to build and polish your skills. You usually are pretty bad at first, but you learn to make it right over time because you have an urge buried down in your heart to make it better. If you are desperate to become a musician, you will become one someday. The same applies to day trading. It can be frustrating at the start. Don't try to give up on a couple of failed trades. You may lose some part of your capital while you desperately attempt to bag profits from a trade. If you have failed, you must push past this pain and keep your gaze fixed at the horizon. You must keep in mind the final destination. Only then you can get over the desperation and the frustration.

When you make up your mind about making a career out of day trading, you should create a tangible and practical plan that you must strictly follow. Every business demands a strategic plan that you must build and evolve along the way. A good plan should contain all aspects of your trading strategy. Without a solid plan, you are not trading but gambling. So, don't just gamble. Follow set rules. Your plan may contain the timing of your trade, the amount of initial investment, the companies you want to invest in, the timing you want to hold a stock, and the time you will have to invest in studying technical reports, charts, and volumes of a given stock.

Do prepare a checklist. A checklist usually is as much important as a trading plan. You need to include your trading rules in the list. You should be satisfied with the checklist before you enter a trade. For example, you can decide how much leverage you need to take and what should be the risk-reward ratio. Going through the checklist each time you make a new trade cuts down your chance of making any kind of silly beginner-level mistakes. Once you have done trading for a couple of months, all the points of the checklist will be fed in your brain, and you will not need them anymore.

The next thing you should do is to follow a strict routine. Day trading is not like a job or physical business that binds you for a set period. Trading is a lonely endeavor and some of you may struggle after finding themselves in a new situation in which they are not under the watch of any kind and they are not being instructed on what to do. It is you who have to make decisions and shape your future.

Therefore, you must have a routine. It will be risky for your capital and your business if you take long breaks from work during active hours of trading. You may miss out on high-probability opportunities. If you have set up a daily routine by clearly defining your goals, you can remain on track and build a successful career as an independent trader.

If at any point you feel that you don't have sufficient learning, you should take time to learn. There is always room for that no matter how much you think you have studied books and online material. You can lose all your money in a matter of hours. The best learning approach is to learn the jargon at first and understand the basic concepts. You must know what a particular word means. Just think of an engineer! Can you call a person an engineer if he or she doesn't know what a particular word in the book of engineering means? What will you do if he had not attended the college of engineering, but call himself an engineer? Would you trust him? Would you like them to build a bridge in your hometown? Would you like them to work on the flyover in your city? You will do everything a bit to keep them away from these projects. You will not hand over your house construction project to an engineer who has just graduated. You will find someone with lots of experience and knowledge. Similarly, you should do that the same when you start trading. Consider yourself as a novice engineer who knows a little and who also has little experience to his credit. When you have traded for a while, you will be able to develop a knowledge base that you can use to gain more knowledge, such as to learn better and faster. Apply these initial concepts to your trading practices and improve your knowledge.

Never at any point should you think that you are expert enough to drop the need for detailed homework. Sometimes, when a person gains enough experience or knowledge, they start feeling proud and superior. This false sense of superiority clouds t judgment and they bitterly fail at a point so badly that they ruin themselves and others as well. Always do your homework before each trade. Doing your homework means that you are researching all aspects of your daily trade. It includes proper analysis of a bunch of companies you will select for day trading, the products they offer, and financial events and their effects on market sentiment. You can find lots of analysis in a cooked form on multiple platforms, but until you can derive your data, you cannot taste true success. The powerful rise in demand has given room to the rise of a breed of analysts that keep cooking analysis all day. You should pay heed to what they say, but you also should do your math. Investigate the rise and fall of stocks and try to understand the factors that triggered a particular sentiment in the market. Listen to these analysts, but follow their advice with great caution. If you blindly follow their advice, you may not be able to understand the reason behind your loss. Make conscious choices.

The Don'ts of Day Trading

Just like the do's, there are some don'ts of day trading as well. Here is a rundown of the things that you don't have to do if you want to survive in this business.

The very first don'ts of day trading is emotional instability. If you feel that you lose emotional control easily and if you get angry or overly happy each time you try to make money, you are not following the recipe to success. A forex trader or stock trader cannot be angry or extremely happy. The best traders across the world are the ones who can part their emotions from trading. As a human, emotions are our weaknesses. We make mistakes when we get emotional. Don't let emotions carry you away and have greater control over what you buy and sell. It often happens when you make a big profit from a sale, you get happy and make a purchase that is triggered by euphoria rather than logic. It can wipe out the gains from your previous trade. If a person pays heed to rumors around him, the best method to deal with him is to ignore him. You will not like to talk to someone who always lends his ear to rumors about politics or other national issues. The same is true in the world of trading as well. You cannot listen to rumors and act on them. Well, it gets tempting to do so sometimes. Some scenarios fan rumors.

For example, you are most likely to believe and act on rumors if you have invested a big amount in a particular stock and have not yet earned anything since then and are desperate to earn before the day ends. You may feel tempted to heed to rumors if you have recently bagged profit by acting on a rumor. Your brain might convince you to repeat the practice. Remember that you don't need to listen to rumors no matter whatever the scenario is. You must do in-depth research before you act on a rumor.

You might have a friend who claims to be a master of trading and who has made lots of money and who is always ready to offer his advice, but it is not wise to always act on what he says. Your financial situation is always different from the situation of your friend. His trading strategy might be different. His capital might be bigger or smaller than yours. You don't always know what his stop-loss is or what his target price at which he would sell is. If he listens to a rumor and you follow suit, both of you will land in serious trouble. Similarly, don't always pay heed to what your broker says to you. The second, don't that you must remember is that you should not isolate yourself from others. It is very natural for you to do so because it is the need for this business. There are two reasons as to why isolation happens in the first place. Day traders have to work from home and keep the focus on the latest analysis coming from different sources. The concentration and amount of study involved demand that you work in isolation. But is it healthy for you and your business? Isolation will take a toll on your mental and physical health hence there is a need to create joint working opportunities.

Try to focus on teaming up with a group of professional traders who will provide each other support throughout the busy day. In this way, you will be able to get a sense of how other traders are approaching their business and how they are solving the problems that arise over the day. You will have the opportunity to collaborate and communicate amidst work, which will allow you to pick a bunch of tips.

You will also be able to share your own experience with others. The last sentence may sound counterintuitive to you, but the fact of the world remains that the more you give away, the more you receive.

Your brain might have started telling you that you never trade your secrets, but that's half true. The things that have worked for you may not work for others because it is not only knowledge that matters in success, but the conviction, the commitment, the focus, and the courage you pour in it that does the magic. Take it in the sense that when you create a culture of sharing, you invite others to share their thoughts as well. In this way, all members of a group can learn and grow.

Don't fall for greed. Many day traders fail because they fall too easily for greed. Volatility in the market is bound to happen, and the best way to deal with it is to remain in control of yourself. As you get consistent in profitable trades, you start buying stocks in high volumes, which increases your risk of loss. I told you at the start that you should make it a rule that you will remain calm and steady while you trade.

Chapter 14: Swing Trading

Swing trading is one of the three core trading strategies that people use, with the other two strategies being day trading and positional trading. This particular strategy keeps traders in their position for a few days up to a couple of weeks, as a way to capitalize on medium-term market trends. A swing trader always looks at the long-term position to validate the quality of their trade, yet only plans on staying in the position long enough to earn profits before exiting their position.

Exercising the swing trading strategy is one of the most effective ways to become a trader and use trading as a way to supplement your income or completely replace your income altogether. The benefits of this strategy are endless, making it an excellent strategy for anyone to get started with.

What Is Trading, Exactly?

Trading is a strategy that investors use to capitalize on the economy by buying and selling a form of securities with other traders. Securities, which are financial instruments, range in type, but typically, they are associated with businesses either through owning shares in a business or through providing some form of loan to a business through your investments.

When you start trading, you will pick a specific type of trading that you are going to use, as well as a financial instrument that you are going to focus on for your trades. You will also choose specific strategies that fit into those two categories so that you can execute each trade. Each trade you conduct is going to follow a different strategy depending on what is going on in the economy, how it is affecting the market, and what positions become available for you based on that information.

Depending on what trading strategy you use, you may have access to a national, international, or even global market that will enable you to conduct your trades. Regardless of what market you are in, the same level of care, caution, and strategy must be exercised to ensure that you are making the best possible moves in your trades, which will help you access the highest possible profits.

There are three different strategies of trading, each of which is used to describe the length of the position you are going to be holding in your trades. This means that these strategies describe whether you are going to be in your trades for a few hours, days, weeks, or months.

Day trading is the shortest trading strategy, with all trades being done within a few hours. Positional trading is the longest strategy, with all trades lasting several weeks, months, and sometimes, even years. Swing trading is the medium-term strategy that is completed within a few days and up to about two or three weeks.

What Is Swing Trading?

Swing trading is one of the three fundamental trading strategies and happens to be one of the most common trading strategies that traders use. This strategy affords people the ability to rapidly increase profits so that they can increase their income while also investing even more into future trades. Over time, the number of investable incomes increases to the point where traders can profit massively off of their trades. As well, they can keep a significant amount of that profit to reach their financial goals, such as replacing their income, retiring, traveling, or affording other more expensive life goals.

When you swing trade, your focus is largely based on identifying patterns in the market that indicate that a shift – or a swing – is about to happen in the direction of the market's prices. Your goal is to get in when that swing is mid-action and then exit when the swing has matured so that you can gain your profits without holding the position for too long. A successful swing trade is one where profits are earned and the market does not swing back into the opposite direction at any point during you holding your position.

This way, you earn maximum profits without having to wait so long for the market to move back into a positive direction for those profits to be earned and cashed out.

The best stocks to trade as a swing trader are those that are known as large-cap stocks, which means they are some of the most active stocks that are being traded on the major stock exchange platforms.

These stocks have well-defined, broad swings between high and low extremes in their price points, which makes them the perfect stock for a swing trader to invest in. Swing traders will decide on their positions and strategies by identifying whether the market is bearish (in a downtrend) or bullish (in an uptrend) and will execute their trades accordingly. By doing so, they ensure that no matter what is taking place in the market, they can earn profits from their trades.

How Do You Start Swing Trading?

An individual can begin swing trading by first identifying what swing trading is and taking the time to accumulate adequate knowledge around how this strategy works. Then, you can begin getting involved in the stock market so that they can earn profits from the swing trading strategy.

When you are ready to leap, a new swing trader will need to locate the tools and platforms required to get started.

These include a brokerage platform that gives the trader access to the exchange as well as tools that can be used to increase their capacity to perform technical analysis, which is a method used to identify and validate trading positions. You will also need at least $2500-$5000 in startup cash to begin trading. In the United States of America, traders must maintain a $2000 minimum in their brokerage account to continue trading. Starting out with more than this will ensure that you never dig into that $2000 and put yourself under the legal minimum, which would force you to stop trading until you could top your funds up. After everything is fixed in place, a trader will require a strong understanding of how to identify positions and use technical analysis to verify those positions so that they can begin a trade. From there, it will be as simple as placing the funds into the investment to open the position and managing that position until they are ready to exit it. Swing trading sounds extremely easy to do when the definition and an example of how it works have been simplified, but rest assured that there is a learning curve to this strategy. You should be prepared to undergo that learning curve so that you know what it will truly take for you to become successful at swing trading.

Buying Long, Selling Short

One crucial thing that every swing trader needs to know before they begin trading is the importance of buying long and selling short.

What this means is that you want to enter positions to hold on to them for some time, meaning that you should conduct the right research and analysis to feel confident that your position will be a fairly low-risk position for the long haul. Ensuring that your position is a good long-term position means that if anything does not go as planned, you are still okay to be in that position for a few days or weeks until your anticipated patterns play out. When you are selling your stocks or exiting positions, you want to have every intention to sell your stocks as fast as possible. This way, you can exit the market immediately, which gives you a greater chance of securing your profits from that trade. If you take too long to sell your stocks, you may find yourself sitting in the position so long that your profits disappear and you have to take the loss to remove yourself from the position. Trading according to the buy long, sell short strategy is critical in helping you lock in a greater sense of security around your trades while minimizing your risk and maximizing your profits. This is a cornerstone in successful swing trading and will be a necessary strategy for you to execute if you are going to earn any profit using this method.

How to Enter Trades

Entering trades as a swing trader will rely on you identifying the right patterns in the market to indicate that a swing is about to take place. There are some incredible patterns that you can look for that you are going to learn about in this very book. Those patterns let you know that a shift is about to take place, meaning that it is a great time for you to get invested in the market.

Which exact pattern you are going to be looking for will depend on what stock you are looking to trade and what is happening with that stock at that particular time. You must learn about all of the different patterns and grow comfortable with identifying them so that you can keep your eyes peeled for when the stocks shift. This way, when you begin to see a pattern taking place, you can identify what trading strategy works best for that pattern and prepare to trade that stock to earn yourself profits. After you have found the right pattern to indicate where the best position is for you, you want to validate the quality of that position using technical analysis. Doing so will ensure that you are trading a stock that is going to be able to supply you with the best potential for earning profits with the lowest possible risk exposure. When you have verified that a position is going to be a strong one for you to take, you can then buy into the stocks associated with that position so that you are officially entered into an open trade. You are considered to be entered in an "open trade" until you sell your stocks and close out that position.

Investment and Margin Accounts

When you start swing trading, you are going to need to open an account with a brokerage so that you can trade.

Most swing traders open accounts with online brokerages so that they can see the market and conduct trades from the convenience of their computer or smartphone, which you are going to want to do. Upon opening your account with a brokerage, there are two types of financial accounts linked to your brokerage that you want to know about.

These two accounts include investment accounts and margin accounts. Investment accounts are the amount of money that you place into your brokerage account to hold as a balance for trading. These are the funds that your trades are going to come out of so that you can begin buying and selling stocks with your account. If you do not place funds into your investment account, or if you do not maintain enough funds in your account, you will not be able to engage in trades on the brokerage's platform. Margin accounts are another form of a brokerage account; however, the way funds are placed into the account is different. In a margin account, the broker lends the customer capital so that they can purchase stocks or other securities on the brokerage's platform. This money is a loan, so the customer needs to be prepared to pay the money back at some point. However, the capital can help you get a bigger start so that you can begin making larger trades and earning larger profits much sooner. This money should be seen as a tool to leverage enabling you to earn larger profits and nothing else.

You should also be prepared to pay it back as soon as possible as this will behave as a loan, meaning that you will owe interest on it so long as the loan balance remains outstanding.

Chapter 15: Swing Trading Rules

As you develop your swing trading style, you might find that you tweak strategies or adapt routines to suit your needs better. Your swing trading plan, which is the blueprint of your business, needs to include several things. For example, it should outline the following:

1. **Your objectives and motivation.** Why have you decided to become a swing trader? Are you interested in having a small side business in addition to your 9-to-5 job so that you can add to your savings? Will you replace your full-time job with swing trading so that you can work from home and take care of your children? Your reasons and goals are personal, so take your time with this.

2. **Your time commitment.** Can you devote 20 hours a week to swing trading? More? Less? Take a realistic look at your lifestyle, responsibilities, and schedule.

3. **Quantify your goals.** Determine what you want your profits to be. The amount you earn will be directly related to how much you put into this business.

4. **Select your risk-reward ratio.** Remember that these potential measures reward per dollar risked. If you have a risk ratio of 1:4, it indicates that you risk $1 because you want to earn $4 potentially. Your risk aversion level and amount of risk capital will help you determine this ratio.

5. **Calculate your capital.** With swing trading, you're working with risk capital - funds that you could lose without negatively affecting your day-to-day lifestyle. Your risk capital is the money you can use for your trading account; you need to know (and record) exactly how much that is.

6. **Gauge your knowledge.** There's a lot to know about markets. Take a detailed inventory of how knowledgeable, comfortable, and confident

you are in all different areas. Acknowledge your strengths and also your learning opportunities. If there are holes in your knowledge base, know what they are so you can fill them.

7. **Keep a trend journal.** This should be an ongoing part of your business plan. Keep detailed notes for your future self.

Swing trading can be a very exhilarating experience; playing the market with so much swift action is exciting. With the numerous available choices for indicators, objectives, and even markets, it's no wonder that no two traders will have identical swing trading business plans. How you operate your business is up to you; however, there are 12 valuable rules that are beneficial, and profitable, to remember.

1. **Write.** Your business plan should be thorough, detailed, and committed to paper. You must take the time and energy to construct your swing trading plan. Include components like your risk tolerance, the market of choice, risk capital, indicators of choice, and limits. Be specific and write a plan that is easy to follow. You should be able to refer to your written plan and successfully find the answer to any "what if" questions that arise. You'll periodically revisit your plan to make revisions, but fight the urge to make adjustments as you go.

2. **Practice.** Before you begin trading on the real market with real money, get yourself a practice account. With your written plan in hand, you can test your strategies before you risk your actual funds. Keep detailed notes of your progress while you practice. Practicing will not only allow you to test your system; it will also allow you to establish your routine and form habits that you'll need as a swing trader. Once you feel you've gotten enough practice, you can begin earning real profits with your actual account.

3. **Know entry points and exit points.** With your practice account, you solidify your trading plan. A component of the plan you develop will be recognizing triggers that signify that it's time to place buy and sell orders. The timing of your entry and exit should never be left to chance. Utilize the tools you've collected, and pinpoint when you will buy and sell. You should have a very clear view of a stock's price beginning to bounce before you buy it. Likewise, you should be

confidently aware that a price has peaked before you make the move to sell. Knowing your entry points and exit points will eliminate the guesswork.

4. **Seek out volatile markets.** With swing trading, we're not interested in stocks with little movement. We need trends of fluctuations so that we can make a profit. For successful swing trading, you'll be looking for stocks that display wide fluctuations in short periods. We can capitalize on a trading range if it's adequately wide; if it's too narrow, though, our trades aren't able to produce enough profit.

5. **Stay consistent.** You've taken a lot of time to devise a solid plan, and you must stick to it. Experimentation and adjustments should be saved for your practice account; you don't want to fiddle around with your construct and risk your real funds. Utilize your practice account; it's what it's there for. Your plan was carefully developed, and it's quite difficult to find your groove if you're changing the rules as you go. Slumps happen, don't confuse them for more than what they are.

6. **Understand support and resistance levels.** These levels are what define your trading area, so you should be familiar and know them well. Support and resistance levels, regardless if they're trending up or trending down, establish your parameters. You'll watch a stock's activity within this range, and as long as you closely follow the movement, you'll be able to monitor the swings adeptly. You'll also be able to recognize a fallout or a breakout.

7. **Comprehend market phases.** As a swing trader, you won't be trading trends, but you need to be extremely familiar with them. Your objective is to be confident about price swings—their duration, the direction they'll take, etc. To accomplish that, you'll need to follow market trends. Become comfortable with knowing the difference between a bull market and a bear market. Understand that upswings and downswings will have varying strengths in each.

8. **Cap the account.** It's not difficult to make money with swing trading; however, it can be very easy to lose it. Sometimes, a trade doesn't go as planned, and you take a loss. It's part of the trading experience, and it comes with the risk. It's a wise idea to have a separate account just for

trading because it will eliminate the urge to trade with additional funds. You should set parameters for yourself so that you're not losing more money than you can afford to lose. Be sure to have a limit and stick to it.

9. **Utilize stop-loss orders.** You should have a full plan in place, including contingencies, before you enter a position. Using stop-loss orders will protect you from being stuck with a stock priced too low. These orders, which will sell your stock if the price dips, should be set a bit below the price at which you purchased it. If the stock price increases, you should adjust your stop-loss order to accommodate that. As the price rises, your stop-loss order should rise so that it closely follows.

10. **Secure your profits.** Sure, it's nice to allow your earnings to accumulate, but it's important to remember that trading comes with inherent risks. Your profits could disappear as quickly as they come if you're not careful. If there is solid upward momentum for your stock, you can pull half the profits when the price nears the level of resistance. Of course, don't forget to adjust your stop-loss order. It should shift upward so that it's just behind the rest of your position.

11. **Cut the losses.** There's no need to hold onto a stock that just isn't performing. You should quickly cut the loss so you can redirect your money toward a different trade. Swing trades sometimes take place for several days, but you should monitor a stock's performance at the end of each trading day. If you have a stock that is losing, and there's no indication that that will quickly change, close it out.

12. **Never leave it to chance.** This is not random gambling, so you shouldn't take wild chances with your money. If you adhere to your plan, you're likely to make money in the long run. Deviating from your course will decrease your chances of success. Swing trading will come with some losing trades; however, your winning trades will outweigh them. Never take a shot in the dark.

Chapter 16: How Does Swing Trading Work?

How Does It Work?

Swing trading is one of the most used and common trading strategies used in almost every market, including forex, futures trading, stocks, and much more. Swing trading is about buying and selling the stock, buying it from the market, and selling it for gains. For this purpose, traders mostly rely on technical analysis to spot good selling and buying opportunities. Subsequently, swing trading mostly relays on fundamental assets since its great determent of significant price movements. Sometimes it will take days and even weeks. It also helps to improve trade analysis. Therefore, a trader can verify where the fundamental assets are favorable or not, or it could potentially improve instead of relying on the bearish patterns. Swing traders use the technical analysis indicator to identify the price of swing trade and determine whether a stock price will rise in the market or drop. By experiencing technical indicators, swing traders are not concerned about the long-term value of the stock.

How to Make Swing Trade With Trends?

Swing trading is one of the best solid trading and it has one of the obvious trends in trading strategies.

For beginners, it is necessary to understand its importance in the market that once you get to know how to invest your money, it will offer a lot of high possibility of trading opportunities with a high upside. For a beginner, it is obligatory to have enough knowledge about the market. The initial step that every beginner should take is to identify the market needs, he should know about the market trends.

For getting a good position in the market, every trader should go with the best trends, any trend that goes on the top of the list that if you show them to a child, they would choose the right one whose prices are getting higher or lower.

Tools and Platforms for Swing Trading

There are countless tools and platforms out there that you can take advantage of when it comes to swing trading; however, you want to make sure that you are on the best of the best. To get started, you are going to need to have the best technical analysis software, the best stock charts with tech analysis, the best broker or platform to trade with, the best technical analysis websites and blogs to follow, and the best platforms for doing market research on.

Regarding technical analysis, there are both software, stock charts, and blogs that you can follow to help you get a complete understanding of what the market is doing, and how it is likely going to behave in the coming days, weeks, and months.

You need to make sure that you are doing technical analysis regularly and that you are paying close attention to what is happening; thus, you know exactly when you should be making your trade deals.

The best technical analysis software for you to start using when you get involved in swing trading is easily Tradespoon. This software features an online trading algorithm that can predict what the prices are going to be in the future and is frequently correct in its predictions. Despite how reliable this platform can be, it is important to cross-reference it by doing your research so that you can feel confident in your decisions. Two excellent stock charts that you can begin following that have technical analysis built-in include Finviz and Stock Consultant. Both of these platforms scan chart patterns, offer you information on what trends are taking place in the stock market and help you pick exactly when you are likely to get the best trade deals. Lastly, you should be following websites like Investopedia, The Pattern Site, and StockTwits to read the information on technical analysis. All of these websites are going to provide you with updates on how the stocks are going, as well as provide you with real-time advice on how to predict stock patterns and determine when your best points of entry and exit are. The more that you follow each of these platforms, the more it will begin to make sense to you. You will also find that you are predicting patterns and developing a greater understanding as to when the best entry and exit points are. The deeper your understanding and awareness around how these patterns become, the more confident you are going to feel in choosing when to make your decision to enter and exit the market.

In addition to technical analysis through actual technical analysis websites and platforms, you should also commit to following a few blogs that are focused on the stock markets. Blogs that are devoted to the stock markets follow not only the market itself but also follow news and current events that can affect stocks, which makes them an excellent resource to help you track possible patterns in the market. Ideally, you should follow no more than two or three regularly updated blogs to make sure that you are now overwhelming yourself with information. If you follow too many blogs, you are going to feel bombarded with information coming in at you, and it may begin to feel like certain trending topics are catastrophic, simply because you have exposed yourself to too many news outlets. Personally, I like to follow Trading with Rayner, Learn to Trade the Market, and Simpler Trading Blog. All three of these provide excellent information that is relevant to the current stocks, as well as advice and guidance on how to make better trades.

Before you begin looking for a platform to trade with, I strongly advise you to fill your trading toolkit with the aforementioned tools and get used to navigating them, first. Giving yourself several days or even a few weeks to begin tracking the market and conducting technical analysis regularly is going to help you acquaint yourself with how the market works.

You will find that taking it one step at a time this way, too, helps to relieve some of the pressure of getting involved with swing trading, which can help you make better trading decisions going forward.

Remember, when it comes to trading, one of the most valuable assets you can have is your confidence, which comes from taking your time and learning how to execute each step of the process properly.

Picking Your Trading Platform

After you have begun to acquaint yourself with the platforms to help you understand and predict market patterns, you can go ahead and look for the right trading platform for you to do business on. When considering picking the right trading platform for you, there are a few factors that you are going to need to consider to make sure that you make the best possible choice. You must choose the right platform for your needs, as this will make all the difference when it comes to making proper trades and earning a profit from your trades. If you are on the wrong platform, you may not set up with what you need to trade properly, which could lead you to struggle to learn the swing of things, so to speak.

The factors that you need to consider when it comes to picking your platform include account size, product, strategy, geography, and cost. You need a platform that is going to accommodate for the amount of capital that you are starting with. Typically, the amount of capital that you are starting with will narrow down your selection size fairly significantly, which can make it easier for you to find what you need. Then, you also need to consider what products you plan to swing trade with, as you are going to need a platform that grants you access to those particular products.

Next, you need to consider what strategy you are going to be using for your swing trading, as there are countless strategies that you can use. There are a few different types you can use, including automated or manual, as well as ones that feature risk management tools and strategies where you do all of the risk management yourself. You also need to pay attention to where you live, as not every trading platform is available in every region. Lastly, you need to consider how much you are willing to spend on fees to use a platform to trade on in the first place.

After you have considered all of this, there is one last thing for you to consider: how many platforms you are going to commit to. At first, you should start by just learning how to trade on a single platform, as this will prevent you from getting overwhelmed and struggling to get the hang of how everything works. However, ideally, you should be working your way up to 3-4 platforms over time to make sure that you have your assets properly diversified to avoid potential risks. If you put all of your trades into one single platform, should anything ever happen to that platform you could lose access to everything you had gained through it. By diversifying the platforms you use, you minimize your risks. You will come to learn that risk management, and minimizing potential risks, is a crucial thing to consider in every single step relating to swing trading, or any form of trading.

With all of this being said, I have four platforms that I use and that I would recommend anyone to use when they get started with swing trading. They are Think or Swim, Interactive Brokers, Trade Navigator, and Ninja Trader. I will explain each one and why I picked it in greater detail below.

Think or Swim is a platform that is extremely simple to use, though it only allows for options trading. Despite its limitations, Think or Swim has several excellent analytics tools built-in for you to use to track the market, as well as an easy to use interface that makes navigating it effortless for people who are new to trading. I highly recommend this as being the platform you start on, as long as you are willing to get started with options.

Interactive Brokers is a fairly simple platform to use as well, and it also has some of the best and efficient margins across nearly any platform. This platform is more challenging for beginners to get started on, so if you choose to use it you need to be ready to endure the learning curve. That being said, if you want to get started with anything other than options, I recommend this platform as the learning curve is not impossible and it will give you plenty more flexibility and freedom in your early days as a trader. As well, once you figure out how to use the platform, it is quite simple and it can make your trading an easy ordeal.

Trade Navigator is another great platform to use, as it offers great technology for backtesting and it has some excellent features that help make trades easier to conduct. That being said, buying a license to use it is a lot more expensive these days, which may make it less than ideal for beginners to start on. Some senior traders also say that unless you are willing to pay the larger license fee down the road, it is not necessary to use this platform to diversify your approach as there are other excellent ones you can use in today's world.

Chapter 17: Swing Trading Vs. Day Trading

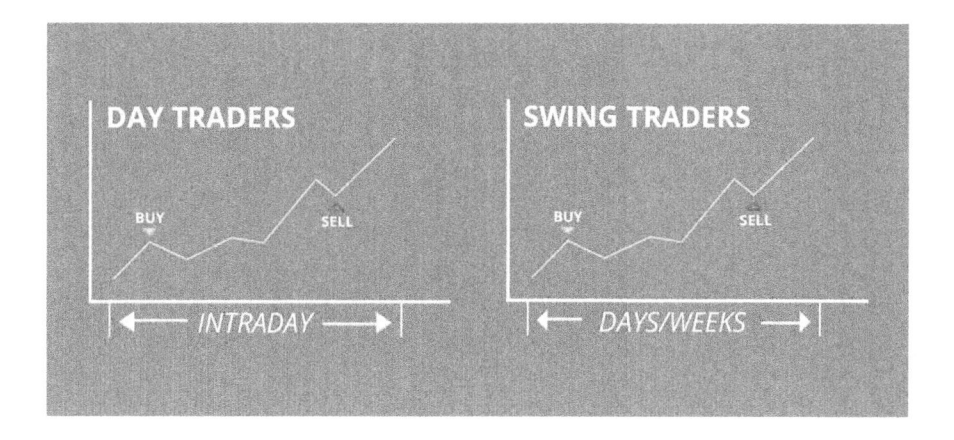

Most companies in the financial markets are familiar with the different schedules that traders might have in the day to day lives; therefore, they made a consideration. All stocks in the market are categorized according to their traders.

Traders are grouped into two categories:

- Swing traders

- Day traders

Swing Traders are those who buy stocks that are not fast perishable and therefore stay on the market longer.

Day Traders are in the market for something fast-moving and has a high volatility rate.

This distinction makes the different types of trading applicable to those in the market. How to identify what stocks are suitable for day trading or swing trading is reliant on the information gotten from the different platforms.

Different website platforms are perfect for this dissemination of information as they are regularly updated and get direct information from those companies and big investors.

Day Trading Vs. Swing Trading

Just when you thought you were getting a grip on day trading, you discover that there is another type of trading. Swing trading is another form of trading that is undertaken by people who have not as much time as the day traders.

Similarities

While there are more stark contrasts, there are also a few similarities between these two modes:

Day trading and swing trading are easily tracked and charted regularly. Their activity on the market is manageable, and statistics are well documented regularly.

There is always a possibility for huge profits based on the stockiest on the market. When the stockist's graph has been on a constant rise, both day and swing traders are bound to reap heavily from it.

There is no limit to the number of stocks. However, you will need to stick to the max dollar stop-loss rule. Both types of trading allow for the purchase of viable stocks, and this is essential as they use different time frames to track.

Both of these types of trading can be done on the same platforms, and the transactions remain the same.

There is a real-time opportunity to keep track of the charting of your stock performance at will in both day and swing trading. There are the limit and timer that can be set by the trader to go off at the time of analysis.

Differences

All traders are grouped into two categories: swing traders and day traders.

Day trading is for people who are impulsive and have a high level of discipline. Swing traders tend to be more cautious and take a long-time making decision, hence the amount of time they use.

Day trading is based mostly on making profits and swing trading is done to identify swings in stocks and occurrences in the forex market over some time.

When it comes to risks, day trading carries the most. Day traders, therefore, have to invest a lot of time in the markets due to the longevity of their stocks. Swing trading only carries the risk of having the amount out on the market for long.

Day trading can be drawn back with a power outage while swing trading will carry on even after the power is back. Therefore, one should constantly have backup internet access or an alternative form of communication on their stocks.

Day trading is full-time, while swing trading doesn't have to be.

Day trading rarely works with high-value stocks and focuses more on small and retail companies, while swing trading mostly stocks belonging to corporate companies.

A swing trader can concentrate on his time off and probably strengthen his trading skills as opposed to a day trader. The day trader is always rushing to make as much profit from the maximum number of stocks he purchased to hone his skills.

Day trading involves more bank transactions than swing trading. This is because, in the buying of stocks, the bank is involved, whereas swing traders do that less often. This is likely to increase the day traders' chances at daily transactions than that of a swing trader.

Day trading involves more charting of stocks and thus a better understanding of fast-moving stocks than swing traders.

Swing traders stand to lose out in case of a market crash than day traders are they are done with everything at the end of the day. This takes a lot of faith in that their stocks will payout and not burn out.

Strategies Used in Swing Trading

Swing trading comes with different opportunities and also frequent scares. These trades are made in shaky markets, and any time the market can crash with all those dollars invested in it.

Its advantage is that it uses longer time frames to track; therefore, one can manage a full-time job as opposed to the shorter time frames on day trading. So, to avoid any pitfalls, one is advised to try it on a demo account first while learning the ropes. While swing trading, there is no need to keep worrying about the trades that you made. The long-time frame allows you to easily pursue other things as you wait to conduct your trade. Such a trade is very convenient since it gives room for flexibility. You would like a trade that gives you freedom. You find that you do not need to keep worrying about the moves that you make since you feel secure in your deals. As a trader, you would like to engage in a deal that grants you your freedom. You want to be at a point where you can carry out your other activities as you keep trading. In this case, swing trading will act as a side job that earns you an income. You get to do other things as you conduct swing trading. It is more like killing two birds with one stone.

Swing trading is also best experienced once one has mastered the art of money management so that you can project your profits wisely. This advanced time on the market will help you identify the patterns in the stocks, and this will improve your decision-making ability. In any business investment, the management of money matters a lot. We have had some businesses start well and ended up failing. You will be amused that they do not fail due to the lack of a good strategy. Instead, they fail due to poor management of finances. Any business that looks forward to making more profits, as the years advance, needs to look at how they manage their finances keenly.

We have heard of cases where businesses started out well only to end up failing before making bigger strides. Money laundering has affected many businesses to the point of closure. Once you know how to engage in swing trading, ensure that you manage your finances. This will ensure that you make better decisions while carrying out various trades. With a good money management strategy, it gets easier to make progress in swing trading. You find that you will easily double your profits with this strategy.

Due to the longer time frames, have a reliable mode of communication as one is bound to forget to make moves on the market, thus ending up with huge losses. Timing is important in all the business deals that you engage in.

The interesting thing about most motivational talks is how they insist on proper time management.

You have probably come across some people that would prefer you to waste their money but not their time.

The importance of time lies in the impact that it has on an individual. The time factor is also necessary while conducting various trades. Ensure that you are keen on the decisions that you make.

For instance, with the long durations in which the trades are carried out, you may forget the time you were required to trade. You find that you have a lot going on and keeping certain dates becomes a challenge. To avoid this, you can set a reminder on when you need to trade. At times, this will require that you are disciplined in carrying out your various activities.

The decisions that you make, no matter how small, hold a big impact in your possibility of succeeding. Utilizing this strategy will help you a lot while trading options. It ensures that you are disciplined in keeping time, and you trade in moments when you can get a big profit.

Observe the trends in the market and steer clear of trading with the trend. This is because its longevity might be questionable, and therefore having a stock that fazed out while you were not tracking it is detrimental. Avoid trading against the most appealing trend and exercise caution by withholding yourself. As a trader, you need to be keen on how the market moves. You cannot achieve success in a certain area unless you fully understand what it entails.

As an individual intending to engage in swing trading, one of the best strategies that you can utilize is knowing how the market operates. You will be surprised by the power of having information. In the world that we currently live in, ignorance will cost you a lot. Nowadays, information is readily available to us that one has no excuse not to learn.

In this era, the internet has done more good than harm to us. You can easily get any information that you want by conducting a simple search. We also have numerous resources within our reach that help us in acquiring the information that we would like. With the many resources, we certainly do not have any excuse for not having the knowledge that we need. Additionally, while learning, we can never finish learning everything. Each day comes with its new things, and we need to embrace that. Have a positive attitude towards learning and see the impact it will have on conducting swing trades.

Strategies used in Day Trading

Know what stocks you are trading by keeping up with the latest using newspapers, financial markets, and trade events. Use reliable sources to keep you up to tabs with the general markets and the high flying financial players. As the market expands, there is more to learn. We need to constantly keep up with the changing terms and factors influencing the market. It is a good thing that there are plenty of resources that we can utilize to have the information that you need.

When you utilize this strategy, it allows you to be well informed. You find that you will even find it possible to make better decisions.

Be mentally prepared to make losses as much as you are prepared to make profits. This is an inevitable step in the trading process. Day trading is unpredictable as a stock can crash at any time during the day. This strategy has been a challenge for most people. You find that you are not open to the possibility of incurring a loss. Asides from the fact that the main purpose of investing is earning a profit, you have to be open to the challenges that come with investments. At times trades go contrary to what we expected. A single mistake can cause you to encounter a loss. At times, we have no control over some factors, and once we encounter a loss. While you engage in day trading, know that you can either win or lose at the end of the day. This will protect you from stress and other challenges that result from being stressed. You get to appreciate your efforts despite failing since you understand that failure is part of the success journey. Not every person can do this, but we need to encourage ourselves.

Chapter 18: Advantages and Disadvantages of Swing Trading

As with all things, swing trading stocks has its good and bad side.

Those that swing trade stocks tend to believe that they are in a less vulnerable position than the positions held by day traders. Although one can understand their thought process, it is believed that they are both equally risky depending upon the experience, psychology, and technical analysis technique employed by the trader. Everyone seems to think that long-term investing is the safest bet, but that is not always valid given the recent statistics. In my opinion, the longer a trade is exposed to the markets, the more risk is evident. Investment brokerages have convinced the general public that investing is too complicated for the average guy and that he should leave his money with the brokerage for 'safe-keeping.'

The Pros of Swing Trading Stocks

Less time-consuming than day trading. A trader is given more time in between trades to perform his/her analysis and could choose better performers.

An initial poor entry has time to recover and return to a positive state dependent upon the direction the trader has chosen.

Long (up) positions will often fair better in this respect than an initial short (down) position.

Swing Traders need not be concerned with meeting the 'Pattern Day Trader' requirements.

Swing traders are given more data to analyze (timeframe wise) than are day traders. A swing trader has more confidence in his/her trade because the current trend is supported by longer-term historical data.

The Cons of Swing Trading Stocks (Double-Edged Swords From the Pros Listed Above)

Con: A swing trader can also get bad information into the mix of their data analysis and choose a less profitable performing stock or a losing stock.

Con: An initial poor entry also has time to keep moving against your trade.

A swing trader, day trader, or any 'trader' must be aware at all times of what they are doing and what they could expect from any given trade. Here is a brief checklist of very basic things to analyze before entering into a trade along with a little tip.

Check Your Confidence Level on the Following:

Psychology of the trade

Are you in control of your fear, greed, patience, and desperation? Make sure your swing trading plan virtually eliminates any of these emotions, or else, you could make a hasty decision. Also, make sure that you are trading only disposable capital to eliminate desperate decision-making.

Up (Long) or Down (Short)

Any trade will return you to the very basic question that you must answer before entering the trade. Do you think the stock is going to go up or down? What analysis has brought you to this conclusion and do you have supporting evidence from outside sources for your answer? If you cannot give your answer some support, then your answer might be just a 'guess,' and you might want to consider not entering the trade at all.

Confidence in Your Strategy

Are your technical indicators proven by YOU? Have you used them before by paper trading or with other trades? Have they worked for you? Simple moving averages and exponential moving averages tend to be one of the most consistent technical indicators available.

Chapter 19: Strategies of Swing Trading

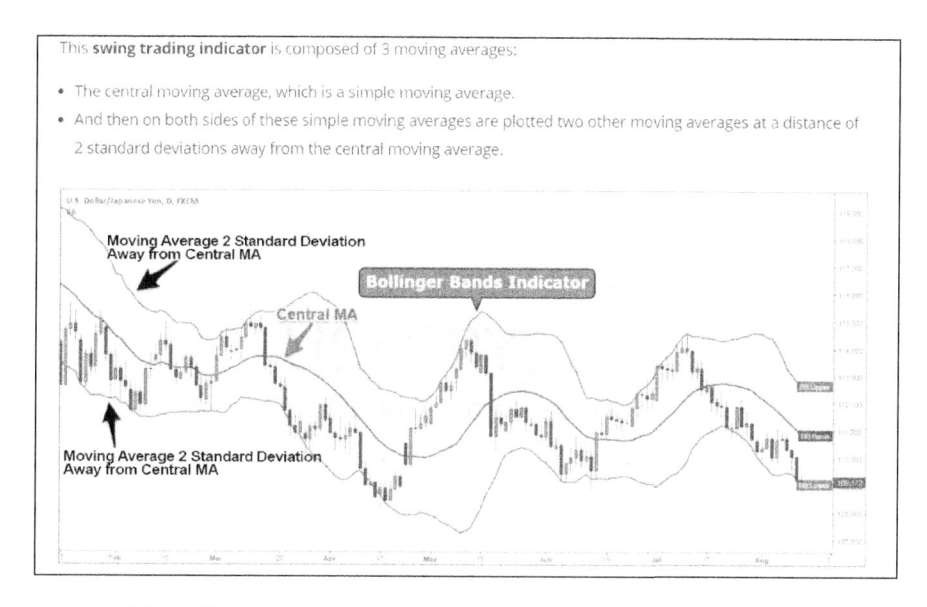

This **swing trading indicator** is composed of 3 moving averages:

- The central moving average, which is a simple moving average.
- And then on both sides of these simple moving averages are plotted two other moving averages at a distance of 2 standard deviations away from the central moving average.

Trading the Trend

The most mainstream swing exchanging system is to exchange with the pattern. At the point when you can locate a stock that is drifting in either course, this is an open door for strong benefits. Truth be told, my recommendation is that you ought to abstain from searching for little benefits doing things like exchanging running markets, and rather, you should stick to just two discovering patterns to exchange. Considering all the stocks that there are in the business sectors, unquestionably you can discover a pattern that would procure you a decent benefit in a matter of a couple of days or weeks. On the outside trade, open your brain to preparing all the monetary forms and not simply the significant money sets.

At the point when you do that, it will be simpler for you to discover patterns that you can ride to benefits.

Pattern Trading

The second strategy is to follow patterns. If you are following the strategy, you need to be fully aware of all the patterns in stock market charts (these also occur on Forex as well) and study them so that you can easily recognize them as they are forming. The Gartley charts are considered some of the best to use. Some swing traders stick to pattern trading and only use that. That might be something to consider if you find all the technical indicators to be too much to worry about.

Dynamic Support and Resistance

This strategy could also be called "the Bollinger bands" strategy. Earlier we talked about how they work. So, in this strategy, you want to rely on the levels of support and resistance that are indicated by the upper and lower bands. If you are looking to profit on an upswing, you wait until the price touches or even goes below the lower Bollinger band. Then, wait until you see signs of a price reversal in the candles or with moving averages. Once you get those indications, you buy your stock and then wait for it to rise in price to the upper Bollinger band. You also use the lower band to set your stop-loss value.

The Super Trend Strategy

The following strategy that we are considering can work with stocks, but it has particularly suited to the Forex market.

There is another indicator we did not talk about what has called the super trend indicator. So, in the strategy, you will use the super trends together with the SAR to identify trends to trade. It is a relatively simple strategy that is very well suited for swing trading.

The Simple Moving Average Strategy

My personal preference is to use exponential moving averages because they put more weight on recent prices as compared to more distant prices. So, in my view, they are going to give more accurate information.

However, I wanted to make readers aware of a strategy called the simple moving average strategy.

In this case, you are going to be looking at swing trading for a week to a month. You are going to want to keep track of your stock using the 10 days and twenty 20-day simple moving averages. Then, you fall the same procedure that we used when discussing the exponential moving averages. If you are looking to enter the position, you look for a golden cross. That is, you look for the 10-day simple moving average to cross above the 20-day simple moving average. This is an indicator of a coming uptrend, just as it was when we considered it discussing exponential moving averages. So then, you enter your position preparing to hold it for a few days out to a month if necessary. Now, you wait until the 10-day moving average moves below the 20 days moving average. This is taken as a strong indication that the price of the stock is going to start declining.

So, at this point, you enter your position by selling the shares. By the way, when the 10-day moving average drops below the 20 days moving average, this is known as the death cross. In my opinion, you should also use this strategy in conjunction with studying candlestick charts. But it is a simple and effective strategy that is well suited to swing trading. And it also does not involve being overloaded by work.

Don't Overanalyze

One of the dangers of technical indicators that I mentioned before is that people tend to get too enamored with them. This can lead to over analyzing your charts and overthinking your trades. You do not want to trade blind, but you also do not want to trade while wasting a bunch of energy on all the curves, and indicators that are available on your stock chart.

Chapter 20: Swing Trading Psychology

Swing trading strategies are very important for swing trading success. However, they just account for half of your potential success. The other half is your swing trading psychology. Without it, even the best trading strategies in the world may not work for you.

Learn to Be Comfortable With Small Losses

As a swing trader, one of the toughest things you'll need to learn to live with is trading losses. No trader, even the best ones in the world, is immune to trading losses. It's a part of life.

However, many traders' emotions can get out of control when they lose trades, especially relatively big ones and when they activate their stop-loss limits then the security changes directions and eventually hits their price targets, making them regret their stop-loss actions. When this happens, many traders tend to let their emotions control their subsequent trades by trading with their emotions, micro-managing their trades, and losing objectivity.

You can minimize your risks for these by learning to take small hits or losses instead of bigger ones. This means a lower stop-loss limit, which is a good swing trading risk management practice. There are good reasons for this.

One is that small losses hurt much less. If they hurt much less, your risks for letting your emotions run your subsequent trades become lower.

Another good reason for learning to accept small losses is that you get to limit the size of your trading losses, particularly if your risk appetite's not that big. This means you get to preserve your trading capital much longer until you start getting the hang of swing trading and begin generating more swing trading profits than losses.

By learning to be comfortable with small losses, you get your skin in the game much longer.

Have a Long-Term Perspective on Your Swing Trades?

You can look at your swing trading efforts from a long-term perspective in two ways. First, you can set your expectations that it'll take you six months to a year to get the hang of it and start earning more trading profits than trading losses. That way, you won't begin and continue your initial swing trading efforts under pressure, which can make you make really bad swing trading decisions out of desperation.

Another way you can swing trade with a long-term perspective is to think in terms of your first 10, 20, 50, or even 100 swing trades! If you start day trading by focusing on the results of every trade, you just might make go swing trading crazy and lead, making foolish and impulsive swing trading decisions.

If you focus on every trade and evaluate your success based one trade at a time, even a small loss, which is expected, can lead you to conclude that your swing trading strategy's a fluke and make you jump from one strategy to another without really giving each strategy enough time and trades to master and validate. By jumping from one strategy to another after every loss or two, you'll never be able to master any swing trading strategy, ever.

Just like how your professors graded you in school based on the average of your multiple quizzes, exams, and recitations, you should also evaluate your swing trading success or shortcomings within the context of many swing trades.

Swing Trade According to Your Risk Appetite

There's no denying the fact that you can risk losing money by swing trading. Remember, the higher the expected return on your investments, the higher your financial risks. Because swing trading can give you potentially superior returns compared to bank deposits and other fixed-income securities, the financial risks are also higher.

Many traders trade emotionally out of fear. Most of the time, the fear comes from the fact that they're not comfortable losing a certain amount of money. Maybe it's because their swing trading capital is an amount of money they'll need in the foreseeable future, which means they can't afford to lose some or all of it. Or maybe they're just not comfortable with losing a certain sum of money.

If you're like that, your best bet would be to limit your swing trading capital to an amount of money that you're comfortable losing, especially when you're just starting out. That way, you can minimize your risks for emotional trading, e.g., fear-driven trading, and optimize your chances of swing trading profitably.

Another important reason for trading based on your risk appetite is fiscal security. If you trade more than what you can afford to lose, you risk sacrificing your ability to meet some or most of your personal or family needs. The amount of money you should dedicate for swing trading must be that which, if lost entirely, will not have a significant impact on your personal or family finances. Never allocate your emergency fund or your kid's tuition fee money next year for swing trading today. Swing trade only your excess money.

Don't Be Greedy

Either way, emotional trading is foolish. On one end of the spectrum is fear-based trading. On the other end is being greedy.

When you're greedy, you'll always go for one-time-big-time profits and will not settle for small ones. The problem with this approach is that one-time-trading profits are very hard to accomplish and opportunities for such rarely come by. Greed can make you lose more trades than you win because even winning trades can eventually become losses when greed keeps you from exiting while ahead because prices eventually drop as you continue waiting for unreasonably higher profits.

This has happened to me before. I took a long position on stocks of a prominent real-estate company and after 2 weeks, I was up 30%. But I truly believed or wanted to believe, that it could still go up and give me at least a

50% return in less than a month.

In the third week, the price dropped such that I was still up but only by 20%. "It doesn't matter, it's just a correction and it'll resume its upward trend in a few days." I thought to myself. In the fourth week, I was only up by 10%, and by the end of the fifth week, I was down 5%. All that time, I kept convincing myself "It's just a correction." I eventually had to liquidate at a loss of 15%. From gold to garbage – and it's all because of my greed.

Set modest swing trading gains and once your security's price hits your target, liquidate your position. At the very least, liquidate a good portion of it, say 50%. That way, you end up breaking even at worst if the price subsequently drops.

Take Smaller Positions

Another way by which you can keep swing trading greed in check is by taking smaller swing trading positions. How does it help you do that?

Setting unrealistic swing trading targets is just a way greed rears its ugly head. The other way it does is through large position sizes. This is because even if you set modest profit price targets, you can magnify your potential trading profits by going for large trading positions. For example, you can earn a trading profit of $1,000 through:

- Profit per share of only $0.50 with a position size of 2,000 shares; or

- Profit per share of $1.00 with a position size of 1,000 shares only.

You can double your potential trading profit by doubling your position size! However, you also risk twice the loss by doing so.

Just because you've allotted a swing trading amount within your risk appetite doesn't mean you should put it all in one security in hopes of raking in a windfall. Aside from setting modest profit price targets, keep your position sizes modest, too, by diversifying your swing trading capital across several securities in smaller position sizes.

Chapter 21: How to Manage Your Funds When Swing Trading

Money management is the practice of supervising an individual's or a group's capital usage. A good manager understands that the first thing to do in money management is to have a budget. A budget is a spending plan. It indicates how much money is coming in, how much is going out, and how it is going out. As a good manager, why should you budget for your money?

To Keep You From Overspending

Most people who do not plan on how to utilize their money always end up overspending. A budget helps you to spend what you have and to avoid getting yourself in debt to cover up for the overspent money.

To Help You Achieve Your Goals

A budget helps you to plan your spending on a priority basis. You direct your money towards the most important things. A budget gives you a plan to stick on and enables you to achieve your goals. It also helps to safeguard your savings.

Enables You to Save Money

Most of the people who do not budget for their money save less or don't save at all. With a budget, you are obliged to put a certain amount of money into savings each month. A budget also keeps you from dipping into the money spent each month. It is because you have already planned for your expenses in advance.

Keeps You From Worrying

Budgets come with restrictions, but the good thing is that you have the right to decide how much to put on each category. It doesn't matter which category you put as a priority, but what is of essence is to stick to your budget.

A Budget Gives You Flexibility

A budget should be flexible enough to enable you to move money, according to your needs in every month. The only amount that you should not touch should be your savings. Other than that, you can adjust the other categories to suit your monthly needs.

A Budget Gives You Control of Your Money

Sometimes we find ourselves in situations where we cannot explain how we utilized our money.

A budget gives you the power to spend and track your spending to know when to stop. It gives you the power to transform your financial future. You make decisions at the beginning of every month on how to manage your money, and you keep monitoring them every day to avoid overspending. It keeps you in control of your money.

Making a budget is as easy as ABC, but the greatest challenge comes in sticking to it. The best way to stick to your budget is to track your expenses. By doing so, you will know when you are within the budget, when you are overspending and when you need to make a change. How can you effectively track your expenses?

A) Record every expense throughout the day

Take time to record each expense regardless of whether you think it is negligible. Also, keep checking the total to have an idea of the amount left in each category for spending. It will help you to keep within your budget and to change your spending habits.

B) Stick to your expense limits

You should train yourself to stop when you run out of money in any category. It will allow you to study your budget and adjust it to suit your spending. Even as you transfer money in different categories, you should keep in mind that paying your debt and savings should top the list.

C) What should you do with the money you did not spend?

Rolling it forward to the next month is the easiest option, but there are also other viable options like saving the amount. To make any of the choices above, you need to understand all the monthly expenses. For instance, it will be wise to roll the amount to the next month in cases where bills keep varying every month like water bills. It will come in handy in months when the bill will be more than budgeted for. In case of unspent amounts in categories like foodstuff, it is advisable to save the amount and work towards achieving other goals or build your emergency fund.

D) Use budgeting software's

Budgeting software is easy to use and helps you to track your expenses easily. There are many varieties, and it is important to choose the option that will suit your needs and one that you can sync with your bank.

E) Use cash only

Some expenses that we incur every month like groceries or eating out, we can opt to pay them with cash. You can have an envelope for each category where you put your budgeted amount. Every time you go to purchase such items, you carry your envelope and keep the receipts after every purchase. The receipts help you to track your expenses all through the month and have a final figure at month-end to know how much you spent.

Other Ways of Managing Your Money

A budget makes your life easier, and we can attest to it with the information that we have shared above. It takes charge of sorting all your financial obligations. We have looked at how a budget helps you to manage your money and track your expenses. However, it is not the only way to utilize to manage your money better. Making a budget and sticking to it is the first step to money management but also other ways to help you in money management. They are:

1. Set a limit for unbudgeted spending

After setting aside your savings and your monthly expenses and you find some amount of money left, how should you utilize it? This money left over can be used for fun, but up to a fixed amount, after all, all work and no play makes Jack a dull boy. In most cases, it is not a huge amount of money, but you should make sure that spending it will not affect your budget.

2. Be aware of all your spending

Some spending might look harmless and negligible, but to a good management system, every coin should count. Save your purchase receipts and record all your spending in a diary.

Observe your spending and take note of the paces that you may be overspending unknowingly. It will open up the 'negligible expenses' that you have not been checking.

3. Be cautious when committing to recurring monthly bills

Banks and other financial lenders will always have enticing offers for their loans, but you should know that you are not obliged to make any commitment even though you are qualified. Remember, the banks only have information on your income and credit report and none on the other obligations. You should always weigh your options to know whether you can afford an extra monthly payment.

4. Pay the best prices

There is nothing wrong with window shopping before making purchases. Different stores have different prices for the same commodity. Always compare the prices and ensure you get the lowest prices for your commodities. Take advantage of discounts and offers whenever possible.

5. Plan for big purchases

You should train yourself to delay gratification to manage your money properly. You should do this by setting aside big purchases to assess whether they are necessary or not.

You also get a chance to compare prices. Saving for such big commodities gives you discipline and saves you from paying interest on credit used to purchase them.

6. Limit purchases made with credit cards

Credit cards are only good and allowable to disciplined people. Credit cards are the stepping stones to debt for bad spenders. You should train yourself to resist the urge to use them just because they are available. They make you not consider your financial position, and purchase something that, otherwise, you would not afford.

7. Set up a savings account

Saving every month gives you good financial habits. Setting aside the amount for yourself can be tricky as you might not take it as a priority and sometimes not remember it. Setting up a savings account and having it checked off from your checking account is always a good move to save monthly.

The more you practice the above habits daily, the more you become better at managing your money.

Conclusion

Trading is a tough endeavor to undertake, but there's no need to complicate it needlessly. By following a structured approach, you too can realize the immense potential it has to improve your life. You might be wondering about exit opportunities and about how capital raising works?

Generally, I would advise beginners not to worry about this just yet. Once you have the results, capital will come. However, there is the danger of you risking far too much capital due to not realizing the amount of investment capital you can potentially raise. Everyone gets into trading for the money and freedom potential it provides in our lives, so it is unwise to ignore it.

So, don't worry about not having enough capital to be able to get rich. As I said, if you can trade well and properly, capital will find you. Trading is one of the few remaining endeavors where you can truly make millions purely based on your abilities.

Many people do not see the results that they're hoping to get just because they don't apply the tips and tricks provided to them. It is essential for you to exercise everything you learn, as that is how you will succeed in your future endeavors.

Nonetheless, the topics we talked about will help you to not only become good at stock investing but to take you to the next level. Even though this book has been geared toward beginner investors, advanced people can still reap the benefits of this book. Making money on stocks doesn't have to be a big mystery. It doesn't have to be a gamble. By being clear on what your needs are as well as the trading strategies available to you, you can put together a plan of action that can help you mix successful trades, not just once in a while, but every single time. Trading takes many forms, and it is dynamic as well. Times change, and with the change, markets and operational methods also change. With the advent of computers, it was logical that trading would become better and faster. This came to pass, and traders now can trade on the go and use programs that make trading easier. It all boils down to the learning curve, and you have to stick to this learning curve. You have to learn what you need to learn and take the necessary risks until you get the hang of it. Put in another way; if it were very easy, then everybody would be a billionaire. That's not the case. You have to stick to it, and you need to put in the time to learn what you need to learn to develop enough expertise to at least trade profitably consistently. Profitable trading, of course, means more than break even. Whether it's a dollar or hundreds of thousands of dollars, it's up to you. I wish you nothing but the highest abundance and success in your trading. The financial markets are full of abundance and all you have to do is work to achieve all of it! I wish you the best of luck with your trading.

Printed in Great Britain
by Amazon